DESTINY CALLING

DESTINY CALLING

How the People Elected Barack Obama

CHARLES M. MADIGAN

Ivan R. Dee · Chicago · 2009

www.ivanrdee.com

Library of Congress Cataloging-in-Publication Data:
Madigan, Charles M.
  Destiny calling : how the people elected Barack Obama / Charles M. Madigan.
    p. cm.
  Includes index.
  ISBN 978-1-56663-778-7 (cloth : alk. paper)
  1. Obama, Barack. 2. Presidential candidates—United States. 3. Presidents—United States—Election—2008. 4. United States—Politics and government—2001- I. Title.
  E901.1.O23M34 2009
  973.932—dc22   2009018373

To my family

CONTENTS

ACKNOWLEDGMENTS

A WRITER owes so much to so many people who are never seen that it is humbling to try to present an adequate list at the beginning of a book. My deepest thanks, however, go to my family, who put up with beastly behavior, tirades about everything from tea bags in the sink to bath towels, fuming silences, and pathetic insecurity. At least I had a book to point to for an excuse. I am sorry for all the days I ignored the needs of my dedicated, patient dog.

Readers are protected from the worst writer behaviors by a thin line of defense that includes an editor. Stephanie Frerich has been a patient and professional guardian, astute at simple commas and psychology. She is also a patient editor of the journalese that is inevitable when an author has spent so many decades, essentially, in journalese.

I am indebted most of all to the people who sat with me and talked about their lives, their hopes, and their thoughts over the course of more than a year of interviewing for *Destiny Calling*. They are not only at the heart of my book, they are at the heart of our democracy. I would have had no story to tell without their help, and I loved the time I spent with them.

I am indebted too to some old friends, the *New York Times*, *Wall Street Journal*, and *Chicago Tribune* among them. I used them to build the chronology for this book. They informed my thoughts and presented a compelling record that was always at hand. In an era so enamored with digital whizbangs, it was a delight to hear the pages turn and to read information that was so lovingly and diligently assembled.

I confess that I too am enamored with whizbangs. I lived on my laptop for the two years of the presidential campaign. PollingReport .com—not fancy but *always* dependable and on time—was a constant source for polling results. CNN.com was my breaking-news favorite. As a measure of the times, I found satire to be immensely informative and entertaining. A night without the *Daily Show* left me feeling I was underinformed.

Finally, I thank my students at Roosevelt University in Chicago, who, trapped in a classroom, watched as I tried to *profess* even as I reported and wrote. Patience, they taught me, is a two-way street.

C. M. M.

Evanston, Illinois
April 2009

I want us to take up the unfinished business of perfecting our union, and building a better America. And if you will join me in this improbable quest, if you feel destiny calling, and see, as I see, a future of endless possibility stretching before us; if you sense, as I sense, that the time is now to shake off our slumber, and slough off our fear, and make good on the debt we owe past and future generations, then I'm ready to take up the cause, and march with you, and work with you.

—Barack Obama, Springfield, Illinois, February 2007

DESTINY CALLING

INTRODUCTION

BARACK OBAMA'S presidential election seems miraculous only to those who have not measured with some precision how it was achieved. If one can move far enough away from the process to view it as a schematic instead of an event, a few realities emerge. There is a pathway through primary and general campaign alike, particularly for Democrats. A candidate must collect the right pieces in the right places at the right time, must find the money and the people to help along the way. The campaign must know the angles and how to take advantage of them. Even as it measures the progress of its opponents, it must studiously avoid conventional wisdom, particularly about black candidates, and stay focused on its goal. In the primary contest it must understand the nature of small matters writ large, and in the general campaign it must translate large matters into thoughts and concepts that are small and easy to digest.

In modern times, no one has done that better than Barack Obama.

With remarkable skill, diligence, and determination, Obama forced his way through the barricades of convention to become that rarest of things, an immensely popular president hardly anyone knew only a few years earlier. He negotiated all of this with questions about voters and their attitudes toward race looming over much of the campaign. His victory was neither quirk nor accident. During the primary and general campaigns, Obama showed us a calculating, intelligent man who was surrounded by calculating intelligent people. They began assembling the parts that would snap together to form a victory before he announced his candidacy, and then they found a way to grow their influence, collect their fortunes, and wage brilliant battle against a formidable primary adversary, Hillary Clinton. They invented novel tactics for running for the White House in the general campaign against John McCain too, collecting more than $700 million along the way, creating end runs around anyone who was not on board and opening a new kind of relationship with individuals who supported Obama with their time, their money, and their votes. They understood from the beginning that success sometimes shows up in disguise in primary elections, that small things—caucuses no one pays much attention to, and close seconds in delegate-rich states— can yield decisive returns. Sometimes a victory doesn't mean what it seems to mean in primary campaigns.

Obama already has carved out a place in presidential annals simply by moving so fluidly through a system that is designed to crush anyone not strong enough to meet its many challenges. Close to two dozen contenders spread across both parties tried for the presidency in 2008. Like one of those car-smashing machines in a junkyard, the crushing process was remarkably efficient. For want of money, for want of inspiration, for want of votes, they were all flattened and hauled off. There was an undeniable aura about Obama even as those around him were failing. He seemed only to grow stronger. In the weeks before he announced his candidacy on a cold day in Springfield in early 2007, hardly anyone would have placed a serious bet on his chances. That began to change when he asked the people who heard "destiny calling," as he phrased it in his announcement, to join him in his mission. He seemed cast to create the eloquent moments that are so moving to people who are eager to listen. On the evening when he claimed his victory in Grant Park, an historic spot in one of the toughest political towns in America, it seemed as though victory had been the most natural and expected thing in the universe. Of course he was elected president. What else could the nation do?

How did this man go from being an unknown on the national stage to being elected President of the United States in an electoral landslide in such a short period of time?

There are two answers to the question. He knew the process well, and he knew the people who would support him even better. It takes vision and passion to draw the attention of the people, particularly in an America that is overwhelmed by noise and exploding with color and stimulated every minute of the day in so many ways. Obama had vision and passion in abundance and put them on display at every opportunity. He knew it was as important to talk to people on You-Tube as it was to talk to them on the evening news, to reach beyond standard political tactics and create a new level of contact by using technology. He knew the influence of conventional media was in steep decline, a drawback he turned into an advantage by creating new pathways to potential voters.

To run head-on into the perceived juggernaut that was Hillary Clinton's campaign took a boldness and knowledge that is rare in politics. She had all the money. She had all the institutional support. Day by day and week by week, he stripped almost all of that away until it became clear that a sliver of advantage had moved to his side. That is similar to what happens when water destroys an earthen dam. The trickle becomes a rivulet. The rivulet becomes a pouring stream. The steam becomes a cascade. And then the dam yields to the power of the water.

The Republicans turned to McCain because, in the wake of George W. Bush's disastrous presidency, he was the most un-Bush-like of the options and had a powerful story to tell, a true warrior's story about honor, bravery, and determination. But, the narrative aside, that left the Republicans with a candidate not beloved at the conservative heart of the party, a man who was obviously bold and little interested in salving the egos of the many party potentates he had offended over the years. McCain, the most heroic presidential candidate in modern history, soon found himself confronted by an irony so great that it helped kill his chances: as a Republican of long standing, he was forced to run a campaign focused on repairing the damage caused by his own party over the previous eight years. All the polling data made it clear that the well was poisoned for any Republican who came along to drink. Obama's eloquence and skill undoubtedly set the campaign standard, but it may have been impossible for any Republican to defeat any Democrat in 2008, no matter how dramatic or creative the campaign. That reality left the valiant McCain scrambling for something, anything that might work, a process clearly beneath him and one that made him seem increasingly desperate as Election Day approached. He tried to counter Obama's momentum by reaching all the way to Alaska to add the feisty Governor Sarah Palin to his ticket. This was soon defined as the clichéd Hail Mary pass that did not work.

Years of Democratic party reform that followed Chicago's tortured 1968 convention were designed to add more voter control to the nominating process. Some in the party recognized that they had created a situation where a candidate who was very good at campaigning, but with no experience in government at all, might win a presidential election. The process undoubtedly had Democratic power brokers wondering exactly what had been achieved.

If anyone had gathered the powers from that era into a room to ponder the consequences of reform and said to them, "Yes, this is true, and it is likely that a black U.S. senator from Chicago will be the man to do it," they would have laughed for days. Just about all loyal Democrats assumed that America would eventually have a black president. But not that it would come so early in the next century. No one could have imagined in the early 1970s that the nation would be ready to make that kind of choice. Race was a wall too thick to break through with much speed. It might take until 2050, maybe even later, for that to happen.

People change. It is naive to suggest that America's problems with race are evaporating, no matter how much one might want that to happen. It is not naive to say, though, that Barack Obama did not run as a black man, and that choice meant everything as the contest played out. Compelling, cool, eloquent, American, father, husband—those would be the descriptions that fit Obama as he chased the nomination and then the presidency.

He never gave anyone the chance to look at him and say he was running because he was black. At the same time he became a source of immense pride, not only for black voters but for white Democrats and Republicans and independents who wanted to show they could back him as a viable candidate, not as a symbol.

Before I began reporting and collecting for this book, I knew I wanted to create my own different pathways to tell the story of the Obama election. I wanted to let people tell much of the story. By looking at the events of the past eight years through the experiences of individuals, I hoped to explain with some clarity how Obama won. People sometimes get lost in conventional media coverage of political campaigns. The process makes a lot of noise, and noise is what gets attention in modern media. Media are also overburdened with useless talk, trinkets, and technical gewgaws—elaborate graphics and digitally created TV realities, for example—that look quite snappy but have no discernible voice. It is wonderful that the world of blogging has given voice to so many people. That doesn't mean they all have something to say. And in the election campaign it sometimes felt that media were only a few technical steps away from creating a holographic voter, an imaginary three-dimensional entity who could play everyman's role. Then a panel of bloviators would have an argument about it with lots of shouting and arm waving. That's politics on TV and the internet. The formula: talk (cheaper than field reporting) plus advertising (robust and expensive in election years) yields profits.

Away from the set stages and the cell-phone updates and the laptops, there was a much more intriguing version of America. The nation is filled with interesting, thoughtful people who have a lot to say if only you just shut up and let them say it for more than a few seconds. What made journalism feel so glorious a few decades ago—that connection with good people of every description who live in a beautiful country—remains as enticing as ever, even as journalism itself collapses. It's hard not to develop an immense crush on the United States during a presidential campaign, and this is one love affair worth repeating as often as possible. A campaign brings passion and thought to the surface and forces the nation to look at itself and make a hopeful decision about the kind of future it wants. The nation writes its own story over many months, a narrative that has its climax in a daylong process that follows the sun across a big country. In 2008 it ended a little after sundown in a Chicago park that should have been cold and lonely and waiting for winter. But even that didn't turn out the way it was supposed to.

FIXING CHICAGO HISTORY, AND THE NATIONS OF PENNSYLVANIA

THE TORTURED GHOSTS of Democratic politics have lived in Chicago's Grant Park since 1968, when the party's presidential nominating convention mutated into a bloody police riot. It is the last place one would expect a rebirth. The staged hoopla of a televised celebration yielded in 1968 to the sense that chaos had captured the Democrats. The boss mayor, Richard J. Daley, took on a thug's mantle. The party, wounded by the assassinations of its heroes, the Vietnam War, and the protest defections from a Southern base that simply could not accept the party's embrace of civil rights, began to fragment. The coalition Franklin D. Roosevelt had constructed to carry the nation successfully through depression and war withered.

Yet there they were late on November 4, 2008—Election Day—a black Chicago Democrat with an unlikely name and tens of thousands of jubilant supporters, celebrating a stunning victory on a warm night that hinted much more of spring than of the approach of another brutal winter. It was a remarkable event that left people

parading and cheering in waves on Michigan Avenue far into the
night. Barack Hussein Obama and his Chicago-based team of election veterans had constructed an electoral landslide: 365 votes for
Obama to 173 votes for Republican John McCain. In the course of
a campaign that seemed to last forever, Obama had beaten back the
persistent demon of prejudice. He had survived a rumor attack built
on ignorance that branded him a Muslim. He had won the votes of
people who could not have conceived of a black presidential candidate just a few months before. He had revived his party's hopes,
defined a new ideology, and forged the strongest political coalition
in the modern era. He had raised more money and fielded more volunteers than anyone in presidential history. He had sprinted as a national unknown from a brand-new spot in the U.S. Senate to victory
in the toughest game in politics, remaining a calm, almost bemused
presence throughout a most unpleasant process. Not McCain, not
Hillary Clinton, not the vitriol of the blogosphere, not the blather
of twenty-four-hour news commentary could stop him. Grant Park
rocked to the thunder of thousands cheering his name, "O-BAM-A . . .
O-BAM-A." It lasted all night long. It banished the ghosts of 1968 and
filled the air with promise.

How did he do that?

Admittedly, that's an obvious question. We tend to measure
presidential elections as popularity contests, forgetting that they are
always reflections of a national consensus defined by the times. There
are many elements at play, but they boil down to an amalgam of the
mood, the presence of the right candidate, and how a campaign con-
nects with voters. It is ultimately always about the people, because
they make the decision. So, there is a better question to ask:

How did *we* do that?

The noisy part of the presidential campaign that fills pages of
newspapers and magazines, hours of broadcasts, and fathoms of bot-
tomless internet space may not be the best place to look for the an-

swer to that question. That is generally what campaigns want you to see. They spend a fortune creating the events that fuel it. Coverage thrives on polling results and interviews with strategists and lots of assessment and commentary from a collection of a few dozen partisans, familiar names all, who have cashed in on this big-top circus of democracy, along with what remains of a rapidly disintegrating journalism. The process fans any spark of controversy—Does a candidate wear a flag lapel pin? Is his wife patriotic enough?—into a flame. Most of it seems to be about media competition and prediction, as though a presidential campaign might be forecast like an impending storm. Beyond all this campaign noise, another America has a story to tell. But you have to go look for it. You never know what you will find.

*

The nation's oldest superhighway, the Pennsylvania Turnpike, cuts across the state, a road that is perpetually under repair but rarely seems to show much improvement. From the Ohio line, where a driver is asked to pay an entrance fee of a few dollars as though the state were an amusement park, it bumps and grinds past Pittsburgh and then shifts a little south to avoid the more determined ridges of the Allegheny Mountains. What it can't avoid it cuts through with a series of remarkable long, ceramic-tile-lined tunnels which are disorienting, particularly when a driver is racing alongside a big truck. They must have been spectacular when they were new. Now tiles are missing and the mountain's limestone waters have leached in, staining the walls and emphasizing the fact that you are, indeed, where a living person should not be, deep inside a mountain.

A short distance east of one of the tunnels, a big wind-power farm churns at the side of the highway. The whirring towers, which march south along the crest toward West Virginia, sit a couple of hundred feet above an untapped fortune in bituminous coal. The highway improves somewhat as it heads toward Harrisburg. Then, worn by trucks and the endless turmoil of commerce, it pushes on after Lancaster, going east toward Philadelphia.

I have driven parts of the Turnpike perhaps a hundred times in my life, and with each visit I marvel at how it transports the traveler through a collection of cultural wonderlands defined by geography, local history, and, strangely, by what one finds on the car radio. An hour east of Pittsburgh the sonorous, serious sound of public radio disappears and a collection of strange new voices drops in to talk to you about God and sin and politics. On this particular April, in 2008, the certainty of the radio preachers is only occasionally broken by political advertising linked to the biggest thing happening in the state, and perhaps in the nation—the presidential primary campaign.

That's why I'm here. I've come to join Barack Obama and Hillary Clinton and their advertising campaigns and entourages on my own unusual mission across the cultural playgrounds of the Keystone State, which I know too well, having grown up there. This is the primary, of course, but Pennsylvania will go on to play a crucial role in the general election too. It always does. It is a useful laboratory for examining presidential campaigns because it has so much of everything, from classical liberals in Pittsburgh and Philadelphia to strongly conservative pragmatists in the rest of the state. Much of the place echoes with gunfire all through several hunting seasons, as everything from doves to bears falls victim to one of America's truly impressive privately owned firearm arsenals. People catch fish, then eat them. It also has a wide array of characters who would not lift a finger to harm a living thing, along with the Mennonites, the Amish, and dozens of other denominations who are by their nature eager to extend a helping hand. There are also people who would steal your last penny and never look back. It has cunning politicians, including one so remorseful about his behavior as secretary of state a while back that he shot himself to death at a TV news conference.

The cliché about Pennsylvania, advanced only a few years ago by
James Carville when he was the strategist behind Bill Clinton's presidential campaigns, was that it was two cities (where the liberals live)
separated by Alabama (the gun-totin', slack-jawed rednecks in the rest
of the state). This was a handy description embraced by just about
every traveling reporter in America and regurgitated many times, including in the current campaign. The look of the place seemed to
support Carville's thought. Pittsburgh and Philadelphia are indeed
filled with liberal Democrats. The rest of the state seems remarkably
distant. In Altoona, an old railroad town that lost its identity a few
years after its massive steam-engine shops closed when the Pennsylvania Railroad turned to diesels, cowboy clothing is common, and
sometimes people line-dance to country music. There is a wilderness
of forestland in the north and rolling farmland in the south, and a
bothersome abundance of whitetail deer everywhere. Carville's description presented a convenient diagram to help explain why one
never really knows what will happen in Pennsylvania elections.

The state can send a nominal reformer like the Philadelphian Mil-
ton J. Shapp to the governor's mansion even as it embraces Republican stalwart Hugh Scott in the U.S. Senate. It can give its electoral
votes to Bill Clinton just after it elects and reelects a Republican governor. It can put a fire-breathing conservative Republican like Rick
Santorum in the Senate and a big-city pragmatist like Philadelphia's
former mayor, Democrat Ed Rendell, in the governor's mansion. It is
a puzzling, ticket-splitting kind of place, six, perhaps seven, unusual
little nations wrapped into one. That's just too difficult to explain in a
small sound bite, so Carville's dictum frequently serves as borrowed
wisdom for journalist visitors, though it greatly diminishes the complexity of the place.

Pennsylvania is the perfect spot to begin the story of an historic
presidential campaign because, like the knobby roots of the trees in its
forests, like its rivers and lakes and the compressed urban confusion

of its cities, its political history is close to the surface. As everyone
in politics eventually learns, it is not a place to be trifled with. The
dream of nationhood was hammered out in Philadelphia, forged by
a revolutionary war, and then tempered like Damascus steel by a civil
war that witnessed one of its bloodiest and most crucial battles in the
quiet fields of Gettysburg, a fruit-farming haven in the middle of the
state. Even though I now live near Chicago, I have always cherished
my Pennsylvania connections, which are as deep as the coal and as
old as I am. When I ramble there, my thoughts ramble with me, like
eager friends who are happy to see me again. The place invites an
almost Quaker level of open-mindedness and thought, a process that
bubbles like a kettle of soup on the stove when presidential politics
is stirred in.

I have been drawn to presidential campaigns since 1972, when, as
a young reporter for United Press International in Philadelphia, I got
my first real taste chasing around a profusion of ambitious Democrats
in what for them would be a disastrous year. I was on a deathwatch for
George McGovern, who was flying into Wilkes-Barre on a snowy, unforgiving morning. The airport sat on top of a mountain that looked
as though a Marine barber had given it a crew cut. There were many
opportunities for disaster, which was why it was so exciting to be
there. I had to do two things. When the press plane landed, I was to
greet UPI's Helen Thomas, even then the reigning senior presence of
the White House press corps, and do whatever she said. McGovern's
entourage was in two big planes. I was to call Philadelphia UPI when
the candidate's plane landed safely to let them know we wouldn't be
writing the big, show-stopping headline disaster story because everyone had not been killed in a fiery crash. In my head I was preparing
the fiery crash story anyhow, because being darkly prepared was part
of the wire service reporter's primitive role, which I loved. Then I
was to wait for Helen Thomas on the second plane.

McGovern's plane floated down from the clouds and glided onto the runway through a light snow while I gabbed with the locals. Then the press plane landed. Helen came blasting down the stairway and swept across the snowy hundred yards to the terminal. When she pushed through the swinging doors, I grabbed her arm and said, "Madigan. What do you need?" "PHONE IN A LEDE," she shouted. "SAY SOMETHING ABOUT THE INDUSTRIAL HEARTLAND!" And then she was gone, spirited away with the other big-name reporters and carried down the mountain by bus. "But it's not the industrial heartland," I shouted into her vortex. "That's the Midwest. This is the Keystone State! Anthracite . . . hard coal!" I called the Philadelphia desk and offered the industrial heartland lede. "What the hell are you talking about? That's the Midwest. We're rust belt," was the response.

Granted, it was a small role. But, like a supernumerary in an opera who goes on to develop a passable baritone and a longing for Italian, I was caught up in the whole process. From that election onward, whenever the nation chose a president I tried to put myself in the way of the process. I missed one. I believe I was in Jamaica on Ronald Reagan's election night. In Kingston I followed it on the BBC and longed to be back in the newsroom, any newsroom, or out on the trail with a hall pass from the office, someone else's credit card, and the order to find out what America is up to.

We live in a spectacular country in so many ways, a place where the people are as interesting as the vistas. Presidential campaigns are like long-running road festivals through these people and places, admittedly perplexing in many ways and frightfully expensive. There is nothing in the world like the breeze in New Hampshire the week before a contested primary election. The static of the cold, dry air takes on even more energy. It fairly snaps when you touch it. It's also one of those places where it's hard to find someone who isn't playing a primary campaign role. New Hampshire bears no resemblance to the rest of the country. Its southern end is populated by tax escapers from Massachusetts. Its down- and wool-encrusted Northerners are great for pithy quotes. Look flinty and act undecided—that's the ticket to media attention in the week before the New Hampshire primary. To draw a crowd, one only need mention "momentum" in close company and a clot will form. A whole battalion of veteran reporters, the Quadrennials, descends on the Merrimack Hotel (and anyplace else one can find a room) to opine, party, fester, mix, mate (sometimes), and even work. People go on for days about anti-tax pledges and who won the last time and why the place is a trendsetter and then, more quickly than the winter snows yield to the daffodils of spring, they are all gone and the locals shift back into the normal rhythms of their lives, which will include no interviews, no media spots for quite a while. Future presidential wannabes will begin showing up years before Election Day just to visit and get known.

Iowa? Who would go to Iowa without its strange presidential caucus system, where normal folks gather in disturbingly small numbers to make a decision that can change the nation's political course? The process, a gussied-up show of hands, draws an immense amount of attention, analysis, and candidate angling. Connecticut senator Chris Dodd moved there to campaign. (This did not work.) It's like prom season on steroids. Nothing compares to talking to a corn farmer who has developed his own foreign policy or a teacher who wants to tell you about the growing national debt and (of course) why teachers are underpaid and underappreciated and underloved. Whatever the problem, be it climbing gas prices or fuel shortages, crop surpluses or famine in Africa, corn seems to be the answer. Put it into a steer and it makes steak. Put it into a car and it's ethanol. Boil it, drown it in butter, serve it on a plate, and it's a summertime picnic institution. Dry it and put it in your corncrib and it will make your livestock happy all winter long. Iowa is a state that does not look like the rest of the country. It might lead a foreign visitor to note: "So, *this* is where America puts all the white people!"

Add to Iowa and New Hampshire any Southern state—say South Carolina, for example—and you have the trifecta of presidential primary campaigning. Victories in the Iowa caucus, the New Hampshire primary, and any Southern state lead to media anointments. Better, when campaigns go off track in the South, it extends this carnival for weeks and makes it all a lot more interesting, as though extra geeks were booked for the midway.

Native Southerners talk so slowly that a reporter's notes actually begin to make sense because there is time to write down every word. "Whaaaaallll. . . . I jist don't know what ahm going to doooo yet. . . . I might be a this or I might be a that . . . I jist don't know. . . . That Fred, he's a good ol' boy, but I do love John McCain's record. . . . I jis don't know. . . ." The eggs, bacon, and toast of New Hampshire and the fritters and cornbread of Iowa yield to the biscuits and gravy of the South. The issues change, along with the varieties of ham available in little restaurants. Inevitably, because the Civil War was only 143 years ago, race somehow becomes an issue, at least in the eyes of the media. Predictions are made about what people are just not ready to do because of lingering animus toward those black folk and their unusual ways or those white folk and their privilege. You can always find some sign of continuing tension or disrespect. Someone will use "uppity," or worse, "nigger," prompting encyclopedic assaults on the language of race. A preacher will show up—not so long ago it would have been the Reverend Jesse Jackson—and talk about life up in the big house and how we all have a dream that Great God Almighty will come to be in our time. The fact that there is a robust and growing black middle class, that sharecropping is rare, that the drinking gourd people follow these days is not the Big Dipper and generally leads to an undergraduate degree and an okay job is somehow set aside.

This is not to argue that the problems of race have been solved in America. Nothing is more brutally revealing than a look at homicide statistics in a city like Chicago, or unemployment statistics in Detroit, or prison statistics anywhere. But to concentrate only on the problems is to miss the passion, work, and determination that have transformed blackness in America over the past few decades. We would be prudent to look to the wisdom of our children and grandchildren, who in many cases seem to have shed the burden of racism that marred the attitudes of their ancestors. The problem in politics is that it is so easy to slip into the cliché.

The Ku Klux Klan indeed still exists, but it's not much more than a clown act with a horrific history now. It's always ready to suit up and march in some places. It will also turn in its own members for a fifty-dollar payment from a cop. I once sat with a federal prosecutor while I was on an assignment to look at a "revival" of the KKK. "How do you get them to talk?" I said, reflecting an attitude that was roughly fifty years behind the time because the problem at that point was that they just would not shut up. "Pay them off. It's what we do. They'll tell you anything for a hundred dollars."

Race, then, is part of the cliché that dominates Southern election coverage. Blacks and whites become props on either side in a campaign-trail Kabuki theater, with all its classical exaggeration. Another cliché includes the inevitable rustic Southern farmer who will say, "The hurtin's come home," referring to either crop prices or production costs. He will be widely quoted by people who ponder agriculture exactly once every four years.

Go out west and drive the long miles from here to there, bladder straining and anxiety building over the fact that stoic Westerners may not actually have anything at all to say to a reporter from the East Coast. I once flew into Fargo, North Dakota (on the eastern edge of the West), for a brief campaign event that drew a couple of dozen people. The wind was so strong I had to hold the candidate's hand to walk from the plane to the terminal. When we got back to Minneapolis, I asked the pilot how he was able to fly in those weather conditions. "Fly! Hell, I nearly killed us on the ground. I think I took off on a runway approach," he said. "Couldn't see a damned thing." Drive for an eternity across Nebraska. Get lost in Colorado up in the mountains. How efficient can it be to try to track down some good quotes in the Dakotas from a place that has all of three electoral votes?

Go write the quadrennial California election story, the one that says there are a lot of crazy people out there but the place is booming and worried all the time about earthquakes. People who build their homes on vacant lots overrun with highly flammable brush seem shocked and amazed each year when fires sweep through, leaving only the fireplace and the plumbing for the built-in espresso maker standing in relief against an ash-filled backdrop. They make for some good campaign-trail interviews. No one ever asks these people, "Why would you build a home here?" The same is true of people who build at sea level, or who prop their mansions up on stilts and gush about the view. When they are sliding down the mountain after a few weeks of rain, it seems location may not have been everything after all.

Maybe you will write about the beauty and laid-back milieu of the marijuana counties, where the nation's drug laws seem ridiculous on the surface and racist and sinister beneath. So many mellow people are making so much money, selling weed to black kids in the city—okay, and to lots of other people too—who are headed for jail on the second or third offense. Doesn't seem right, does it? Try *that* issue on the trail if you want to shorten your campaign.

I have visited many of these places because of my affection for presidential politics. I don't love it as much as I love visiting every corner of my country, but it means a lot to me just the same. There is something bracing about the potential for change, in individuals and in nations too. Thomas Jefferson was brilliant to understand that a little revolution is good every few years. The Founders' jaws would drop, wooden teeth and all, if they could see what this has become in the modern campaign season. But if one keeps an open mind about America, retains some affection for its people, and holds on to the thought that the place continues to evolve after two centuries, everything that happens in a political campaign makes perfect sense, even when the outcome seems senseless.

Such thoughts fill your head when you are chasing across the universes of Pennsylvania in pursuit of Senator Hillary Clinton of New York, who just doesn't wish to admit that she has been snookered by a newcomer from Chicago and will not be the first woman president in history, at least not now. One has to hand it to Obama, who was most certainly going to lose the Pennsylvania primary on April 22 but did not seem at all worried about it. In fact he didn't seem worried by much of anything. We have never seen a candidate so cool. It could be his poker experience. Anyone who plays cards well—and Obama plays cards well—knows numbers. The presidential primary is a game of numbers for the Democrats, who now pay the price for trying so mightily to reform the process since the primary and election debacles of 1968 and 1972. A Republican must collect only a majority of votes to "win" a state's convention delegates. With the Democrats, it's proportional. You can lose, lose, lose—and still pick up a respectable chunk of delegates. Obama's strategist, Chicagoan David Axelrod, knew that, of course. Like a Cubs baseball game, it doesn't actually matter if you win the nomination by assembling a lot of dingy little parts and some unexpected home runs. It's still a victory. No one gets anywhere by arguing that they won eight important innings and then luck came along for the other side in the ninth.

Here is how the primary season looks when you think about it zipping along the Pennsylvania Turnpike, avoiding its three main threats—trucks, potholes, and troopers: Obama will collect enough of the small, unattractive pieces so that Senator Clinton will find that not enough is left when she tries to make her own math work. She will run out of options and money at about the same time because she made one fatal political mistake before it all began: she assumed she had been anointed. She will win all the big, glamorous places that feel they carry such weight in the process (because that is where the institutional party is strongest, and she is the institutional party's favorite), only to be slapped in the end by a reality: people from Chicago have always known how the numbers game works, perhaps better than anyone else in politics. She will crow about the number of votes she has collected, but it still won't matter. Democratic primaries are all about delegates. It is the most fragmented challenge anyone can face in politics. If you have twenty delegates available in a given state and you can only take nine, then take the nine and move along to the next contest.

To the Obama campaign, the nation looked just like a bigger, more complicated Cook County, or perhaps the counties of Illinois. But math spread all over the nation is still math, and that's where you win in the primaries. Grab the caucus states no one pays much attention to. Grab those sparsely populated places that don't seem to have much to offer. Roll up what you can elsewhere.

Don't yield anything. It all adds up if you are David Axelrod.

The presidential campaign is not the same for me this time around. I am no longer a newspaper reporter or columnist. That road ended for me where it ended for a lot of my colleagues, at a newspaper rapidly running out of money and longing like a streetwalker on a cold night to sell itself to the most eager bidder. I'm a professor now. That has not changed my longing for presidential campaigns, but it has wrecked my chances to hook up with one. One of the modern era's great political writers, Jon Margolis, formerly of the *Chicago Tribune*, once told me that the worst thing a reporter can do is "cheapen the beat" he's covering because it will wreck the budget for the person who follows him next time around. "Think of the presidential campaign this way," he said. "It's only money, and it's not mine." It costs a media company perhaps two thousand dollars a day to send a reporter (maybe lots more if you are sending a whole crew) to run with the campaign crowd, and what you get is what everyone else in the flying chartered titanium airplane tube gets—the quotes the candidates want you to have from the places the candidate wants you to visit. You trade your freedom and a lot of your company's money for some access.

I don't have any money, and I don't have a newspaper anymore, and I have no access at all. No one returns my calls, not even Axelrod, an old friend from my early *Tribune* reporting days. (If the truth be known, he did return some emails, including one in which he said he bet I was happy not to be at the *Tribune* anymore after the paper had announced more people had been defenestrated. I did finally get a call back as Axelrod was on his way to the White House after the Inauguration.) Instead, though, I have a great deal of freedom. This time I am taking a different direction. I am seeing most of this campaign the same way everyone else sees this campaign. A little over two years ago, when it became clear to me that I would have to find another way to pay attention to this election, a thought settled on me: What if everything I have been doing for the past forty years or so has been wrong? I think this might be a little like deciding late in life that you should have been a Quaker, or maybe a woman instead of a man, or maybe single instead of married for nearly four decades. Or maybe Republican instead of Democrat. What if chasing campaigns around was not the way to write about a presidential election? Basically the media aspects of these events are planned by people who are interested in taking no risks. I have several hundred pounds of good newspapers filed in orderly piles to prove this. They are the record of this long, long campaign, from its inception until well after the November 4 election. I look at them often and think, "Well, isn't this just like before?" Even down to the candidate crisis stories, the primary elec-

tion night guessing, the dramatic "convention bounce" stories, the
wild-speculation-about-vice-president stories, the "both sides claim
victory in debate" stories, and everything else. And the polls. Almost
every day a different poll. But basically the same story: who is ahead
right now. ("If the election were held today . . ." Guess what? It's not
today!) It's depressing. It makes you think, "No wonder these media
institutions are collapsing. They're doing exactly what everyone did
ten, twenty, forty years ago."

Because of that, you could put these campaigns together with
your eyes closed. At some point the candidate must go to Europe,
either to sneer at the French, bond with a new collection of Brits, or
drop in on the Germans because you need to let them know we're
quite sorry about former Defense Secretary Don Rumsfeld's slanders
and actually *do* view them as important and not at all Old Europe.
There will be plenty of photo opportunities. Perhaps a visit to the
troops or, at the very least, a stop at the tomb of whichever country's
lost soldiers remain so sadly unknown. Look solemn and put a wreath
there. Common sense dictates one should ask, "How could you have
wasted so many lives in 1916?" but taste and diplomacy tell you to
keep your mouth shut.

Reporters are like pet monkeys on these foreign trips, entertaining but always under control. They do exactly what they are allowed
to do. The same is true of those who are on the campaign trail with a
candidate. There's a reason why so much of what the media deliver
looks exactly the same: everyone is going to the same place and working with the same set of "facts." Maybe I'm just jealous that I'm not on
anyone's plane. But on a sunny April day with three hundred miles
of Pennsylvania ahead of me, a presidential primary to ponder, and
stops in Philadelphia, Harrisburg, Altoona, and a lonely cabin deep
in the woods with no cell-phone service and no deadlines for months,
somehow I don't think so. I am on my own campaign trail. It will

carry me not to places so much as to people with stories to tell about politics and their lives.

In some cases the people I met looked to government for help in their darkest moment and found nothing. They are patriots who have led soldiers into battle but worry about the futility of our current wars. They have played by all the rules but can't find work. They have struggled to change government and politics but find the beast absorbs all their energy and moves only a tiny distance. They have won and lost at this political game and still can't break away from it. They are at the whip's end of vast forces in the nation's economy and have no clue about what a derivative is or why their 401(k) has collapsed. They are young people just starting out, hopeful and optimistic that they can change the direction of their nation.

These are big stories that live in the shadow of politics, away from sound bites and manufactured events. They are only vaguely represented in polling statistics. They are not the face of statistical samplings but of life and the way it plays out in the world's most important democracy. I chose this sampling of people carefully for what their stories show about us and about politics. I am chasing the campaign, then, around these important people the public knows nothing about and everything about at the same time. They are, in so many ways, *us*.

Pennsylvania is just a part of this mission, but it is crucial to what I am trying to understand about America and the way it selects its presidents. This state simply was not supposed to matter in Election 2008. Most of the other big states rushed to hop on the February 5 Super Tuesday train (with primaries in twenty-four states) so they could play an early role in settling this battle. All they did was add more confusion. Super Tuesday managed to resolve nothing and everything at the same time. Michigan and Florida were so eager they bounced themselves right out of the Democratic game by pushing their primaries up to the front of the schedule. It didn't matter. When the day was over, it was clear that Senator Clinton's inevitability was a myth. John McCain, on the other hand, gathered what he needed on the Republican side to brush away a host of other challengers and become the likely nominee of the GOP. So while the Democrats were still struggling before the Pennsylvania vote, the Republicans, with their "winner takes all" primaries, were already shifting into "coast" and watching from a distance to see what kind of ammunition they could collect as their Democratic enemies became more and more aggressive toward one another.

Like an army that leaps too quickly into battle and finds itself moving all over the map at a moment's notice, the Democrats were leaving ammunition all over the place. Obama took heat for the wacky comments of his pastor (he then shifted churches), for a little side deal on a strip of real estate with one of those seamy Chicago fixers, for brushing up against some now toothless 1960s radicals who lived in his neighborhood and traveled in the same political circles, for being either too black or not black enough, and for a couple of other little bumps on his short pathway of experience. These "issues" would chase him all the way to November, but never to much effect.

I am headed for a debate, for a big Obama rally in Harrisburg and whatever else life presents as the Pennsylvania primary campaign plays out. Like any thinking person in April 2008, I have questions, the biggest being, "Are we really going to have a black guy as the Democratic candidate?" Somehow that feels good. It also feels good that it is Obama, a gifted speaker and compelling man who has managed his broken-field run through the minefield of Chicago politics without getting too bruised.

A confession: I like Chicago politics. I still admire the Daleys, even the old man. I may well be the only one left who will say that, but there you are. I had dinner with the family once, where a daughter said the boss would leave his boss hat at work and come home each day to be a dedicated father. He would spend fifteen minutes talking to each child. I can admire a man like that. I wish I had had the sense to do that for my own children. The Daleys have figured out how to make a big city look good and run, if not well, then at least effectively for most people. It is frequently not a pretty process. I know that to survive in that system you have to be more than just average. If you are bad, you have to be the worst. If you are good, you have to be the best. Everyone else gets stuck somewhere in the Chicago/Cook County process, and you hear from them only occasionally and maybe not pleasantly. It's a system that seems to thrive on creating characters who will at some point spend time in jail or just find themselves in deep water, surfacing only on occasion, like seals. Or perhaps they will find themselves at the pinnacle of American politics.

People build newspaper careers in Chicago moaning about the behavior of the locals, who oblige by doing things that are just a little more outrageous than what they did yesterday. There is always, then, plenty of muck to rake up. Some of it is much more sophisticated now than the bold graft and political behavior that made the place seem like Sodom on Lake Michigan in the old days. Muck these days more likely resides in the complex world of bonding, development, and finance, perhaps masquerading as progress. Former Illinois governor Rod Blagojevich stands as evidence that elected officials remain as venal as ever, blatantly primitive and aggressive about their narcissism. He became a theatrically awful governor, with a whole nation as the audience. Even without clowns and corruption, there is enough going on in Chicago in plain view to distract a whole city of souls.

After years of sparring with the business elite, who viewed small Meigs Field as a personal downtown airfield for their jets and helicopters, did Mayor Daley actually send bulldozers out in the middle of the night to chop that runway into big chunks to clear the way for a park? Yes, indeed. Was the former governor of Illinois sent to prison for being somehow involved in a scheme to sell truck-driver licenses to people who should not have been on the road? Yes, indeed. Are the alleys so clean you can ride a bike from Howard Street, the city line, in the north to downtown, traveling ten miles through an extended Streets and Sanitation Department wonderland? Not quite, but just about. Did someone actually create a gigantic kidney bean out of sparkling steel and plop it right in the heart of a park on the city's most crucial thoroughfare? Yes, indeed. Can a smart black man actually go from "community organizing" to the state legislature to the U.S. Senate and to the top of the Democratic ticket in a couple of years? Yes, indeed.

Now he's here in Pennsylvania, trying to convince people who didn't know him more than a few months ago that he's the real deal. In this place, where Hillary Clinton is beloved, just as her husband was beloved, he is selling another outrageous Chicago political thought—that a black man with not much weight to his résumé might be the nominee of the Democratic party for President of the United States. This is a lot bigger than chopping up an airport or putting a shiny giant kidney bean in a park, and it's not going down at all well in this place Hillary called her own.

What can I learn from the local news about what's happening in this brutal Democratic party struggle? Radio reception is spotty in the hills and mountains, not because I'm using AM but because there's just no radio around. I finally locate a station past the Harrisburg exit off the Turnpike. I have no idea what this station is, but I know exactly what it looks like: a little cinder-block studio with a big antenna outside, maybe windows, maybe not, air-conditioning, and someone sitting in an ozone-saturated studio inside, working the programs. I head south to Chambersburg on Route 30, the Lincoln Highway, mainly because if you are thinking about the presidency and Pennsylvania and you don't go to Gettysburg, you haven't thought enough. It's not just a tourist trap. The nation was saved at Gettysburg. In memory of that battle, Abraham Lincoln delivered perhaps the most profound speech in anyone's history. Look past the commercial infestation that is the scourge of every important tourist spot in the nation, past the golden arches and trinket shops, and you see fields consecrated by the blood of soldiers. Gettysburg is like a mecca for people who love America. You go to Chambersburg, turn left, head east, and the Lincoln Highway takes you into the heart of it. Finally, I find radio.

I wouldn't know Rush Limbaugh from SpongeBob Square-Pants on the radio because I don't use radio much for my political commentary. I am old-fashioned: I like the papers. Whoever is on the radio as I head toward the Lincoln Highway is deep into a rant about Obama's comment at a private fund-raiser in San Francisco, of all places, about bitter, worried people and how they hold on to their guns and their religion. I hate this type of radio because it fuels the kind of demagoguery the Founding Fathers were shy about (fearing uneducated masses would be easily misled by demagogues, thus their votes could be manipulated) back when they thought only male white property owners should be allowed to make political decisions. I don't get to hear it for long because, as is often the case when you leave the big roads in Pennsylvania, I am driving straight up the side of a mountain. But even after the signal goes away, I'm stuck in a thought about the truth of what Obama said.

I know all about bitter people and guns. I keep translating "bitter" into a word I think is more fitting—"frightened." Obama was and is right about gun possession in some cases, and it drives people crazy here. There may also be a hidden part of the reaction, a part that touches on how people in some rural areas feel about black men. Thirty-five years ago I lived in a little town not very far from the mountain I am driving over. Guns were common. The fear among some people—and it wasn't everyone by a large measure—was that the black people in Harrisburg (my wife and I were so shocked to hear the word "nigger" used to describe them that we boycotted one bigot's shop and put anyone who said it on the "avoid at all costs" list) might band together and come out to steal . . . what? Bad furniture and autumn-harvest-gold window treatments from Sears? Color televisions? There was not much of material value in our little river town, if the truth be known, though anyone with any soul at all would have loved the place.

A local character once showed me his arsenal, which included a 9mm pistol he kept under the pillow he slept on each night. I stopped counting at seven guns. They were everywhere, generally within reach. Anyone who walked into that place uninvited was getting plugged. He was showing me around a two-bedroom ranch house on the side of a hill in a town so poor it had no stoplights and no parking meters and only the state police to swoop in and protect people from one another. What did he think he was guarding against?

Beyond "fear," I don't know that anyone can produce an answer to that question. At the time, his was "niggers in Harrisburg." It would be pointless to try to explain why the black people in Harrisburg would have no reason to band together and decide to come roaring up the Susquehanna River to take his avocado-green refrigerator or the Barcalounger. Perhaps he is now dead, his arsenal distributed among family members. But for many people, attitudes toward guns are not about to change. Maybe frightened, bitter people believe a gun will save them from the pace of change, from neighbors they dislike, from unwanted visitors, from old age, from disease, from . . . I don't know what.

One of the reasons I came to Pennsylvania was to test whether these kinds of attitudes toward race had changed over thirty-five years, and I was in just the right place to do so. I wanted to see what kind of support Obama could raise in counties along the southern border of the state. I knew he wouldn't win, but how badly would he lose? The gun argument goes beyond conversations about bitterness and fear, though. In this part of Pennsylvania are many, many hunters, and for hunters, guns are tools. I am certain they do not like being described as bitter or frightened of anything, so Obama would not win many new friends in the hunting community with his unintended announcement about firearms and religion. That was going to make it difficult to determine whether it was the guns comment or race that undercut support for Obama in those southern counties. I concluded I would just look at raw numbers and try not to guess, because of course you could never really know.

What I was hearing on the radio was a rant against what seemed to me to be a defensible statement about firearms and fears. The religion part—that's a bit of a stretch, but I can make an argument on that too. I am fond of religious radio in rural America, mainly because the people who preach there are so certain about everything. I live in a world full of doubt about God, about me, about whether my dog actually likes me, about everything, so certainty to me is like the green grass on the other side of the fence. A gospel hour appeared on the radio farther up the side of the mountain, but this particular sermon was not about a gospel. It was about cancer. You want something to be afraid of? Cancer is a good thing to be afraid of. The preacher believed, he said, that God reached out and cured his cancer because he had a Christian doctor who at some point said "Praise God!" after he learned the preacher's cancer, assaulted by chemotherapy, had gone into remission. The preacher was excited and of course certain. He concluded from this experience that he would never have anything but a Christian doctor by his side. No Jews from New York need apply. No Muslims from Pakistan or Hindus from India. He said he would never allow anyone but a Christian doctor to touch him, and a Christian could do whatever he wanted.

Applauding his certainty, I came at this case from a different direction. My big question for the preacher was why had God given him the cancer in the first place if he was just going to wait until some Bible-thumping doctor came along to cure it with a prayer? A God who does this is obviously not a thinking God who plans ahead. And what had the preacher done to warrant scaring the bejabbers out of him by giving him cancer? Why would God, with all the business he has on his agenda, single him out? Why wasn't God just giving tumors to the Taliban? I concluded he was clinging to a religious explanation because he was terrified by the experience he had just survived. Obama, as I said, was right about that too. For people who feel the need to be clingy, guns and God are good things to be clingy about. The question is why they need to feel clingy, and what in the name of all that is good and holy does *that* have to do with a presidential campaign? Politics is such a very strange business that it finds a way to stretch across even what seem to be unrelated events.

My guns and God and Obama thoughts simply would not leave me. All the way down the south side of the mountain and onto the Lincoln Highway they were there, as though they had been planted and taken root.

Presumably the preacher had an audience for his story about Christianity and science. But what interested me most about his radio story was the fear behind the message. The preacher was looking into the face of death. Medicine saved him, but he immediately attributed it to an act of God. In his moment of greatest fear, he embraced religion. All he needed was a pistol in his pocket, I thought, and he could be the poster boy for Obama's message about bitterness—fear in my view—and what it does to people. The troubling part about presidential campaigning is that it's so easy for people to misunderstand what is said. It sounded to me as though Obama was sending a message about helping ease the troubles in people's lives so they don't have to turn to firearms or an unforgiving, judgmental version of the Christian message to find a sense of security. But you have to think about the situation a bit, without the help of a crowing collection of bloviators and partisans, to get to that stage. Also, a candidate doesn't want to be saying something like that at a cocktail party in

California. Hearing that in Pennsylvania would be the equivalent of pinning a big "Kick my ass all the way to Punxsutawney" sign on your butt. Fortunately for Obama, he had no chance of winning the Keystone state in the primary election anyway. But the guns-and-religion comment surely fueled conversation about him.

I pulled into Caledonia State Park at dusk and headed back into the state forest to the cabin I would be using overnight. It's family property, a comfortable cabin that has been sitting in the deep forest for more than sixty years. The seven dwarfs would have fit well there with all the moss and dampness and the sound of a trickling stream, reminding me of the kind of place they would have taken the virginal Snow White for vacation. I dropped off my stuff and headed out to meet people for dinner at an old inn in Cashtown, about five miles east on Route 30.

Just outside the park I ran into the fear-and-gun problem again, but this time not on the radio. Three state troopers' cars were parked end to end along the south side of the highway. Hats off, the troopers were leaning hard over the front of their patrol cars, shotguns pointed at a cabin about a hundred yards off the road. I had no idea what was happening. The reporter wanted to stay and watch, but the thoughtful professor said, "Get the hell out of here fast," so I sped thoughtfully on down the highway. I turned on the radio. More preachers, advertising for mattresses, local events announcements, the news, but nothing about what I had just driven by. Hillary Clinton was tapping into the Obama guns-and-religion comment in her ads. Her message: we don't need an elitist snob as the Democratic candidate. Nothing, however, about the troopers' standoff.

I ate dinner and headed back to the cabin for the night at 8:30. The Lincoln Highway was blocked a full five miles from the point of the standoff by fire trucks and ambulances. I tried to find a back way in, and after an hour of driving I finally reached the western end of the blockade, with more fire trucks and ambulances stopping all Route

30 traffic. There was just one chance to get back into the woods, and that would involve talking my way through a police line. "It's a hostage situation," a state fire policeman told me. "The guy has guns. He's threatening to kill himself and anyone else who comes near." I explained I needed to get back to the cabin. He said, "The troopers don't want anyone back there." This was not a pleasant thought. My suspicion was that the state police had sent snipers to approach the cabin from the back and didn't want unrelated innocents crashing through the woods. But the officer was persuadable and moved the barricade, giving me access to the cabin road. I slept that night in a room that faces the deep woods with the curtains wide open and a knife by the bed. There was no moon, nothing but blackness outside the window and not too many miles away a battalion of state troopers and a crazy person issuing threats. It felt like being in a Stephen King novel. For the first time in many years and in many circumstances most people would view as dangerous, I was completely alone and frightened.

I wished I had a gun, and I said a prayer before I went to sleep.

In the morning I headed east on Route 30, then up to Harrisburg to get on the Turnpike for the drive to Philadelphia. Except for the little piles of white ash from the phosphorous highway flares, I saw no sign anything had happened. Nothing on the radio. Nothing in the local papers. A few days later I tracked down a story that said a man had been taken to an institution after threatening to kill himself, an event that had blocked traffic on the Lincoln Highway for a standoff that lasted until a little after midnight. No one was injured.

Without much traffic on Route 30 I zipped into Gettysburg and stopped for breakfast. Scrapple is what you eat here. Scrapple is what's left after the more pleasant parts of the pig have been processed. You cook down the remains, add lots of spices, strain them, add cornmeal or oatmeal depending on your scrapple religion, and let them "set," as the locals say, to form what I have always thought of as "pig fudge."

Then you cut off a slice, fry it, and eat it with maple syrup or ketchup. It is somehow wonderful, but not delicious. It is not healthy. It is not compelling, like buckwheat pancakes. It is scrapple, and it stays with you for quite a while. Once a year, I believe, is quite enough.

I stopped in Gettysburg to take a walk, as I always do there. My Gettysburg walks generally carry me to a cemetery or to a building with a sign announcing its historic role, or more sadly to the monuments recounting what units fought here, who died, who is still missing, and how many were wounded. I do not know about the veracity of the local legends that claim there are ghosts here. I do believe there are spirits that somehow draw us into thought.

For me, visiting Gettysburg is like going to church in the cathedral of democracy. There is no doubt in Gettysburg about the importance of the presidency, an element of the campaign season that can get lost in all the hyperbole, nastiness, finger-pointing, and bluster. As tough Americans, we like to think that all politicians carry some fraud in their souls, some dishonesty, and maybe we accept that. But in these rolling fields Lincoln's eloquence echoes forever. It reminds us that alongside all presidential campaigns runs a noble thought about nationhood. I always leave the place loving the ideal of my country again, recognizing completely how distant people can be from the better angels of our nature as we tumble across the battlefields of presidential politics.

Hillary Clinton was the big news in the Gettysburg paper. She was in Harrisburg. Obama was in Philadelphia getting ready for the debate, of which the primary Democrats had already had way too many. The debates of my youth were classical events: one question per side. Statement: "The United States should support Israel at all costs." Research and then go at it in a very formal way, with nuns and priests slapping at you when you mess up. But modern political debates are not like that. They are not properly named. They are actually public relations mash-ups where candidates who cannot win under any circumstances get some attention and, perhaps more important for career purposes, anchor people, reporters, and columnists get national face time on television. Mostly for reporters, debates involve sitting in a big hall with the rest of the media, waiting for someone to make a fatal mistake, which usually does not happen.

I decided I would watch the Pennsylvania debate in Philadelphia with a friend, Tom Ferrick, a great metro columnist before the *Philadelphia Inquirer* joined the rest of big-city journalism in collapsing into a steaming, troubling heap. We worked together at UPI in Philadelphia and Harrisburg in the 1970s, bonded like brothers, and had a fabulous time writing about politics. Ferrick had taken a buyout (as I had from the *Chicago Tribune*) and was working on his own developing media plans at the time of the Clinton-Obama debate. Ferrick knows volumes about Philadelphia history and politics. Thirty-eight years ago, during an early-morning walk after a night of serious journalism partying, he told me, based on the patterns in brickwork on the houses in his neighborhood, which ethnic groups had put the bricks in place two centuries earlier. Our partying skills have melted away with time, but not his knowledge of Philadelphia and its history. Ferrick knows how race works in city politics too. Every big city in America with a healthy black population presents its own story: what works in looking at the question in Chicago would not work in looking at the question in Philadelphia, New York, Los Angeles, Atlanta, or Miami.

Race would be important for Obama and Clinton in Pennsylvania. Obama was counting on a strong enough showing in Philadelphia and Pittsburgh and some of their suburbs to offset Clinton's strength in the other four universes, regions outside the big cities that define the state. Both cities and the suburbs around them have robust black populations. Maybe because the stakes were so high, the candidates were tired, and the debate formula had run its course, the conclusion in the Ferrick living room was that the debate did nothing for anyone. It was boring.

Hillary seemed stronger. Obama was halting and said nothing one would carry away from the event. No one did damage, but no magnificent bridges were built to the brilliant future. ABC questioners Charlie Gibson and George Stephanopoulos (who should have been banned from the set because of his close earlier connections to the Clintons) were terrible. The first half of the debate focused on questions aimed at marching Obama back into a collection of brush-fires about his former pastor, about wearing flag lapel pins, and a host of other smoldering embers. You could not tell from the questions that the nation was at war in two places, that its presidential incumbent was in a slide, or that the economy was beginning to slip. As I had with two dozen or so other Democratic primary debates, I found myself thinking, "What is the point of this?" The media people involved all argue it gives "the people" a chance to see how candidates function under pressure. What pressure?

I got into my car the next morning, turned on the radio, and headed west for the April 22 election. It was good to see Tom again and Philadelphia was lovely, but I wanted to get to Altoona. Catholic high school kids had canvassed for Obama there, and even though it had only a tiny black population and was filled with Republicans, I thought the outcome in Altoona might be interesting. One of my sisters who lives in Altoona said that if Obama didn't carry the state, race would be the reason. I wanted to see what that meant locally. But first I wanted to talk to some Democratic friends in Harrisburg and go to an Obama rally in front of the state capitol.

The state capitol in Harrisburg is the most fantastic building in town. A renovation was completed in 2006 to mark its centennial. It sits on a small hill, and from the steps you can look toward the Susquehanna River. The capitol is one of those pre–World War I buildings in which the inherent corruption of old-style politics meshes perfectly with neo-Roman architecture, sending the message that this is where government resides and it's not going away, ever. It could just as well house the pope. Some of the spectacular fittings inside were purchased by the pound, so thieving contractors made certain there was a lot of lead inside the light fixtures. It may be the only capitol in America that has a spot in its Moravian-tile lobby floor memorializing the common housefly. It carries the label "House Fly." Perhaps the contractor was paid by the insect.

As with all Obama rallies, you had to get there three hours before the candidate. For this particular event, Obama would be coming from the biggest rally of his campaign in Philadelphia the night before. My friends and I grabbed some Subway sandwiches about a block from the capitol and then walked over to the rally. It was a revealing scene. Button and hat salespeople roamed the lines. The Obama people had farmed out lots of work to button and hat people, with the campaign getting a cut and the salespeople pocketing the rest. I did not see what would become my favorite button of the campaign, "Another Middle-Aged White Woman for Obama," which was created by Toni Gilpin, an Obama fieldworker in Illinois, who had grown tired of hearing media reports of how well Hillary was doing with middle-aged white women. But there were lots of others. People were buying them by the handful. The campaign was careful to stack the crowds on the capitol steps behind the podium so the TV cameras would show only an overwhelming wall of supporters of all ages, races, and costumes behind the candidate. Lots of rock music, lots of celebrating, and lots of time standing on the steps waiting.

Obama entered down the steps of the capitol, stopping all along the lengthy walkway to shake hands. He looked tired and not very happy, but he has perhaps the best smile outside of Hollywood and he uses it well, so some people were flashed as he walked along. He was met on the podium by U.S. senator Bob Casey, Jr., who has deep roots in Pennsylvania Democratic politics and who, in Washington, was a freshman senator with Obama. This was an important moment for the Democrats, for there may have been no more tortured relationship in recent party history than the one between the senator's father, the late Governor Robert Casey, and the Democratic party. Bob Casey, a New Deal Democrat and pragmatist of the highest order, was perhaps the most ardent foe of abortion rights in the history of modern Democratic politics. He was also not at all enthusiastic about Bill Clinton in 1991 when the future president was working through his first tough campaign. The rancor reached a level at which the Pennsylvania governor was essentially banned from speaking at the Democratic National Convention that nominated Clinton. An Obama-Casey relationship this time around, should Obama become president, would bury remaining doubts about the Casey family and its connection to the party.

Harrisburg had everything a rally needed to have. Because people were not allowed to bring their own signs to events for security reasons, the Obama staff was busy passing out hundreds of standard "Change" blue-and-whites, and lots of multicolored posters that from a distance looked as though they had been made by committed humans, perhaps in their kitchens. That's not so. The Republicans do the same thing; the whole objective is getting the right look for the day's campaign coverage on TV. It has to appear as though everyone is about to explode from the event and rush into the street to do campaign work. And that is just about how it always comes off. Another sister who lives in Lancaster tried to bring her own sign to an Obama rally. It said, "UR MORE THAN A RAY OF HOPE, UR SUNSHINE!" It was nice. It was confiscated. They gave it back to her after the rally, and the Obama crew liked it so much one of their vans stopped after the rally and someone got out and took a picture and asked for her name.

Obama went through the motions at the rally, but it was clear by this time that he knew he would not get the percentage points he needed to close the gap with Hillary Clinton. Her ties to the party, to Governor Ed Rendell, to blue-collar workers were just too strong. Still, he called his forces out and told them to make Tuesday one to remember. Then he went off into the night, heading west for more campaign stops. You might well know you are going to lose a primary election, but you never want to show it. People have worked hard for you, and you don't want to disappoint them.

Obama and Clinton had made their mandatory stops in Altoona as the campaign played out. I went to look at the bowling alley where he rolled up a whopping 37. (If you can't bowl, don't bowl. That's the lesson of that visit.)

After he tried bowling, Obama stopped at Texas Weiners out on Fifty-eighth Street to get a hot dog. This is a reflection of how deep into local culture a candidate must dive to appear friendly. A Texas weiner bears no resemblance to the hot dogs Obama left behind in Chicago, which have peppers and pickles and tomatoes and Lord knows what else, along with celery salt on a poppy-seed bun. They are construction-project hot dogs. A Texas hot weiner is a marvel of simplicity, having just an unadorned bun, soft from being steamed, the weiner, which is cooked along with hundreds of its weiner brothers on a rolling machine, and its defining touch, the sauce. Maybe chopped onions if you really want to torture yourself.

Sources close to Texas Weiners report the sauce is made from yesterday's hot dogs, chopped up into a fine mush, and altered with garlic powder, chili powder, and paprika. Another recipe calls for one pound of hamburger, covered with water and cooked until brown, a half-teaspoon of garlic powder, three tablespoons of chili powder, three tablespoons of paprika, and one teaspoon of pepper. Simmer for an hour and don't drain the water. A reddish brown mush results, which you then spoon, lengthwise of course, down the hot dog. Which of these is the authentic recipe? The weiner people won't say. The "yesterday's hot dogs" recipe goes all the way back to people who worked there decades ago, so it reeks of history, among other things. The hamburger recipe is more recent and has less romance. You have to really want to be president to eat this. The sauce and the onions together have a good six-, maybe eight-hour breath life.

The election weather was good in Pennsylvania, particularly for Hillary Clinton, who beat Obama by ten percentage points. I had a strong suspicion that would happen. Tom Ferrick had told me that some areas of Philadelphia clearly voted overwhelmingly white, which he had expected. History partially justifies the argument that it was racial, but Hillary Clinton was a good candidate too, so that has to be an important part of the formula. Besides, an Obama victory wasn't what I was looking for.

If you take your finger and drag it along the southern border of Pennsylvania, the Mason-Dixon Line, from, say, York County westward, you find Obama got 45 percent of the Democratic vote in York County, 42 percent in Adams County, 41 percent in Franklin County, 32 percent in Fulton County, 30 percent in Bedford County, and 35 percent in Blair County, which includes Altoona. In Perry County, where we lived in the 1970s, he collected 38 percent of the vote. Those numbers present two remarkable realities, by my measure. The first is how many people in those southern counties were actually voting for a black candidate. I couldn't have imagined that not so long ago. And perhaps as surprising, all the rest of them voted for a woman.

All elections are historic, but some are more historic than others. Long before Pennsylvania's primary election, it was clear the nation was heading for a contest that might define a new era, realign the nation's politics, and change the very philosophy that had dominated so much of federal policy for so many years.

The idea that white folks wouldn't vote for a black candidate collapsed initially in Iowa and rolled across the nation in caucuses and primaries everywhere. It was a sign that a huge change was under way. Political scientists argue that these kinds of elections can shift a nation from an era dominated by ideals—programs to make people behave better, sometimes informed by religious values but generally driven by conservatives—to an era of civic behavior in which the common good becomes more clearly defined and addressed.

Such changes are important and characterize eras. In one world you get a political dynamic that emphasizes issues like abortion and gay marriage. In the other you get health care, infrastructure improvements, and more emphasis on what government might do to help people. Franklin Roosevelt presided over that kind of a civic era, as did John F. Kennedy and Lyndon Johnson. Theories about these shifts remain the focus of heated debates among specialists.

What is not debatable is that President George W. Bush and the Republicans had done such a terrible job that their party's candidate, John McCain, had to run as a reformer. And he had to go all the way to Alaska to find someone who was untainted by the festering corruption of fact and spirit that attached itself to President Bush's administration. The most important clue about what was coming was presented when McCain and running mate Sarah Palin decided they too would be the candidates of change.

The administration created the backdrop for the 2008 contest with four key failures of Bush's eight years in office: the 9/11 terrorist attacks that claimed so many lives in New York, Washington, and Pennsylvania, which came in the wake of many warnings that Osama bin Laden was targeting our nation; the foolish and wasteful war in Iraq, constructed on a foundation of exaggeration and lies, which drained resources from the real war on terror; the biggest financial crisis since the Great Depression, a product at least in some measure of intentionally lax or declining regulation and plain ignorance, and something humankind could do nothing to stop: weather that moved into the Gulf of Mexico after it had picked up a woman's lovely name that a lot of people will never forget, Katrina.

2

THE GREAT STORM

CARMEN DEDEAUX'S new house sits up in the air on Hiern Avenue in Pass Christian, Mississippi. This is prudent, because when the weather turns bad there, it's worse than almost anyplace else in the United States. Pass Christian stretches out along the coast on the Gulf of Mexico, just a bit west of Gulfport. For saltwater lovers, sitting down by the breakwater and watching the pelicans gliding like modern-day pterodactyls low over the Gulf and taking an occasional plunge to grab a fish is a delight. A wide, inviting beach stretches along the Gulf. It is one of America's beautiful places.

Before the Civil War, wealthy people from New Orleans came to build vacation homes, which sat on a slight rise and faced the full, sparkling glory and breezes of the Gulf. Pass Christian, named for a nearby deep channel and known as the Pass, was the most popular regional resort of the prewar era. West, a couple of miles down the coast, sits Louisiana and its compelling, troubling, magnetic gem, New Orleans. To the east sits a harbor filled with well-kept fishing and pleasure boats, all protected from the Gulf by the breakwater. A seaside bar stands up in the air on well-tarred legs, and a seafood-processing plant dominates the east end of the harbor.

Because she loves it down by the water, Carmen Dedeaux sat here one afternoon in August 2005, marveling at how calm the Gulf of Mexico can be. She was comfortable. She often spent summer nights at the beach, sitting on the seawall. She knew that the calm wouldn't last because the Gulf was preparing to fuel one of the hurricanes that work their way past Cuba, turn in the wrong direction, and suck tremendous amounts of energy from the warm surface waters. They thunder in the Gulf for days, growing bigger and bigger, then slam into the shoreline, sometimes just making a mess, sometimes wrecking everything in their way, and sometimes making a disaster.

When the big storms come in, Carmen is not to be found in Pass Christian. There is too much history there. She was ten years old in 1969 when the storm of all storms, Camille, pushed its eye up through the Gulf and landed in Pass Christian. Just east on the coast, before you drive past the casino near Gulfport, is an old shrimp boat that sits as a rusting monument to Camille—not that she needed one, because that is one storm no one can forget. The ruined boat is on dry land and faces the Gulf. Everyone uses Camille to set the measure for storms that followed. It was a Category Five hurricane that killed 259 people and at its peak had sustained wind speed of 190 miles per hour. It left $1.4 billion in damages, measured in those sturdy old 1969 dollars that actually had some value. Until recently, nothing quite compared. It is easy to understand why people who lived through that one concluded they could live through anything. What could possibly be worse?

Carmen remembered climbing into one of two cars—one for her father and one for her mother—with some brothers and heading for "the country" as Camille approached. "The country" is not as exotic a destination as it might sound. Seven miles inland, just over the bridge, it was far enough to move the family out of the face of the storm, away from all the energy that would be expended when the leading edge hit land. Carmen's family had kin inland, with houses sturdy enough to stand bravely in the face of wind and rain without folding up like soggy cardboard boxes. Inland was where most everyone with any sense went when the storms came. A few stayed behind—young men and women, fueled by barbecue and beer, who rode it out and can brag forever about partying through the apocalypse. Escaping was a particularly good idea in Pass Christian, which has water of one kind or another all around it. It may well have been protected by Providence through all these years of storms, but certainly not by geography. It is as exposed as a town can be.

Camille blasted in, did her worst, and then was downgraded, first to tropical storm status and then just to a lot of rain. Such is the fate of all hurricanes, which, deprived of their warm-water energy source, cannot thrive for long on land. It took Carmen and her dad, Uncle Dansler, and the rest of the family three days to move those seven miles back home, sawing their way through the downed trees and driving through Camille's wreckage. At home Carmen remembers riding on her dad's shoulders and surveying the damage to her lovely little town. The memory of men tossing bodies like logs into the back of a truck next to Trinity Church, bodies of whole families she had known, will never leave her. Many people had sought protection there, believing that if the building had weathered other hurricanes, it would survive Camille too. It was a common mistake along the coast. You can imagine the scene, praying first for God to deliver them, and then for God to forgive them, and then for God to welcome them home. Most of those who stayed behind to party were killed too.

I sat with Carmen and listened to her Camille story and realized that when you are fortunate enough to be with a person who remembers and recounts everything so clearly, you should just shut up and listen. I wanted to talk with her about politics, about the presidency, about what happens when you realize at the darkest moment that you are actually alone and that your government will not help you, cannot help you, doesn't even know you exist. Instead I just sat there, lost in her story and looking at her high cheekbones, crystal-clear eyes, and bronze skin, occasionally dampened by a tear. She was so comfortable that when I gave her a handkerchief to blow her nose, she used it and started to hand it back before she said, "Whoops!" and laughed through her tears, snatched it into the palm of her hand, and kept on talking. Her face was unusual, with such strong features, that I asked her where she came from. The simple answer was "right here," in Pass Christian, where her family had been forever. But that, of course, was not what I meant.

She retrieved her family album, assembled with great detail and affection for a reunion a couple of decades earlier. It went all the way back to the days of slavery. Looking at it was like following a genetic map. First there were slaves who bore children to plantation owners. Then there were some big postslavery families. Then there were Seminole Indians, whites, Creoles—just about every type of person who settled from the Gulf north to, say, the middle of Mississippi. Time passed and more generations came along, and then there was Carmen, delivered by her ancestors as the ultimate American, sitting here in her house in the sky and talking about politics.

Someone once said, if you want to find spirit in the Deep South, head for saltwater. Soulful, brave people are drawn to the water. Cautious, frightened people live inland or up north, where there is less risk but much less reward. This truth works all along the Gulf Coast. It helps explain why New Orleans is such a wonderfully wild venue, even when it is *not* Mardi Gras, and why folks along the coast seem to have maybe a little more passion closer to the surface.

You would have to love it to live in Pass Christian. Many people enjoy visiting the beaches of the Atlantic and the Gulf for a few weeks during the summer, when it's hot and the prospect of a splash in saltwater makes sand in your pants a small price to pay. They park themselves in air-conditioned comfort, sip fruity beverages, chomp on fat boiled shrimp, and think about how nice it would be on permanent vacation by the sea. Discomfort for the visitor is getting sand in your sunscreen, or maybe a lobster-red sunburn, or running into a jellyfish, or being stung by a yellow jacket exploring your cantaloupe. The price is a lot higher for the people who live along the water all the time. If you live by the ocean or the Gulf, it pays to keep a close eye on the water, particularly when the barometric pressure is dropping, it's late summer, and the waters off the African coast are stirring up big trouble that inevitably makes its way westward. There may be no power in the Western Hemisphere to match the fury of those hurricanes.

In my head I kept thanking Providence that I had made several calls to find Carmen Dedeaux, because she was such a perfect example of a point I wanted to make about the unfolding presidential campaign. So much of what we pay attention to in media coverage of politics is meaningless, a drumbeat of name-calling, polling results, speculation, endless strategy, and gamesmanship. The mechanics of campaigns fascinate media, but they do not touch voters. The experiences in voters' lives inform their voting decisions. If food critics wrote this way, their stories would be all about spats in the kitchen, bloody paring-knife accidents, who has the most potatoes, and surveys about who is likely to eat meat or fish (with vegetarians playing the role of the independents). You would never know that the meal was great. To be sure, presidential campaigns have never been the place to turn to for uplifting behavior and inspiration. But life goes on, sometimes quite bitterly, outside the confines of media attention or campaign rhetoric. It will certainly matter to most people who wins the presidential election, but not to the extent that the process defines the waking moments of each day. There are many other things—some of them small and some of them vast—beyond the frantic news reports about the latest bump on the presidential campaign trail.

Life-changing events burst on the scene. They will define forever how a person views politicians and government. We are told it's all about the economy or all about health care, but down where the people actually live, it might be all about the day they almost died, the day they could find no help, or the day they fell into the viselike embrace of despair and gave up.

We pay little attention to government in America until we need it, which is actually a blessing when you think about what it would be like if the presidential campaign were going on all the time. Imagine being that political! It would be like living in Europe, where everyone is political all the time. Generally for most Americans, government is highways, tax collection, military spending, distant wars, parking meters, pothole repairs, and bothering an alderman until someone comes to cut the trees on the parkway. But when we need it—when disaster or disease or our enemies strike us—the level of expectation rises fast. We want government to respond to our needs, which is in no way out of line. It's what we pay for. It's why we are a society, not just a sprawling land of disconnected individuals.

For a time Carmen Dedeaux was a lost American in the wake of a disaster that helped shift public opinion not only against President Bush but also against the thought that the federal government was competent, that it might be able to help people who are oppressed, impoverished, wave-tossed by the great storms of life. That was, perhaps, an unfair assessment. New Orleans's problems with Katrina, and Pass Christian's too, were not created by the Bush administration. They stretched all the way back to the construction of a city below sea level that would be administered for generations by dubious political characters and live in the shadow of threat from weather, from the Gulf, and from the Mississippi River. The assumption behind federal disaster planning for New Orleans was that the first three days would be the province of the locals. The feds would gear up and move in once the first responders had done their jobs. No one thought to ask what might happen if lines of communication and transit were so crippled by a hurricane that the locals simply couldn't respond, which in many places is what happened.

Then again, Bush's first visit to the disaster wasn't really a visit. It was a flyover in *Air Force One*. That simply added emphasis to the thought that he didn't care. Flying over a disaster is truly a faceless, bloodless exercise—up there it's cool and clean. Down on the ground, where fuel oil and muck and loss mix in a smelly profusion, it's not. It's much worse when a president is flying over an area like New Orleans that has been all but abandoned by people of means, who had the wherewithal to get away, as opposed to poor people, many of them black, who did not. It would be wrong to argue that President Bush did not care, but it's not wrong to argue that his behavior made it seem as though he didn't care.

Across the region the reaction to government was not uniform. Mississippi governor Haley Barbour got high marks for responding immediately to Katrina. Louisiana and its former governor, Kathleen Blanco, did not. All around, for government the problem was one of appearances. People didn't get to see all of the heroic Coast Guard rescues. They didn't get to see the Mississippi Fish and Game agents out in their motorboats saving lives. They didn't get to see the cops who didn't flee, who stayed behind to serve and protect, just as always. What they saw of Katrina looked bad from the first day, stayed looking bad for quite some time, and then glued itself to President Bush as part of his troubling legacy. The inevitable bureaucracy that moved in to help with rebuilding and salvage, with its confusion and trailers with their formaldehyde gas and endless paperwork, didn't help.

When you look at Carmen Dedeaux, you can see all the souls who found themselves crushed by Katrina. She is not a poor person who was left behind, nor were the other storm victims in Pass Christian, where most people owned their own homes or lived in houses that had been passed down through generations. A storm of unprec-

edented fury, Katrina destroyed Pass Christian and many other communities along the Gulf, and flooded and ruined New Orleans, one
of America's most romantic cities. Perhaps most important, the storm
laid bare the painful reality that race and poverty still march hand in
hand, particularly in the Deep South. It is no wonder then, pondering Carmen's story, that so many Americans have concluded their
country is going in the wrong direction.

That thought is like tinder in the political process, just waiting
for the right spark. Katrina might not have been a direct issue on the
campaign trail, though every candidate who could visited the disaster
area during the primaries. But it was an important part of the backdrop, perhaps the most visible of all the reasons that explained the
nation's angst about its direction. Arguments about whether fixing
blame is fair or timely simply don't matter when the pain of disaster
is delivered to the living rooms of America with such clarity. That the
coverage was filled with rumors and slanders doesn't matter much
either. A big slice of presidential politics is about perception. The
ghost of one of our most determined humanitarian presidents, Her-
bert Hoover, could tell you all about that. Hoover saved millions of
lives heading famine relief for Russia when he was the U.S. commerce
secretary in the early 1920s, but he became forever linked in the public mind with the Great Depression that followed his presidency.

The perception after Katrina was that President Bush's federal
government screwed up just about everything. Because of that, Republicans were running for reelection in an atmosphere that somehow blamed them even for the weather, which was perhaps the only
undebatable, concrete, and obvious culprit in the case of Katrina.

When I met Carmen Dedeaux, the storm was long over, rebuilding was under way in most places, and the Democrats and Republicans were on their primary campaign romp, a festival of finger-
pointing and too many debates for anyone to follow with much

interest. It was about halfway through a campaign that had already
been in progress for a year.

New York senator Hillary Clinton, the likely and presumptive
(at least *she* presumed it) Democratic nominee, faced a strong challenge from Illinois senator Barack Obama, a black Chicagoan whose
middle name was Hussein and whose dad was black and Kenyan,
and his mom not Kenyan and white. (These facts alone would have
wrecked his chances by conventional political measure. But it would
become apparent that Obama and his campaign people were not using conventional political measures much at all.) Former North Carolina senator John Edwards was the best-looking of the Democrats.
A wealthy man and onetime vice-presidential candidate (with John
Kerry last time around), on the 2008 trail he had taken to channeling
Woody Guthrie and an array of 1950s social and labor reformers in
reaching back to his father's factory roots. But his trial-lawyer profes-
sion, affection for four-hundred-dollar haircuts, and preening raised
questions about his bona fides. This was no Joe Hill.

The rest of them signed up as also-rans—even veteran senators
Joe Biden of Delaware and Chris Dodd of Connecticut. Alaskan
Mike Gravel might actually have had a contribution to make, but due
to so much campaign noise, no one could tell. New Mexico governor
Bill Richardson seemed by far the smartest of the lot and the most
experienced too. He had been reelected in 2006 with the support of
seven in ten voters and had a deep background as U.S. ambassador to
the United Nations and a long record of public service. To his credit,
Dennis Kucinich, with never even a tiny chance of winning the nomination, served well as the voice of reason amid the babbling, battling
Democrats. He received attention for marrying well. For most of the
Democrats the problem was the same: money. Senator Clinton had
sucked up all the early dollars from all the usual Democratic sources.
She and her husband, the former president, had made it clear one

way or another that the question on the table was loyalty, however that might be expressed, and early money was certainly a good way.

The Republicans, it seemed, had somehow gone crazy and had no voice of reason of their own. "Not President Bush" seemed to be their most important qualification. It was impossible to tell whom they might nominate. It appeared the options would include former New York mayor Rudy Giuliani, who was so Big Apple that he had dressed as a woman on national TV and was the perfect model of insensitivity in divorce proceedings. The thrice-wed Giuliani had announced one of his marital breakups at a news conference. His wife didn't know it was coming. This bumped another Republican who was not running, Newt Gingrich—who had discussed terms for divorce with a hospitalized wife recuperating from cancer—out of first place in the Outrageous Republican Behavior in the Face of Family Values Rhetoric competition.

Mitt Romney, the former progressive Massachusetts governor and Mormon, had turned away from moderation and embraced a string of highly conservative positions in a bold attempt to make himself attractive to the Republican base. Romney came from certified Michigan Republican blood. His father was former Michigan governor George Romney, which was both an asset and a liability. The modern Republican party bore no resemblance to the party of George Romney, whose own presidential campaign collapsed after he claimed he had been "brainwashed" to support the Vietnam War. Also, was the nation ready for a Mormon president? What makes the unusual rituals of Catholicism (bread and wine become body and blood, and then they eat and drink it) and the defining lifestyles and culture of Judaism and the unabashed spirituality of fundamentalism (casting out demons and speaking in tongues in some cases) acceptable in American culture is familiarity. Few people, I suspect, could identify the Angel Moroni or his role in Mormon belief. They might also find puzzling the fact that the church is run by a prophet and a whole posterful of white men who, for the most part, seem old. Mormons are no longer polygamous and haven't been for many years, though that keeps coming up as spin-off groups and breakaway believers adopt some very old, controversial ways. All that aside, though, one thing was certain: the Republicans were ready for a man who could bankroll his own campaign, and Romney, Angel Moroni or not, had the money for that.

Mike Huckabee, the former Arkansas governor and Baptist preacher—who, it was later revealed, thought it would be good if the Constitution were a little bit more like the Bible—popped up and drew a lot of attention from the party's most fervent believers, conservative Christians. In addition to speaking to the Christian conservatives of the party's base, he also played garage-band-level electric bass, which made him seem unusually cool for a Republican. Once the size of a small manatee, he had lost a hundred pounds through diet and exercise. Media, which generally shy away from ardent believers for their perceived lack of coolness, found a cool character indeed in the former governor. He was intensively profiled and interviewed, and for a while showed up everywhere. Here was a Christian conservative Republican who would be a good guy to hang out with, it seemed. But he was such a product of just one sliver of Republicanism that it also seemed clear he would not be able to gather much of a Republican following. He segued handily into an engaging talking-head role after it became apparent his candidacy was going nowhere.

Fred Thompson, the phlegmatic former Tennessee senator and actor who managed to muster the demeanor of a hound dog on a hot, hot afternoon, was a candidate for a while and got a lot of media attention for a few weeks as the party's great white hope. The media buzz may have been a measure of how desperate the Republicans looked, even to their own supporters. You weren't about to find Fred Thompson in drag, that's for sure. But it seemed he was not interested in heavy political lifting. The media blather receded after Thompson's passive debate and public performances, a sign that most of his support came from newspaper, magazine, and internet kingmaker wannabes who misinterpreted star power for staying power.

And, with no chance at all, Arizona senator John McCain, war hero, veteran troublemaker, and sometimes cranky character, announced his candidacy. He was soundly disliked by many Republicans who still believed President Bush was doing a fine job (which was many of them when this long, long primary season got under way). McCain gassed up his Straight Talk Express bus, gathered up a gaggle of friendly reporters, and hit the road, fueling his media entourage with donuts, humor, and a rare authenticity, dispensed during sessions around a table at the back of the bus. For quite some time the media, he said, were his constituency, which was fine with him. Liability traveled with the senator. He was in his eighth decade, making him quite old for the White House. His battles with melanoma had left him scarred and appearing vulnerable. The torture and mistreatment he had suffered as a prisoner of war in Vietnam had left him unable to raise his arms over his head. He was indeed a maverick, and Republicans pay a price for that kind of behavior. McCain had skeletons in his past too, one of the most troubling being the role he had played in the savings-and-loan scandal of the late 1980s. But he was that most unusual of things in politics, a genuine hero who had given almost all his life to his country. One level of presidential campaigning is about the story a candidate tells, and McCain had the most powerful story in the Republican field, perhaps in any field. He had wrapped himself in the demands of his nation and put his life on the line many times, so he did not need to wrap himself in its flag to look patriotic on the campaign trail.

Some others were in the mix too, but no one put much of a dent in the process. Texas congressman Ron Paul entered the race, but probably as a Libertarian more than a Republican because, well, where else can a Libertarian run in a primary contest? He was the most determined among those destined to lose. Long after his time had passed, his lawn signs still sprouted like daffodils in fields around America.

Add them up in both parties and in the beginning there were twenty-three people running for president. All but one would lose the race, but no one thinks much about that when they first burst from the starting gate. They all seem so fresh and full of . . . rhetoric? Yes, rhetoric. Enough for a total of twenty-eight primary and general election debates and joint appearances beginning in April 2007, and two town halls from inception to Election Day, the most memorable ones occurring only at the end, after the field had been well cleared of losers.

The 2008 Democratic primary campaign had actually opened at the Democratic National Convention in Boston in 2004, where Obama had delivered the keynote address and left everyone with any sense at all wondering when he would run for the White House. It was that good. It would not take many months to answer that question, which put Senator Clinton and her key supporter, former President Bill, into high gear in a bid to stop Obama. The rest of the field was watching from the sidelines, or at least diminished as either a Greek chorus or a peanut gallery, depending on the issue.

The Republican primary campaign began as soon as it became apparent that President Bush could turn anything he touched into dirt. The wars went badly, and word was delivered that the more disastrous of the two had been launched on dubious evidence of weapons of mass destruction that no one ever found. A troubling drumbeat of ethical misbehavior across his administration sounded. An administration that delighted in secrecy also apparently delighted in leaks, particularly when they were used to torpedo political enemies like gabby former ambassadors and their spooky CIA wives. Then Vice President Cheney, the most secretive but powerful vice president in modern history, shot a lawyer friend in the face on one

of those bird hunts where people ride to the kill in limos. This unleashed cascades of jokes, not only about Cheney, who is not a funny
character, but about hunting seasons for lawyers, and so on. These
were just the preliminaries.

The Bush administration was in steep decline almost from the
day it began its second term. What a change. President Bush had
enjoyed the strongest approval ratings in history just after the 9/11
terrorist assaults that claimed victims in New York, Washington, and
Pennsylvania. In times of trouble it would appear that Americans
rally around flags and presidents. But the numbers over time made it
look as though someone had poked a hole in the bottom of his ship
of state. Bush was sinking so quickly that even his remaining supporters were in despair as the nation moved toward choosing a new
president.

That brought out the best and the worst in the Republican party
as ethical visionaries jousted with opportunistic grave dancers to
see who would win the right to walk into an Oval Office that had
been trashed by its previous occupant. The nation's standing in the
world, so bright just a few years back when it was muscling Slobodan
Milosevic into prison in The Hague, was in the tank, undercut by reports of sanctioned torture in Iraqi prisons and the shipment of prisoners to torture-happy allies for interrogation. Its debts and deficits
had ballooned. A perception was afoot that this particular presidency
was all about rich people and preserving their wealth through tax cuts,
no matter the expense. It was as though the clock that had begun tick-
ing when Ronald Reagan ran on the message that government *was*
the problem, not the solution, had run out. If the conservative objective had been to wreck the reputation of the federal government, the
fates were lining up to show just how well Bush and his predecessors,
going all the way back to Reagan's first year in office, had done their
job. The war in Iraq was constructed on lies. The war in Afghanistan was being shortchanged. All of that set the stage for one of the

strangest Republican campaigns in modern times. Ultimately the dominant theme, even on the Republican side, would be reform, an immense irony in the wake of eight years of Republican control of the White House and six of Congress.

Beyond politics, nature was gearing up in August 2005 to send a powerful message that would expose weaknesses that reached to the very core of the Bush administration. Certainly there were people who fared worse than Carmen Dedeaux as that message played out. She lived to tell the story, and many of them did not.

It takes good weather sense to live in Pass Christian, particularly in late summer when the storms that build off the west coast of Africa work their way across the Atlantic and slam into the Caribbean, along the coast of the southeastern United States or in the Gulf of Mexico. I have been through two hurricanes. The first was at the northern end of a storm called Agnes in 1972 that dropped so much rain on Pennsylvania that the Susquehanna River looked like it would explode. It remains the worst storm in Pennsylvania history. It carried away boats, cars, houses, people—whatever got in its way. It poured over embankments and floodwalls alike, sending cappuccino-like waters into towns all along the river. Straining to find the right metaphor, one of my journalist friends described the river towns as "muddied beads on a necklace of devastation."

My second storm was Hurricane Allen, a Category Five that bounced around the Gulf of Mexico in 1980. I chased it from Corpus Christi all the way down to Brownsville in a Pontiac I had rented from Rent-A-Wreck because none of the mainline car rental companies would let you take a new car into the storm. And I do mean chased. In the days before cable news executives sent pretty young men and women in handsome slickers to stand in the high winds and shout "*It's very windy!*" reporters tracked hurricanes by phone and on the road. Because you could never tell where they would land, you had to be fleet, courageous (or just stupid? in retrospect, it seems stupid), and, most of all, mobile. If every other car on the road was heading north, the hurricane reporter headed south, hoping to settle in before landfall to witness and then recount the full fury of the storm and talk to people nowhere near a rail line who would say it sounded either just like a freight train coming or maybe the end of the world. After the back fell off my hotel in Corpus Christi and splashed into the bay, I headed south to spend a night in Refugio with a retired judge and her family, eating ham-and-cheese sandwiches in a boarded-up house, singing Hank Williams songs, and waiting for the storm to hit. But it missed. So I drove south through tornadoes and blinding rain past the vast King Ranch to Brownsville, where I helped a guy named Skipper tape up the windows at a hotel where the only guests were a bunch of Israeli tourists.

We drank beer and watched cabanas from the swimming pool fly through the air past the huge plate glass windows. Skipper recommended we move promptly to the center of the building. There wasn't a dry space in the place. My brand-new blue Korean sneakers started wicking dye up my sand-colored Levi's. The worse the storm got, the bluer my pants got. I was a dye-fueled hurricane pant gauge, perhaps the very first. Heading back north, I hitched a ride with a telephone company repairman who wore a pistol because rattlesnakes, seeking refuge from all that rain, tended to gather around the elevated dirt bases of telephone poles. He drove down a highway that was submerged. You could see nothing but water. He said, "Just luck, I guess" when I asked him how he knew where the road was. I was very happy to leave that storm.

But I had learned two things. First, if you want to be a hurricane reporter, don't wear cheap Korean sneakers, and if there is any possible way to escape before the storm hits, get out.

Raised in a region that faced a couple of big storms every season, Carmen Dedeaux knew this intuitively, so in late August 2005, when a big storm began taking shape out in the Caribbean, she knew she would probably have to leave. She didn't know where she would go, but she knew she had to get her kids, her mother, all her kin who would go, out of town. Two of her brothers, obviously full of the balls-out *joie de vivre* that describes so many people who live that far south in Louisiana and Mississippi, decided to ride it out. They were among just a small collection of Pass Christian's 6,500 citizens who stayed behind. They would stand full in the face of this Katrina storm with beer and barbecue in hand, because that's what you did when you were a young man in hurricane land. Legends grow from those kinds of experiences. They planned to start the barbecue on Monday morning and be drinking and eating by the time the storm hit. They had emergency supplies on hand, batteries and lights and the like. They were prepared.

Carmen said she hadn't known where to go to weather this storm. The old option, the country, was as gone as all of those 1969 relatives were gone. She was such a local girl that she was a little lost when she got too many miles from Pass Christian, which is a simple, thin kind of place to get around in as it stretches out along the Gulf. But you didn't want to be there if it was about to get rough. At least Carmen didn't want to be there. The images of those Camille bodies had never left her. A young girl seeing such a thing carries that nightmare for life.

Pass Christian boarded itself up and waited for the storm. It was Saturday, August 27, 2005. Carmen got a call from her ex-husband, Michael, who wanted to know whether she and the children had a place to stay. Carmen told him she knew they all had to leave because it was going to be a bad storm, but she didn't know where to go. The people she might typically go to stay with were also leaving. Sometimes things had been tense between Carmen and her ex, but this time she thought it would be prudent to take him up on his offer of housing in Jackson, 140 miles north. He worked there for the Veterans Administration. It would be safe and comfortable. And because

one of her children had attended school at Jackson, she knew at least
how to get to the school. But she was afraid if she depended on her
own strained sense of directions, "I would probably end up somewhere in Georgia." Michael told her he would meet her at Jackson
State University so the trip would be familiar for her. Carmen called
her mother and told her they were all going to Jackson, that Michael
would provide the food, that they were to bring only their necessities.
Her mother had been through so many hurricanes in her life that
packing to go was almost automatic. At 5 a.m. on Sunday, August
28, Carmen, her mother, and her children squeezed into the car and
headed for Jackson. It was not yet raining in Pass Christian, but the
wind was picking up. Her brothers Rodney and Michael—Nay and
Pike in the family—checked up on their barbecue provisions at Pike's
house and prepared to weather what would become a storm deadlier
than Camille, which Pike's house had escaped. It would be the worst
storm ever to hit Pass Christian.

Carmen and the family got to Jackson in just a few hours. She
called her brothers Sunday night. They reported rain and some
wind, but nothing too bad. Maybe this was another one of those false
alarms. A hurricane can look like it's coming right at you from the
satellite photos and then mysteriously shift direction a bit and miss
completely. By Monday morning everyone would know, but the satellite photos on the weather channels did not look good. Katrina had
grown to fill much of the top of the Gulf. She was Category Four at
some points, but the winds were up and down. Out in the Gulf, National Oceanic and Atmospheric Administration buoys had recorded
forty-two-foot waves. Over time the storm made three landfalls, the
first being at 6:10 a.m. at Buras on the Mississippi Delta. Katrina's
eastern-eye wall, the strongest part of the storm, made landfall in the
same place hit by Camille in 1969, Pass Christian.

President Bush and his entourage were out west on a political
trip when Katrina pushed its way into Mississippi and Louisiana. It

had a twenty-four-foot-high wall of water in front of it by the time it reached the beaches at Pass Christian. There was nothing to stop it. The water swept over the seawall and destroyed the fish-icing plant and the harbor structures. It tossed fishing trawlers around like toys. Then it moved up onto the rise that overlooks the Gulf and wrecked a long line of once-pristine mansions, the pride of Pass Christian, that looked out onto the Gulf. Then it moved inland and destroyed roughly four of every five homes. It brought water from the canals around Pass Christian into the disaster too. Businesses. Banks. Restaurants. Hardware stores. It was almost all gone.

Meanwhile the president dropped in at Phoenix to take a birthday picture with John McCain, who was turning sixty-nine. It was sunny, and they were smiling like the old buddies they weren't. Then Bush went off to answer Medicare questions at a public forum at a senior center. If he was aware of the scale of disaster playing out on the Gulf Coast, he wasn't showing it. He had been briefed by an array of disaster officials who told him they were prepared for the storm, though they were worried about its size and particularly concerned about its consequences for New Orleans. He asked no questions. Within hours they knew they did not have what they needed to respond to Katrina.

By the time Katrina made landfall, Pike was making breakfast for him and Nay at Pike's house. At 6:20 a.m. Monday, and with no warning, a wall of water hit the house, bursting through the storm doors. They grabbed the dog and the generator and raced upstairs as the water burst through the doors. They had no time to get their emergency supplies. They had no food, no water. Behind them on the steps to the attic, the water was sloshing and creating waves, rising and falling like waves on a beach. Carmen had been on the phone with them off and on for hours. They told her water came up suddenly and then a terrific wind started to blow. From the peephole in the roof of the attic they could see nothing but water and some rooftops where Pass Christian had been. Houses, cars, vans—they were all floating on the wave that came in with Katrina. The boys joked and picked on each other, she said, but later they would tell her they were both terrified that they were going to die in that house. Pike was filled with remorse. He had persuaded his brother to stay with him for a party, and instead he was looking at death for both of them.

They could hear the house shifting and cracking, and furniture and appliances banging around downstairs, but there was nothing they could do. The force of the water tore the front porch from the house. Pike's shed of his mechanic's tools disappeared. They watched his van float by. Nearby the priest's house from the Catholic church floated from its foundation and disappeared. Two houses across the street lifted from their foundations and began slamming into each other until they cracked apart and disappeared. Carmen stayed on the phone with her brothers until 9:30 a.m. She told them the weather reports in Jackson said the worst would be over by 12:30 p.m. Pike told her, "12:30? I don't know if we can last until 12:30!" Then the phones went dead and stayed dead.

When Carmen turned to the media to find out what was happening, she was disappointed. Most of the news was about the fact that Katrina had missed New Orleans. Then the news was about people trapped in the Superdome with no food or water. A day later the news was all about the levies and the flooding of New Orleans. She was looking at a city that had a flood but thinking of a hometown just up the coast that was probably gone. Were her brothers still alive? Was the house still standing? What about her house down on Hiern Avenue on the other side of the railroad tracks? Did the wind and water get back in there? She had a thousand questions.

The only way to answer any of them was to coax her ex-husband to get into the car and drive back to Pass Christian as soon as she could. She would try to find her brothers, check out her mother's house, and stop at her house to pick up some clothing for the kids.

They would have to go to school in Jackson, and she did not want to
have to buy new clothing for them.

After a conversation, Carmen and Michael got in the car and
headed south. Remembering her own experience after Camille, she
decided her children should stay in Jackson. She didn't know what
she would find at her brother's house. The chance they might see
their uncles drowned, crushed, or who knows what was not worth
risking. But she knew she had to go herself. She did not want strang-
ers finding the remains of her brothers. Years later these thoughts
remained so vivid for her that she wept when she told the story. "I
really did think my brothers were dead," she said.

The closer they came to the coast, the more apparent was the
extent of the disaster. Finally they arrived at Pass Christian. The town
was still open. People were struggling to get to what remained of their
homes, cutting trees, moving debris. She described a scene that was
only vaguely familiar to her. The park with its big iron swings was
uprooted and gone. The Beach Road, Route 90, was destroyed. The
massive live oak that graced the park was uprooted. She remembered
climbing over debris and then looking down the street. Only two
houses remained. One of them was Pike's. The house that had been
on the corner was gone. The minute she saw her brother's house,
Carmen started to run, slipping and sliding in the muck and mud on
the street. She could make out two figures standing on what was left
of the porch. It was Pike and Nay. Both of them wore cutoffs. One of
them wore two different shoes, one a slipper and one a flip-flop. She
ran to them, hugged them, and told them she loved them.

"Girl," said Nay, "what are you doing here?" She said she had
to come, that she knew she had to come when they stopped answer-
ing the phone. She asked about the houses of her other brothers, of
her mother. They were all gone. The boys told her they had not had
a chance to go down the tracks to Hiern Avenue to see her house.
Carmen took her ex-husband and headed down the tracks. What

she found was confusing. All her points of reference were gone. Mrs. Rose's house and the Sauciers' house had disappeared.

She remembers walking down the track, but she can't recall what was there as she passed through the wreckage. It's even hard for her to recall what was there before Katrina. Vast piles of wreckage with houses broken in half filled the area. In the survey conducted by authorities in the wake of the storm, Pass Christian was described simply as "destroyed," with nothing much left. How could a house just disappear? Suspend it in seawater and add a 140-mile-per-hour wind and there is no telling what happens to a house. Some of them were never found. Bodies were found miles from town. For more than a year, obituaries listed August 29 as the likely date of death. Remains, belongings, the precious things people use to build their lives were spread all over the Gulf Coast. More than 500 people were killed in Mississippi alone.

Carmen's heart almost stopped when she saw her lot. What remained were some cement blocks the house had been sitting on. Nothing else. Big trees were knocked over. She climbed the side of one to look around. She saw her house about a hundred yards down Hiern Avenue, wedged up against a utility pole. She and Michael rushed to the house. As a measure of the shock she was suffering, she searched for her keys to open the front door, even though the picture window had been broken from the front of the home and anyone could just step in. Everything in the house was ruined. She managed to collect some clothing to take back to Jackson for her children. The trophies and prizes she had saved, the legacies of four smart children and one focused, determined mother, were all swept away. They got what they could collect and left.

It would be weeks before Carmen could return to Pass Christian. By the time she came back to her house, which she assumed would be open to her, she found that someone had bulldozed straight through the building. Part of it was on one side of the street, part of it on the other. She began digging in the collapsed structure, trying to find signs that would tell her what room she was in. Every weekend for four weeks she went back to look for her belongings in the wreckage. She slept in her car. She wanted the trophies and the shiny little crowns her daughter had won in beauty contests. She wanted all those mementos she had collected over her lifetime, the reminders she had used in her home to bring back happy memories of her children. She found one baby shoe, one of a pair she had planned to bronze.

That was the political, the emotional, the personal breaking point for Carmen Dedeaux. She remembers what she shouted to an empty sky: "Why, God, why would you do this to the kind of people who live out here? There cannot be a God who would allow this to happen."

It was the darkest moment of her life, she recalled later, a moment of hopelessness and despair. She had reached bottom. She had lived for her children, sacrificed for them, pushed them to do well in school. She had tried always to be kind. She prayed. She went to church. The injustice of it all overwhelmed her.

She went back to Jackson and stopped praying. Stopped going to church. Stopped believing. She didn't like it in Jackson. In the first place, she said, it was the only time her in life she was ever made to feel "black." It might be hard to believe, given its history, but in the saga of race relations Mississippi is now a bright spot in the South. In Pass Christian, Carmen said, she never felt as though she was anyone but Carmen Dedeaux, an individual, and her children were never viewed as anything other than bright, well-behaved kids. Jackson, with its big-city divisions, even with divisions within the black community, was simply not like that. A woman whose life had been defined by the confines of tiny Pass Christian, she knew she couldn't stay there.

What happened to her next made the situation that much more complex. In the process of applying for what assistance she could find, someone in a federal office had checked the "has residence" box on an application instead of "no residence." That closed the door on $2,300 in emergency assistance for people who had lost their homes. It took four months to get that corrected. Then she became enmeshed in the "It's a flood—no, it's a hurricane" debate that insurance companies were using to deny benefits all along the coast. If a person had flood insurance and it wasn't called a flood, it wasn't covered. If a person had hurricane insurance and it was called a flood instead, same problem. She spent hours standing in line to apply for help, only to find she couldn't qualify and would have to go wait in another line. People wanted documents that had been destroyed. Banks wanted houses as collateral for people who were at the bank because they had lost their homes. In one success, Carmen finally managed to convince her insurance company to pay off the mortgage on her home on the grounds that, by anyone's measure, thirty-five feet of water over your house was a flood. But there was no money left to build a new home. Her credit rating was weak too. Over the years, anytime her children needed anything, she just went into debt. It built up. Now she was looking at a life in a small FEMA trailer on her lot.

This all began to change months after the disaster. She had sent a pleading email to just about everyone she could think of, telling about her predicament. One day she came home from work to find a card from a woman at Samaritan's Purse stuck in her trailer door. It offered a number. When she called, the Samaritan's Purse people said they were ready to help. Samaritan's Purse is a charity run by Billy Graham's son, Franklin Graham. Its work is generally international, but along with many other charitable organizations it was swept into post-Katrina recovery efforts by the sheer volume of need caused by the storm.

There was a conversation. First, a talk about God. Then, about need. She connected with people from the First Baptist Church of Simpsonville, South Carolina. God was just screaming out to try to convince people to get their lives together, they told her. God had to do something to get people's attention, she replied. "We were just good people that got caught up in the bad stuff." Carmen found herself going back to church, not in any way coerced to return but gently urged to go back to see whether that part of her broken life could be repaired. It could. Then some other unexpected people showed up: Mennonites who had been dispatched from Pennsylvania, where the church's disaster relief operation has its headquarters near an outlet mall in Lancaster. The Mennonites, simple people by choice but tremendously efficient and skilled at home building, announced they would frame a new house for her. Carmen said she had no money. They told her that didn't matter, that it was just an honor for them to be able to help. So they built her a house up in the sky, eighteen feet above sea level, and a porch so high it is unlikely any future hurricane would be able to harm it. The house is anchored to a thick concrete slab. Steel cables run through the pillars all the way up to the roof. If they cut themselves, the Mennonites left thumbprints in blood on the framing. They wrote scripture there too. This house will not float away, and it is unlikely to be blown away either. Carmen and the Mennonites became fast friends, but the Mennonites would not take so much as a sandwich from her. She found herself going to her new house at night, just to sit there on the framed-out floors, with the framed-out walls around her and the beginning of a roof above her head.

When that framing was complete, the First Baptist Church of Simpsonville, which dedicates itself to an annual mission of rebuilding a home in Appalachia, shifted its focus and moved in to finish the inside of Carmen's house. They put up the drywall and the finish work and helped her fix her beliefs at the same time. Carmen calls it the house that love built.

I found Carmen through Kevin King, who heads the Mennonite Disaster Relief Service. He and his daughter have visited her a few times, and she has attended various Mennonite seminars to thank them for their help and pray with them. I had talked to him earlier about the church effort in the face of such a huge disaster. "Mennonites don't sit well when there's trouble," King said. At the peak of the Katrina crisis, when the federal government was still trying to figure out how to get water to New Orleans, King had 250 Canadian Mennonites waiting in line to head to the Deep South to help wherever they were needed. He had a lot more on site with their chainsaws, clearing trees from houses, fixing what could be fixed, feeding people who were hungry, loading up trailer trucks, and heading toward trouble. The local Mennonite bishops surveyed and reported on the need, and volunteers showed up to help.

It was sunny and warm when I met Carmen at her new house, one of the few reconstructed buildings on her street. But the Mennonites, the Baptists, and a host of other volunteers from various denominations were still at work all over town. It was a little distracting to see what appeared to be Old Order Amish women in black dresses with bright blue aprons and fine linen bonnets in the streets of Pass Christian. Gospel singers and Catholics were also in the area. In fact it looked as though some kind of ecumenical construction company had moved in to rebuild the place. Some people wouldn't be coming home for sure. There were still many ghostly lots in town, with nothing left but some cement steps and pipes coming up from the ground for utilities and big, sprawling live oaks standing as silent witnesses to what had happened.

I talked politics for an hour or so with Carmen, but nothing we could say compared to the story she had already told. She is very traditional. As a young woman, like everyone else in her family, someone else helped her decide. "Bubba said vote for the Democrats. That's how it was," she said. If you ask her whether she is conservative or liberal, the most you can get out of her is "in between." She doesn't like the idea of people getting money for nothing, but she knows food stamps and Medicaid benefits are crucial for some people. She despises the war in Iraq and believes it was constructed on lies. She has a son in the air force, and she worries he will be drawn into battle. But when the conversation moves toward Katrina, her affect changes. This is about her, her kin, her life.

"I feel like we should have gotten our immediate needs met. That should not have depended on the Mennonites or on volunteers or anyone else. Maybe it was just like 9/11 in New York—immediately afterward, no one knew what to do. It was that big. But we couldn't get food or water or a place to stay. They came in and cleared the streets, but what did they do that for? They didn't do anything for us after that. We needed food and water and a place to live, and they couldn't do anything for us. I am sorry for saying this, but I believe our president is full of shit. I'm sorry. I mean, I never did like him in the first place, but I didn't know he could do so much damage and do so little for the people."

Carmen wanted a sandwich, so we decided to go to the Harbor View Café, which used to be on the harbor in Pass Christian but was destroyed by Katrina and rebuilt far from the Gulf, for oyster and shrimp po' boys. A po' boy is a crusty bun, about half the size of a French baguette, with something delightful crammed into it. In this case it consisted of tartar sauce, sliced tomatoes, some cukes on the bottom, and about a pound of freshly fried oysters and shrimp on top. Somehow it seemed bad for me and yet, not! It didn't matter. Sweet tea made up the rest of the lunch.

Carmen planned to vote for Barack Obama in the Mississippi primary and said if she had to, she would vote for Hillary Clinton in November "because she's not as great as Bill Clinton, she's a hard ass, but I can support her."

When we finished our sandwiches, I told her I had a tough question for her, one that would take her back to her darkest moment, when she was sitting in the mud with the remains of her bulldozed house all around her. It was a tough question for me to ask too. What is government for if not to help people who are in great need? How else are we to measure ourselves as a nation? Maybe it was her story, I don't know. I was overwhelmed when I asked it, and she was overwhelmed when she answered it.

"If the President of the United States walked up beside you when you were sitting there in the ruins, what would you want him to say?" I asked her.

"'I will help you fix it. I will do everything I can to help you fix it.'"

Another big hurricane pumped itself up just off Pass Christian in late summer 2008, threatening just as the Republicans were planning to open their nominating convention in Minneapolis. They responded with a gesture. Apparently having learned the lesson of how things look, they canceled the opening of their convention until it was clear that Gustav was no Katrina. New Orleans mayor Ray Nagin ordered an evacuation, calling Gustav "the mother of all storms," then a few days later admitted his hyperbole and said he should have called it "the mother-in-law of all storms." You just can't shake the jester out of New Orleans politicians, unfortunately. No one needed reminders of how poorly the federal government had responded. The Republicans went back on schedule as soon as it was clear this storm was no monster.

Carmen left town as Gustav threatened, because she always does. When she got back, she found her shed flooded and water in her yard, but her house up in the sky was safe.

The response to Katrina shattered the thought that President Bush was commander in chief of an effective federal government, another crack in the political visage of the Republican party. Bush would not be running again, but the record he constructed over eight years would define the public's view toward the Republicans more strongly than any campaign themes the party could create for a new candidate.

*

Elections come down to an abysmally simple question that has an answer only in the days after the ballots have been cast: exactly who voted? It's not a question most people pay much attention to, but for the people who run campaigns, it's essential. If you know who voted last time around in a presidential cycle, you have the perfect starting point for a new campaign. You don't even have to know what candidate people voted for. The fact they showed up or didn't is enough.

I know a lot about the question of who voted. One of the realities of working as a reporter is that you never really let anything go. It's like having a passion for junk. Not antiques, not precious treasures of the past, but junk, items like meat-grinder handles or power-line glass insulators or old pliers. My folly is delivered every couple of years after a presidential election by the U.S. Department of Commerce, Economics and Statistics Administration, and U.S. Bureau of the Census. "Voting and Registration in the Election" is perfect campaign junk for a reporter. By the time it appears, most people, and certainly most journalists, have lost interest. Not me. It's like having a derelict box of Christmas cookies show up in the mail in February. It's not Christmas anymore, but they're still cookies!

Just before the 2008 campaign began to heat up, I gathered all my statistics and went on a mission to Moscow to explain the "who voted" question to an unlikely audience, the Russians. They wanted to debate about it. I just wanted all the statistics in my head to prepare for this campaign, and I thought Russia would be as good a place as any to test myself in advance of the election.

While you can learn a lot about the future by looking at the past, you can't know everything. Who will win is always an open question. But who makes the decisions is not.

What it says about us is surprising, uplifting, shocking, and maybe even a little depressing, all at once.

3

MOSCOW, AMERICA,
AND THE LAY OF THE LAND

"WHEN WILL DEMOCRACY COME TO THE UNITED STATES?" Admittedly a loaded question aimed at a specific audience, this one being Russian "intellectuals" who wished to engage in a "debate" about American politics. Just before the American presidential campaign burst into flower, two years before anyone was to vote, I was invited to Moscow through a friend, Georgii, a former Soviet academic who ended up as a professor in the United States after his doctoral thesis was dumped because it was not sufficiently Leninist. He is that rarest of things, a genuine intellectual with a platinum education but with an engaging manner and spectacular sense of humor. The Russians, he said, wanted to know what was happening in American politics and what was likely to happen in the 2008 presidential race, so the Russian Debates, as the organization is called, sent an invitation.

Russians love to jab at American politics, particularly at some of its more glaring hypocrisies. Poverty, health care, job security, foreign policy, the system's lust for big money, corruption—it all becomes cannon fodder, particularly for the most argumentative people, the kind drawn to debate programs. The same things that make

Americans angry about politics make Russians angry too. It's just that Russians are unyieldingly arrogant about it. Communism is gone, but in its wake the deep skepticism of everything American is always ready to thrive in Russia. I had to go prepared for just about anything, including the question that generally closed all conversations with Russians about conditions in the United States in the old days: What about your black people? Foreigners who are intent on slamming the United States have always had that question as an ace in the hole, because it was one that caused even great defenders of the nation to stumble. "Well, they are doing better and better" just would not suffice. Neither could you say, "They aren't *my* black people, Lincoln ended all of that," because they wouldn't get it. As I headed off to Moscow, no one could have anticipated that the United States was on the eve of presenting the perfect response to the question.

My challenge in preparing for my Russian hosts was to find out what we can actually know about what happens on Election Day. As the nation prepared for what would become a contest with an unexpected and historic outcome, prudent people were taking a close measure of what had happened the last time around. I believed the keys to understanding what would happen in 2008 were embedded in the data created by the 2004 election. We are such a measuring culture that every collectable aspect of election information gets chopped up, weighted, assessed, and tabulated. That kind of information is off-putting for Americans, who have raised short attention spans to the status of a national character trait. But for Russians, particularly Russians who look for any contradiction or conflict they can find about America, it's like a hot bowl of kasha with some chicken skin cooked in just to add fat. Marxists, with their passion for science, love statistics, and even though Marx did not have Russians in mind when he was composing his thoughts on how the world should be, today's liberated Russians still have Soviet Marxist insides, especially the older ones. It was how they were taught for generations. Everything becomes scientific in Marxism. They just love those numbers. And I had them.

As time would show, data on the 2004 election and a grasp of how people felt as the 2008 contest got under way were the perfect scene-setters for what would play out in the United States. Diving into the numbers to prepare for my Russian visit gave me a whole spread of charts and statistics to ponder. In the absence of anything actually happening in an election cycle, charts and statistics are the next best thing. They tell you about age and voting, income and voting, geography and voting, marital status and voting—almost any category you can imagine. They tell you how people say they feel as a campaign begins. Anyone planning an election campaign with an understanding of these numbers will be ahead of the game long before the gate opens and everyone rushes to Iowa or New Hampshire to bond, struggle for media face time, and make friends. It is even possible to measure who doesn't vote and why that decision came about. These are columns of numbers full of surprises because what they represent is not campaign strategy or position papers but how people actually behave.

If you know that your opponent has a solid base and you need to look for votes, you search in areas of potential where the voting base has not already been tapped. For 2008, based on what happened four years earlier, that would mean Hispanics, and most important of all, young people, who represented a huge pool of potential voters. You want to draw them in on your side. You can expand support in other groups—senior citizens, for example—but not without a lot of work because they already vote in big numbers and tend to be set in their voting behavior.

I had a simple image in my mind of being able to view the United States from a high altitude. I could see where the votes were, where the potential votes were, and where there were not enough people to spend much time hunting for support. Beyond that, I could also see who was happy, who was sad, and who was nearly livid about the way things were going. But this was a vision constructed of statistics, not of images. I knew the Russians would find that interesting.

I had lived in Moscow from 1977 to 1979, fueling myself for the UPI assignment by crash coursing on Russian language and economics. These were not complete wastes of time, but nearly. It was a difficult place to be a reporter. I was not sad about leaving after two years.

But when the Russian Debates asked me to come back in 2006, I simply could not resist. I wanted to see the place again, first, and second, the assignment fed directly into my long-running interests in presidential campaigns. My objective was simple. I wanted to explain who had voted in the 2004 presidential election and who had not voted and make some cautious predictions about the 2008 race. Ever the democrat, I have always been puzzled why participation in presidential elections generally involved about 60 percent of eligible voters and sometimes less, and a lot less than that in congressional election years, usually below 50 percent. Russia seemed like a great place to present this information since its own experiment in democracy had gone so wildly off track. Recall the 1990s, when we were going to help the Russians become just like us by showing them how to be democratic! Now flush that thought. By 2006 the Russians had invented a faux democracy that amounted to nouveau-tsardom, with former KGB boss Vladimir Putin on the throne. You can make an election seem democratic but still assure the outcome by intimidating anyone else who wants to run and by controlling the media. That seemed to be the new Russian model. The place was swimming in oil money, though, so not many Russians were complaining.

Sometimes getting far away from the United States is the best way to look at American political behavior. In the States it's too easy to be drawn into the media message, an agenda that changes at least once a day during an active campaign.

When I went to Moscow in December 2006, an official presidential campaign hadn't begun yet. But people were already polling, and the conclusion had planted itself that New York senator Hillary Clinton would be the Democratic nominee and take the whole cake early in the game. This initial guesswork bore no resemblance to what eventually played out, which means a lot of people wasted a lot of money polling too early. But such is media life.

Meanwhile Barack Obama was just one in the bunch. The Republicans were certain to tap either the fabulously popular Rudy Giuliani or the properly wealthy and deeply Mormon Mitt Romney. John McCain was viewed as cranky and still angry at how badly he had been treated in 2000 in South Carolina by the Bush people, who, legend has it, planted the thought he fathered a child to a black woman. It was not a subtle smear.

The big issue was the war in Iraq, which was not going well. Republicans had just been booted hard in the 2006 congressional elections, paying the price for the building anger toward Bush and his presidency. Some early clues about 2008 could be found in those numbers. Young people were trending more Democratic, and so were Hispanics. "God" as a demographic was beginning to work against the Republicans after many years of blessings. Still, it was pretty early to project presidential election stuff. It's always best to carry the "Dewey Defeats Truman" headline in your heart to keep you from becoming too arrogant too early.

Moscow remained grey and brown, overwhelmingly common colors even when I lived there thirty years earlier in the Soviet era, when the place was famous for its earth tones. There was little snow before Christmas in 2006, and that robbed a big, filthy city of its only chance to look romantic. Blanketing everything in white is a nice touch. I noticed some remarkable differences from my earlier stay, the big one being that the place looked like someone had poured a lot of money on a lot of people. Gucci stores, in fact every kind of top-dollar store, were common. Very broad six- and eight-lane streets were crammed with traffic. There were traffic jams on the sidewalks and a lot of neon lights. You could get quality coffee at 4 a.m. Mercedes-Benz had the biggest rotating Mercedes symbol I have ever seen on the top floor of one of its dealerships. The food stores had food! True, the Russians in the street still had their "Russians-on-the-street" look, which would intimidate even an aggressive dog. The Russian Orthodox church had been revived, complete with newly gold-leafed onion domes, icons galore, and an abundance of religious trinkets. Just outside the metro stop at Red Square, a tape loop played Orthodox chants. People crossed themselves as they left the metro. I kept expecting the arrival of either the tsar or St. George, the beloved dragon slayer.

Moscow was preparing for its jolly Christmas. This happened in the Communist years too but was usually disguised as a New Year celebration when a suspiciously Santa-like man named Grandfather Frost and his hot young associate, the Snow Maiden, brought gifts on a sled drawn by three white horses. On Red Square, where Lenin rests under glass in his brown (of course) tomb, a gigantic plastic Christmas tree had sprouted from the grey cobblestones. An inflatable hockey rink was nearby. From the wall of GUM, once the world's most wretched department store but now very snappy and au courant, a mosaic Blessed Virgin Mary gazed across the courtyard toward Lenin's tomb. The tomb itself reflected the Christmas tree lights. For someone who walked frequently here during the Cold War, the scene was surreal.

Down on what had once been an avenue named after some forgotten five-year planner, the brown buildings still carried an interesting Soviet legacy, the bas-relief of old heroes of labor, economics, science, whatever the Soviets could claim good news on, all trapped in stone. Undoubtedly this was the proper thing to do in the 1960s, when the store windows displayed empty shelves or a few cans of fish or sauerkraut. Now they had been taken over by something like a Victoria's Secret gone wild. That left one old Soviet hero in stone in the position of staring at mannequins dressed in hot red silk panties, tiny bras, and black masks. They carried whips.

It takes a sense of irony to enjoy modern Moscow.

Two challenges were in my head as I wandered around in the dark, because it's almost always dark in Moscow in the winter. The first: What do with the money? The Russians gave me two thousand dollars in twenty-dollar bills to talk about American politics. I felt like a drug dealer, getting a bundle like that in brand-new bills. It troubled me. Just a few weeks before I arrived, the investigative reporter Anna Politkovskaya had been shot to death walking into her Moscow apartment. The killers were not amateurs. She had become a huge pain for the Russian government because of her aggressive questioning of human rights abuses in Chechnya. It could have been a government hit, or it could have been an organized-crime hit, or it could have just been a favor for someone. The money from the Russian Debates had nothing to do with the slaying, but the sourcing of the two thousand dollars was murky enough that I could quite easily imagine a connection to the government. I tried hard for the past decade to think of the Russians as reformed members of the world community, but their official behavior kept raising questions. People were being killed. Who killed that reporter? It felt like bad money to me.

The other thought was about our own democracy and how we elect presidents. I had been down this road many times before. I was worried about the decline in civics education in America and about how few people participated. I was standing in the center of a city that always leans toward the totalitarian side of life, worrying about why everyone in my own country doesn't rush out and vote as often as possible simply because they can and because it almost always means something. The low participation rates of young people were particularly troubling. No matter how difficult they might seem to their elders, young people are in charge of true passion in America, and one might think a lot of that could be focused on politics. But it wasn't happening much. People have their reasons for showing up and for not showing up. You only have to ask.

That is exactly what the federal government does during every presidential election year. What an amazing effort the census is, an ongoing measure of America by the numbers, certainly not perfect but good enough to carve some sharp edges out of the unknowable collection of disconnected events that make up the typical Election Day. One tidbit that comes from this immense batch of data is the news that Barack Obama was born in the lightest-voting state of them all, Hawaii, where maybe half the voting-age people go to the polls. The Republicans held their 2008 convention in the state with the strongest voting record, Minnesota, where more than 80 percent of the electorate shows up. Most states seem to fall in the 60 to 70 percent range.

One might spin these little references out for many hours. In my own favorite measure, which I call the American Standard, I have concluded that the more vitreous china you have in your house in the form of toilets and sinks, the greater is the chance you will vote. I am not the first person to make this claim, but certainly among the most recent. It is a function of income. The more money you make, the more likely you are to vote. The more money you make, the more bathrooms you have. That of course is an assumption, but supportable. It's all in the data.

The Census Bureau, then, gave me my heaviest artillery in the confrontation with the Russian debaters. I had other ammunition too. I planned to lean heavily on maps created by the University of Michigan that offer a much more accurate picture of what happens on Election Day than the standard red state–blue state cliché that defines almost all Election Day TV coverage. I also planned to draw from "Reported Rates of Voting and Registration by Selected Characteristics, 2004" in the Census Bureau's "Voting and Registration" report. Admittedly these studies seem designed to frighten away anyone without a stomach for numbers. But they are like pornography for election-obsessed reporters, and best of all, anyone with a computer anywhere in the world can get them. I thought I would just prime the Russians' pumps and let them search for more on their own. My final source of information was the website PollingReport.com, a not-too-webby daily collection of polling information on just about everything from everywhere. The Polling Report people don't dress up what they collect. They just copy it, identify it well, and present it. Fancier places exist, but nowhere with information as direct and simple to digest.

Sitting in my tiny hotel room on Pushkin Place, with its wee, square bathtub and orange water coming out of the faucets, with its overheated radiators and the sense that the hotel might well erupt at any moment should anyone touch a flame to the kitsch that decorated it, I realized I was ready for battle. The debate people would welcome me the next day. I was the big item on the agenda. (I learned later that the other American they considered inviting was Barack Obama, the new senator from Illinois, but decided he was not high enough in the political pecking order. My head did not swell with this news. It merely fueled my conclusion that the Russians don't actually *know* anything about us.)

The presentation would play out in a large meeting room at a downtown hotel, one of those places that are well guarded and apparently well connected too. My only remaining worry was what to do about that money. I could spend it all on souvenirs, furs, jewelry, and the like, but no one in my family cares about any of that. A collection of teas would do on the home front. I hid the bills under the carpet in my hotel room because Moscow remains one of those places where some very needy people can just smell money and will not hesitate to take it from you. Even hidden, it continued to bother me. I couldn't give it back, and keeping it would fuel the endless collections of dark speculations I already carried in my head about everything Russian, this time putting me at the center of them.

I would like to report the next day dawned bright and full of potential, but in Moscow you couldn't tell. I was up at six in the morning, four hours before daylight illuminated the topside of the thick clouds that blanketed the city. I went for a walk. I had breakfast at Kafemania, always open and, unlike Russian restaurants in the old days, always ready to serve. I read English-language newspapers and learned that dozens of women had died in a fire in a ward for drug addicts in Moscow after someone left for the night and locked all the doors. I read that dozens of people had died in a nursing-home fire in another town because the government had not funded repairs of the fire safety station just down the street and there were no firefighters to attack the blaze. I continued to wonder about why we were ever worried about these people in the Soviet days, when nothing worked well either. I went over my presentation. I waited for sunlight that would never arrive. Then I went to speak.

Somewhere in the archives of the Russian Debates there is a record of the event. I began with my University of Michigan maps. These brilliant cartograms by Mark Newman, Michael Gastner, and Cosma Shalizi represent election results based on population and several other measures. This leads to wild distortions of geography and a collection of artistic wonders that deliver a truth that would turn out to be very important as 2008 played out. George Bush had indeed won the 2004 election, so he didn't need a friendly Supreme Court to keep him in office. But the impression that the nation was solidly Republican was wrong. People who thought a new Republican era was evolving were not looking closely at real numbers. The cartograms made it clear that the nation was almost evenly divided. Where the red-and-blue Election Night TV map indicated a huge Republican presence, in the West for example, there were not many people, so those states dissolved to tiny places on the cartogram. But New York and Pennsylvania, where there is big population and a big Democratic presence, added dollops of blue to the map of election results. The whole West Coast was one big blue Democratic blob.

I asked the Russians to think a bit about what depth of victory might mean in an American election. Votes are counted by precinct, I told them. Change a few votes in each precinct, and some of these red states would become blue states. What happens on the ground on Election Day, then, is crucial. If you can identify enough likely voters and get them to the polls, you can change the outcome. The nation was not so much red and blue as it was purple, I argued, with not too many votes deciding changes of fortune.

The Russians seemed to like the complexity of this argument, which is challenging, I will admit, even for Americans. What it tells us is that things are hardly ever as they seem. They are filled with complexity, unpredictability, or, put another way, opportunity. These are the numbers that bring down overconfident people and partisans on the right and left on radio talk shows. What I had to say next did not help matters. I noted that the Founding Fathers had never intended American democracy to be a process for everyone. Women were clearly out of the picture, as were slaves. White landowning males—now there was a dependable collection of voters. The Fathers had worried about the rabble and its capacity to be swayed by any demagogue who came along. It took a couple of centuries of evolution for American democracy to open its doors to every citizen over the age of eighteen, and there were still plenty of impediments in the system that kept people away from the polls, I said.

I turned to the Census data for 2004 to show the Russians who actually voted. There are many revealing ways to measure the number. For example, there are 24.8 million American citizens between the ages of 18 and 24. About 11.6 million voted, or 46 percent of the number that could vote if they wanted to. As you move up the age

scale, participation becomes heavier. Of 32.8 million people in the
25- to 34-year-old category, 55.7 percent voted. Of the 35- to 44-
year-old population, 38 million people, 64 percent voted. In the 45-
to 54-year-old group, 39 million people, 68.7 percent voted. Above
age 55, a vast group with 62 million members, 71.8 percent voted.

The older you are in America, the more likely you are to vote.
And that was just one measure. The one that created the most interest
for the Russians was the wealth measure. Fifteen million voting-age
citizens come from families with incomes of $20,000 or less. Just 48
percent of them voted in 2004. That means 52 percent of the people
who lived in poverty did not vote. That made them a likely target
for voter registration and get-out-the-vote campaigns, particularly for
Democrats making economic arguments. Going right up the wage
scale, the percentage of people who vote goes up. By the time you get
to the $100,000-and-over (in family income) group, with 29 million
people, the voting rate is 81 percent. They vote at a much higher rate
than people at lower income levels. I told the Russians the Founding
Fathers may have been prescient on that point. The people who benefit most from democracy are its most ardent participants.

One of the other most compelling comparisons in 2004 looked
at voting by educational status. There are some 25 million voting-age
Americans with less than a high school education. Only about 40
percent of them voted in 2004. Participation moved right up the scale
along with education. Almost 85 percent of the 16 million citizens
with advanced college degrees went to the polls. The greater the level
of education, the more likely you are to vote.

How people voted was a question that didn't interest me much
at that point. George Bush won, and unlike the farcical outcome in
the 2000 contest when Al Gore had the numbers but the Supreme
Court handed Bush the prize, there was no debating that. How people felt about it two years later was another matter because those statistics carried you right onto the battlefield for the 2008 presidential

campaign. The Democrats picked up thirty-one House seats and six Senate seats in the 2006 mid-term elections, handily bumping the Republicans out of control. The Republicans gained nothing from the 2006 contests. It was an important sign of a turn in direction and a telling measure of the Republican plummet from favor under President Bush.

If generals are always fighting the last war, political strategists are, in a way, always fighting the last election. They either want to repeat what happened or reverse it, and the public's perception of the president's track record is what determines which of those strategies will be at play.

I told the Russians that on the eve of the 2008 presidential race George Bush was in deep trouble. His performance ratings, once so strong in the days of unity after the 9/11 terrorist attacks, had shattered. His policies were widely disliked. He continued to hold on to about a quarter of the electorate, but that was not a healthy place for a Republican president to be as his party looked down the road at the next contest and a new candidate. He was not quite a pariah yet, but anyone with plans to invite him to fund-raisers was most likely reconsidering as 2006 played out. Iraq had not yet benefited from the "surge" that would make it a little more peaceful. It remained a visible failure. Afghanistan was slipping back into chaos as the Taliban began flexing its muscles in areas not under tight control. Something was wrong with the economy, though it wasn't quite clear yet what that might be. People of all kinds were way out on a limb with their mortgages and investments. The issues that seemed to be etched into the landscape—health care, the economy, jobs, education—were still dominant.

At PollingReport.com the December 2006 figures were in. Some 58 percent of the people believed the nation was on the wrong track. Just 28 percent thought things were going in the right direction. If you looked at that number over time, it was clear that public perception was in a steep slide. You had to go all the way back to 2003 to find a point where a majority thought the nation was on the right track. I presented all these numbers to the Russians and then opened up the session for questions.

You never know what you will get when you ask for questions from a roomful of Russians. It's best to prepare for someone tossing a rock. That way anything less seems benign. They wanted to know why Americans are always so critical of Russia and its democracy. Well, you try to be polite, you know? I told them it took the United States more than a century to give the vote and property rights to women, longer still to give voting rights to black people, and it continued to get itself into occasional messes like the Florida vote count in 2000; so it could take the Russians a while to get their democracy in order. I said I thought the lack of participation in American elections was a scandal (a point the U.S. embassy representative at the session strongly disagreed with, but not in public). I was babbling on about what might happen in the 2008 election when, from the back of the room, an American journalist who worked for either *Forbes* or *Fortune* popped up to say that everyone knew Hillary Clinton would be the Democratic candidate.

That stopped me. I had spent a lot of time looking at Hillary Clinton's numbers and even went to the trouble of calling polling people in key primary states quietly to check her out. What they found in places like New Hampshire was not so promising. She had plenty of support, as one might expect for someone so tightly connected to the power structure of the party. She might even win primaries. But not many people liked her. In fact a good number of Democrats who usually said they would support the party's choice said there was no condition under which they would vote for her. Her "negatives" were almost in balance with her positives, and you don't want those things to be equal in a presidential campaign.

So I made a bold prediction. I said if she got the nomination, she would not win the election, and that I did not believe she would get the nomination. The *Fortune/Forbes* guy offered a bet. I think I put one hundred dollars on Clinton not being the nominee. She just came with too many reasons not to vote for her. Maybe being the first woman nominee would be important to the part of the Democratic party that was behind her, but was it important enough to make that gesture and then lose the most winnable presidential campaign in recent memory? Would putting her on the ticket revive the whole Randy Bill the Bad Husband President episode, with all its embarrassing side trips down infidelity lane? Of course it would. Before you knew it, that Arkansas cabaret singer Gennifer Flowers (now billing herself as a charismatic comedienne, singer, and actress—she gives you a big kiss when you enter her website, though the audio sounds a bit like a fart) would be doing commentary on Fox. The Republicans would make sure of that.

It wasn't going to be Hillary Clinton. Then who?

I wish I could report that I had said, "Barack Obama," but I could not make the leap at that point. I should have been more astute because I had everything I needed in my head to make a bold prediction. People were longing for change; I knew that from the polling results. Young people were an increasing presence and had added 11 percent to their voting strength with a get-out-the-vote effort in 2004, though they could not swing it for John Kerry. There were still a lot of young votes to gather, but the spark was there. Middle-aged people and those beyond middle age were increasingly angry about health care. The more people found out about the war in Iraq, the more angry they became as the casualty count mounted. Obama was a lonely voice against the war early on. Much of the blame was falling on the Republican party.

At that point no one knew that the economy would be falling off a cliff so dramatically or that the Republicans would turn to John

McCain, a valiant man who is awkward in his own party, and Alaska governor Sarah Palin, who came with an excess of spunk but a load of baggage. The thought that government was the enemy would be replaced with the thought that incompetent government was actually the culprit. Katrina helped seal that, along with the government's failure to anticipate an economic crisis.

All the pieces were in place for a big change. But it would take time for that message to settle. It was still difficult to see how a nation riddled by so many questions of race could vote for a black man. What no one could have anticipated at that point was that Obama had no intention of running as a black man (that had already been done unsuccessfully, by Jesse Jackson), that he would run instead as an American, a strategy that made him attractive to a wide range of voters and enabled him to talk about what was on the nation's mind, not about the color of his skin. It would also make him magnetic for the black voters who are at the core of the Democratic constituency. All they needed to know was that he could succeed with white voters. Besides, as 2006 ended and the campaign for the White House began to take shape, only one issue was at the top of the list: What were we doing in Iraq, and how were we going to get out of there?

I left Moscow in a snowstorm that at least made the place look a little fluffy, which was nice. I landed in New York with the two thousand dollars screaming at me from my coat pocket. When I got home, I put it in the bank and sent it to the Committee to Protect Journalists. I said a prayer of apology to the reporter Anna Politkovskaya for the way her life ended.

Within two months Obama mounted one of the most audacious presidential campaigns in American history. He kicked it off on a cold Saturday morning in Springfield—Abraham Lincoln's Springfield. He went looking for exactly what the 2004 election results told him was available: young people, poor people, black people, Hispanics, people who were angry at how the Bush administration had played out (a huge collection of potential voters), people who were troubled by the war.

"I want us to take up the unfinished business of perfecting our union, and building a better America," he said. "And if you will join me in this improbable quest, if you feel destiny calling, and see, as I see, a future of endless possibility stretching before us; if you sense, as I sense, that the time is now to shake off our slumber, and slough off our fear, and make good on the debt we owe past and future generations, then I'm ready to take up the cause, and march with you, and work with you."

It would be a long, long haul, filled with problems, as every presidential campaign is. A piece of me wanted to hop on the bus, plane, whatever, and follow Obama wherever the campaign went. But there would be dozens of people already on board, eager to hear this interesting man say the same thing a dozen times a day in different locations. Too crowded, I thought. Besides, I was thinking about the wars when I watched his speech, about whether a nation ever gets over that kind of loss.

4

THE WARS

"The most priceless thing we own as a nation is our soldiers, and to throw them away and allow them to be killed and maimed on purpose is a crime. . . . The country hasn't even begun to measure what the cost will be." —Colonel E. W. Chamberlain III, U.S. Army (Ret.)

IT WOULD NOT TAKE LONG for the Iraq War to claim first its hundreds and then its thousands of soldier and Marine casualties. For a time newspapers, networks, and websites published the pictures of the dead soldiers, with stories about how and where they had been killed. But in many cases that eventually ended, either because publishers felt it was too negative or because it took up too much space and time. Of course the war was a central issue from the beginning of the presidential campaign. "Win the war or cut and run." It was that simply expressed in the vernacular of politics, which boils even the most complex issues into sound bites and PowerPoint presentations. The complications of either choice were too difficult for campaign-trail specifics. Maybe we had forgotten what a war actually costs.

Vietnam was measured in tens of thousands of deaths, lost purpose, and a lingering confusion about the projection of force. Korea put us face-to-face with the ideological struggle that would define decades of Cold War, but stopped without a resolution. World War II was measured in hundreds of thousands of American deaths but ended with a sense that the nation's sacrifice had been noble, heroic. World War I, which was supposed to end all wars with its introduction of truly murderous technology in the form of machine guns and poison gas, was all but forgotten.

Support for the war in Iraq, built on a foundation of charges that Saddam Hussein had weapons of mass destruction and was willing to use them, was strong as American forces were unleashed in 2003. Historians are likely to use the months before the war as a case study in building momentum for military action. The memories of the 9/11 terrorist attacks in New York, Pennsylvania, and Washington were still fresh; we had hit the Taliban hard in Afghanistan; and President Bush, with the help of the media and his allies in Congress, had made an apparently strong argument for the move into Iraq. That was clear in polling results, never very far from the minds of people who mount, run, and win or lose presidential campaigns.

Two months after the terrorists attacked, 78 percent of the people questioned said the United States should invade Iraq and force Saddam Hussein from power. On the eve of the invasion that number still approached 70 percent. Bush's approval rating was higher than ever in the days after the war started, a time of valiant news, flashing bombs, and rockets taking out the Iraqi infrastructure. It made for disturbingly great television. "Embedded" reporters told the stories of the military as it swept, almost unimpeded, toward Baghdad. The Iraqi army, humiliated in the first Persian Gulf War, retreated, ran away, gave up, or just didn't fight in vast numbers. "Mission Accomplished" was the banner hanging from the aircraft carrier *Abraham Lincoln* that was used as a backdrop for President Bush (arriving by combat jet, he wore a flight suit), who came to announce, quite prematurely, the end of major hostilities.

With Afghanistan being a war spawned by the 9/11 attack, Iraq was the first military campaign under Bush's newly implemented foreign policy that called for using warfare to defuse national threats wherever they might develop. This was the first significant change in defense strategy since the collapse of the Soviet Union, a decline that followed decades of strategy built on containment of communism and the threat of mutually assured destruction for any nation that would use nuclear weapons against us.

It would take two years of brutal insurgency, mounting losses, and a string of revelations about U.S. behavior to change the national mood, which in politics is an eternity. The Bush administration's management of the war, its dishonesty about the causes, its manipulation, and its embrace of torture and behaviors that seemed not at all American would help set the stage for what was to play out in the 2008 presidential campaign. People who were fairly aggressive about military action in the wake of 9/11 changed those positions once it became clear that the war would be tough and that the reasons advanced for our invasion were not true. Plus, the war would become particularly important as an issue for people between the ages of 18 and 24, especially college students, that vast pool of almost untapped potential political support. Fewer than half of them had voted in 2004. A full 6.8 million said they weren't even registered, with the biggest slice of that group saying it was just not interested in politics or politicians.

The foundation of a political movement was developing, particularly among liberals and young people. A slight majority of liberals thought the war was a bad idea from the beginning. The certainty of the worthiness of the cause, so essential in calling a nation into a conflict that will take its sons and daughters and mothers and fathers, and ask them to inflict and suffer horrific violence, seemed to dissipate and then disappear as every day brought another revelation about the motives behind the conflict, the abuses of prisoners, and the deaths of civilians. A nation that had been a beacon for human rights in the world only a few years ago found itself defending charges it was using torture in interrogating prisoners.

The jubilation at the defeat of the Iraqi army was replaced by an awareness that American forces were trapped in, at the very least, an insurgency with a vague but persistent enemy, or at worst, the first rounds of a civil war. Our young men and women weren't facing Iraqi soldiers but car bombs, booby traps, snipers, and hit-and-run rocket assaults. No one in politics wanted to walk away from American troops, but the nature of the mission in Iraq grew unclear. Catching and later hanging Saddam Hussein seemed almost like a sideshow. What had begun as a romp in the desert had changed as Iraq became a magnet for terrorists from throughout the Arab world who had easy access to its hundreds of thousands of tons of abandoned Iraqi ordnance and explosives.

Inevitably the White House could no longer hide the images of returning coffins, lined up in big transports at Dover, Delaware, each valiant soldier's remains covered by a flag. The erosion of support for the war was swift, even as the casualty count mounted and the Bush administration's motives and behavior came under closer scrutiny. The advice to visit Disney World or go shopping, President Bush's feeble attempt after 9/11 to encourage normalcy, was viewed in retrospect as more and more outrageous. Bush had missed his chance to rally a nation to the cause, so there was very little patriotic fervor in the bank to draw on when casualty numbers began building. Even the treatment of the returning soldiers became an issue. For a Republican administration that was so hawkish about sending troops into battle, to allow wounded veterans to suffer when they came home was scandalous.

The thought that there was some nobility behind the effort in Iraq evaporated too, as the nation learned more about what was happening on the battlefront.

As the presidential campaign developed in 2007 and early 2008, Iraq was at the top of the list of issues, but it was not clear how it would play out on the campaign trial. Only Barack Obama among the top-tier Democrats could claim that he had been against the war, placing him in the vanguard of that slim majority of liberals who rejected the war from its inception. But his opposition had been expressed from the Illinois legislature long before he became a candidate. On the trail he was pushing for a time frame for withdrawal of American forces. Most of the other Democrats, with Senator Hillary Clinton being the strongest among them, had cast votes or taken positions supporting the war effort in one way or another. It was hard not to, particularly in the face of White House requests for expanded budgets and permissions to wage an ever more aggressive campaign. When war budgets were cast as litmus tests on support for American troops, a politician was left with few options but to vote "yes."

On the Republican side, Arizona senator John McCain had a clarion voice on the subject. He was frank in charging that the Bush administration, with Donald Rumsfeld as secretary of defense, had created a debacle in Iraq. But McCain and most of the other Republicans were not opposing the war, just the way it was being fought. (Ron Paul, the persistent but second-tier Texas Republican candidate, opposed the war from the start on constitutional grounds. He also said Iraq had nothing to do with the 9/11 attacks. Paul campaigned on the theme that the Republicans had lost their way.) From the beginning, McCain pushed for more troops. With the exception of Paul, the rest of the field seemed to have settled on an argument that we should win—very safe ground for a Republican. Support for the war put the Republicans in a difficult spot. They had to be hawks to draw backing from their most ardent primary voters, but shifting in that direction carried them away from the evolving public mood about the war. The more deeply they forged into territory comfortable for GOP primary voters, the riskier the bigger journey to the

White House became. It was one of those win-the-battle, lose-the-war situations, but political.

Independents would be crucial in the general election campaign, but on the war they were in a different world from the stalwart conservatives who voted in Republican primary elections. By the time the presidential campaign began to build momentum, 63 percent of Americans believed the United States had made a mistake in going to war in Iraq, almost as many as had supported invasion a few years earlier.

The debate was developing on one side into the Democratic argument that the nation needed an agenda and time frame for withdrawal of troops (eventually the position of most Democrats), and on the other, the Republican argument that we could not cut and run or we would be viewed as weak in our resolve to confront terrorism. These themes heated up during the primaries, when candidates on both sides were aggressively pushing to connect with their party's liberal or conservative bases.

The parties were reflecting the attitudes of their own most important constituents, even though it made the campaign feel as though the Democrats and Republicans were running in different countries (and maybe they were). Knowing about the kinds of people who show up in primaries, the posturing was obvious. The only candidate who had substantial credibility on military issues was McCain. He had paid a high price as a pilot and Vietnam prisoner of war. When he said he opposed torture, one important reason was that he had been tortured. But he was not a patsy for the administration on Iraq. He advocated for the troops and was unyielding in his opinion that Bush had not sent enough people to get the job done and had misdirected the war. Bush's dismissal of Rumsfeld—too long in coming in the view of many, but inevitable given the defense secretary's standing in the polls—seemed to affirm that criticism.

The war was important to Republicans and Democrats for opposite reasons. The Republicans, particularly the substantial portion of the party that still stood beside the embattled president, wanted it to be won, or, more important, wanted it to be viewed as a war that *could* be won. The Democrats, particularly the senators in the presidential field who had initially bought into the war package, needed to get as far away from that support as they could. The Democratic party's primary campaign voters are unusually liberal, even within a liberal party. The war was toxic for them. So the candidates did what they could to dance away from their previous positions. Because I have always liked McCain and because I thought Obama was prescient on the subject, I decided those were the only two people I would pay much attention to on war issues, though Ron Paul was certainly more interesting than the rest of the pack.

As a voter in Illinois, I lived in a virtual campaign vacuum. The state is at the epicenter of Democratic politics with its many Daleys and Obama and Senator Dick Durbin. There is enough weight in that trio almost to offset the fact that Governor Rod Blagojevich seemed to have lost his mind and mutated into an auctioneer of state business. This place was going for Obama in the primary and Obama in the general, so no candidate saw any need to come here, except in Obama's case, to have a home life when he was off the trail. The lean toward him in Illinois was sufficient to loft an endless stream of shameless requests for money on the internet. Want an Obama button? You had to buy it. A lawn sign was ten dollars. A bumper sticker for a buck. A T-shirt could set you back twenty dollars unless you bought one from the "defective" stack, as I did at Evanston Democratic Headquarters.

I had my own Iraq War shorthand: Republicans, for; Democrats, against. That didn't mean I wasn't still interested in the war. But with the exception of McCain, it was politicians talking tough about something so few of them had experienced, and worse, talking to the limited audience that would vote in primary elections.

I wanted to find a soldier to talk to me about warfare and politics. If you want the truth on the subject of war, soldiers are the only credible sources. Everyone else, from campaigning politicians and policymakers to think tankers and opinion writers, to draft-dodging presidents and historians, might make brave arguments for or against war, but only someone who has been under fire can be truly well informed.

I learned that lesson when the Iraq War began, and I raced off to Bedford, Virginia, to see what kind of lasting impact a war would have on a hometown. The talk, particularly in journalism, angered me at the beginning of the war. People would throw around numbers of casualties in the thousands and debate how much loss was acceptable. They would talk about losses in World War II or World War I, how we had to get used to thinking in terms of thousands of dead, just like generals did. Somehow I could not see myself accepting a couple of hundred thousand dead Americans in the prosecution of this war. I thought about my own sons. I would not want George Bush deciding their fate on some distant battlefield. I wouldn't want them on a battlefield at all.

Bedford is a good place to go to think about the consequences of those kinds of political decisions. It is home to the Peaks of Otter Rifles, a Virginia National Guard unit whose roots reach back to Stonewall Jackson. They are named after the tops of the mountains that look down on the town. The unit signed up in 1941 to go off to fight the Germans and played a significant and heartbreaking role on D-Day in 1944 at Omaha Beach. In the first hours on the beach, nineteen of the town's young men were killed. I talked to some of their girlfriends, some of their widows, now gracious women of a certain age with accents soft as the fuzz on a peach and many sad memories. This is how it is going to be someday for a lot of young women who have wept at the news that a boyfriend was killed in Iraq—or, in this war, young men who lost girlfriends, I thought. As a nation we will forget the names of every one of those dead soldiers, but their loved ones will spend the rest of their lives recalling what they can of just one name, one face, one moment.

War may not create an instant generation of pacifists, but it does leave in its wake people who place a high value on peace and have little time for ineffective commanders-in-chief. Boyd Carl Wilson, who was eighty-one when I met him, visited the Omaha Beach D-Day memorial in Bedford every day because he said he felt he owed it to the nation's war dead. He was flat on his belly on the beach when the Germans opened fire. He still has a hunk of shrapnel in him from D-Day, along with a bullet in his right hip from Africa. He watched nine of his ten friends die at Omaha. Senior officers should lead all such assaults, he concluded. Everyone knew the Rifles faced a hopeless, doomed mission at Omaha. But they put them in the boat and landed them on the beach anyhow. Someone had to be first. As for Iraq, he suggested pulling the Americans out and dropping an atomic bomb. "We don't need to lose any troops," he said.

Maybe that's how you will always feel once you have seen most of your friends die in war. It was hard enough to talk to people who were fighting and losing loved ones half a century ago. But the women of Bedford were kind and open. One told me she went to the train station when the boys were shipped out and kissed each one goodbye. Another ran the Western Union booth at Green's Drugstore. "We have casualties. . . . The Secretary of War regrets to report . . . " She read every one of those messages each morning, each death notice naming a friend, then glued them onto telegram forms and sent them along to the families. The men told their stories in clipped, well-practiced versions. The twin who never had a chance to say goodbye. The wounded soldier left on a beach for transfer to a hospital ship, who drowned when the tide came in.

I knew when the presidential campaign began that I would have to talk to a modern soldier about this war too, about its casualties, about the connection between politics and the military. I knew who

I wanted—a retired colonel who had written a holiday essay for me when I was editing a newspaper section. It was a touching story about feeding the troops he commanded in the first Persian Gulf War a turkey dinner on Thanksgiving during a sandstorm.

I met Colonel E. W. Chamberlain III through Joe Galloway. There may be no journalist in America who is closer to soldiers or speaks about the Iraq War with more passion than Galloway. He was decorated for bravery by the Defense Department for the role he played in the first big battle in the Vietnam War. A UPI reporter, he helped evacuate wounded troops and picked up an M-16 and used it at the peak of a North Vietnamese army assault. He is the reporter at the center of the movie *We Were Soldiers Once . . . ,* which was based on a book he co-wrote. His battlefield valor, which would raise an eyebrow in journalism circles among people who had never been shot at, won him friends and sources who stick with him to this day. Galloway is a stern critic of the Iraq War and of how it has been managed. He is most aggressive on the subject of the treatment of wounded veterans. He is not beyond asking the Bush administration, "Have you no shame?" on the question of treatment of the troops and meaning it. I worked with him in Moscow for two years.

I told him when the war began that I needed a soldier to write for me about Afghanistan and Iraq. I didn't particularly care about the politics, but I needed a literate correspondent who could present and defend a point of view. Without a moment's hesitation Galloway said, "Bill Chamberlain," and opened my relationship with the colonel.

Colonel Bill Chamberlain, U.S. Army (Ret.), is a furniture builder, father, husband, author, and whatever else he wants to be in the places he lives, which when we talked included Florida and Maryland. I visited him while he was rebuilding his father's house a couple of hours south of Washington, down where Maryland no longer looks so prosperous and official, with strong hints of the Chesapeake Bay. He was looking at a wrecked kitchen floor when I walked in, because his renters had trashed the place before they slithered away, and now he had to fix it. His tools filled the garage—table saws, planes, the carpentry sidearms that some men find so necessary and comforting. Not a tall man but powerfully built, solid, he looks like he would be out of place in an office, a discomfort that plagued many generations of Chamberlains, he told me. Chamberlain is fourth-generation army, and he looks and talks it. He is the kind of man who could drop out of high school, enter West Point, and graduate somewhere near the middle of the class, generally because he thrived in "The History of the Military Art," a dreaded course in strategy and tactics that he loved. His education did not stop there. He also holds a master's degree in education from Duke University and a master's degree in arts from the Naval War College. He is a scholar soldier.

A lifelong Republican, Chamberlain does not vote the party line. If you had to put a label on him, it would most likely be "progressive," though he would argue that point. He has thoughts about forming a new political party. He would probably still be in the army were it not for a heart problem that led to his retirement, but even after he left he kept working as a consultant on current warfare. The only label he ever wanted said "ARMY" on it, and it has been that way since he was a young man, when his high school attempt to follow his father to Vietnam took some twists and turns and landed him an appointment to West Point.

All the Chamberlains eventually were officers of one kind or another, some up through the ranks and some through officer candidate school. They were not to be fooled with. Bill's great-grandfather Jack Corbett beat Douglas MacArthur in rifle and pistol competitions on the Mexican border. Corbett was MacArthur's 1st sergeant when MacArthur was a company commander at Fort Leavenworth, Kansas. When World War II came along, he had been retired for years but basically squeezed back into the army as a captain by dyeing his hair and fudging his age. Chamberlain's grandfather was near the top of his class at West Point and served in the Coastal Artillery. His father and two uncles went to officer candidate school. One uncle was killed in Korea and the second was awarded a Distinguished Service Cross (a combat award one step beneath a Medal of Honor) in Vietnam. His father won three silver stars (awarded for gallantry in the face of enemy action) and was heavily decorated in Vietnam. Chamberlain delights in these infantry stories. When he tells them they seem to bond him to everything from the pursuit of Pancho Villa through the great wars, into icy Korea, and on to sweltering, frustrating Vietnam. He comes from a long line of heroes, so what he says about war and politics seems to carry substantial weight. Even though he is retired, if you stuck him with a pin he would most likely bleed army green.

Chamberlain is not a pacifist. He is a warrior. The colonel is an expert in applying force of whatever kind—artillery, air cover, side-arms, rifles, machine guns, grenade launchers, bare hands, anything you can imagine—to destroy his enemies and protect his troops.

Sitting at a table in Maryland with bowls of hot chili and corn bread baked by his wife, Sherry, he measured his age, fifty-seven, against the number of times he has moved in his life, fifty. In his thirty-four-year marriage to Sherry, she has moved twenty-two times. "In the army, it's what you do," he said. In the kitchen listening, Sherry offered just the slightest hint of a knowing smile at that comment.

There may well be no dull conversations with Chamberlain. He has enough thoughts and memories in his head to have filled two novels about war. When the talk shifts to the war in Iraq, it is as though he were led to a podium and asked to lecture.

"We're not after bin Laden and the boys. We're not fighting Islamic Jihad or Islamic terrorism, like they would say it a couple of months ago. Where they got that is absolutely crap. We're not getting to the heart of the matter, which is that we were attacked for very specific reasons by a very specific group of people. We know where they are. They are hanging out between Afghanistan and Pakistan. And yet our focus is Iraq. Gasoline was $1.46 a gallon when we started the war. It will be $4 a gallon before the end of the summer. So who is winning? Certainly not us. And what has it done to our economy? It is destroying our economy. Three trillion dollars. And they say, 'Well, you can't count this and you can't count that.' But guess what? Yeah, you can. And look at our own country. Is everything okay here? No. Is our infrastructure where it ought to be? No. Is our education system where it ought to be? No. Is our medical care system where it ought to be? No. Is our crime where it ought to be? No. Is drug use where it ought to be? No. But we can afford to spend three trillion dollars in a rat hole in the Middle East. It does absolutely nothing for the average American."

That is how conversations go with the colonel. You are clipping along and then you hit an exposed nerve and he talks as though he has been thinking about a subject for years. It might be tempting to line him up with all the other loquacious folks at the bar at the American Legion, but Chamberlain is not a man to be written off. He represents a whole class of soldier-scholars who are experienced at warfare, overwhelmingly loyal to their soldiers, and not happy with the Bush administration's pursuit of the war.

Long after the war began, it was revealed that the Pentagon had an arsenal of retired officers, most of them generals, who were regularly briefed about what was happening in Iraq so they could carry the message to the media and show up for talk shows to explain war strategy and how it was working. Chamberlain was not part of that group. He would better be viewed as part of a group of retired officers who were critical of the war from its inception and the target of return criticism from the office of the secretary of defense under Donald Rumsfeld. The official message was to be as loud about the war as you wanted to be—as long as you were shouting what the Pentagon wanted to hear. Yet the Department of Defense had nothing but time for Chamberlain when it needed him the last time around, when another President Bush was determined to force Saddam Hussein out of Kuwait.

Chamberlain was one of the men the army put up front in the First Gulf War. Think of a big red arrow sweeping across the desert on a map. Then go about thirty miles ahead of the arrow into dangerous territory where most of the army has not yet arrived. That's where you would find Chamberlain and his troops. He is exactly what the army wants in its commanders on the battlefield.

I asked him about that.

"The Persian Gulf was the last great war. We did right. We did it for the right reasons, with the right amount of force, and the right instinct. We knew going in that we weren't staying. At one point—I will brag a little bit—my battalion conducted the longest continuous mounted attack in the history of warfare. We were the boys that cut the highway in the Euphrates River Valley on the Hail Mary. I led that, me and my guys."

A great war story followed.

"We had been augmented with everything you could imagine except artillery, which is what I needed. But I couldn't get my brigade commander, who was an idiot and an amateur, to understand it. I was the main effort and was going to be in front of the brigade main body. In fact I ended up thirty miles in front because the rest of them were slow. I had no artillery support. So when we went in and attacked the Republican Guard [believed to be Hussein's strongest and most loyal troops] in the Euphrates River Valley, we did that all by ourselves. We had no air support. No artillery support. No intelligence support. We had no support at all other than my task force."

He had fourteen tanks and four companies of mechanized infantry in M113 armored personnel carriers from the 1960s—as it turned out, not armored well enough. An AK-47 round, which was what the Iraqis used, would penetrate not only the side of the vehicle but also the sloping front, which is supposed to be the armored part. But

Chamberlain had lots of grenade launchers. He had fifteen hundred troops in all kinds of vehicles. He was racing across the desert, heading toward Baghdad but still on the Kuwait side when he ran into some fifteen hundred Republican Guard troops who found themselves dug in, in a very bad place.

The way Chamberlain tells it, the Guard had made a mistake in the placement of the anti-aircraft guns it was using. When he and his racing desert army approached, all the tracers and rounds were going over the heads of the American troops, which was fortunate because the anti-aircraft guns would have made quick work of the M113s. The second good piece of luck came when the commanders of the Republican Guard, a general and his staff, stepped into the open to see what was happening and lit up the sights of one of the machine gunners in a tank in Chamberlain's unit. The young lieutenant shot them all, just like that, in less than ten seconds. All the Republican Guard officers were wounded and captured the next day, among them the only general who was wounded in the conflict. They were badly hurt but survived.

The Iraqis had been trained by Soviet military advisers over the years and hence were a top-down organization that allowed no independent thinking and had no idea what to do after the loss of their officers. Chamberlain's troops lobbed their grenades along the trenches. "We just walked it down. And these guys would pop up at the other end of the trench with their hands up. And if they didn't have their hands up, then we shot them." Four hundred Iraqis and two Americans were wounded in the fight. Leaderless, the Iraqis eventually surrendered. Chamberlain became the momentary owner of fifteen hundred Iraqi prisoners of war.

"We started treating them, and that made me feel good, because these were good people, the Iraqis, they really were. I had a whole bunch of them come up to me and say, 'Now, you go kill Saddam.' I told them, 'No, here's the deal. I will give you your rifles back and *you* go kill Saddam.'" One point after the battle along the highway, Chamberlain, already 250 miles inside Iraq, was looking at a sign pointing toward Baghdad, no more than a couple of hundred miles across the Euphrates River. "I turned to my executive officer, a real nervous kind of fellow, and asked him, 'How much gas do we have?' and he said, 'Oh, shit, sir, you're not.' And I said, 'I'm thinking about it.'" Chamberlain said he told General Barry McCaffrey about that later and McCaffrey said, "Bill, you would have been my hero for the rest of my life, but I would have court-martialed you."

Chamberlain talked about soldiers, families, and that war all afternoon. When we shifted to primary campaign politics and the current war, his mood changed.

"The election this year is wonderful. There are three contenders right now, you know—Hillary, Obama, and McCain. And I don't like any of them. If you want to sit here and say, okay, out of 300 million people this is the best we can put forward to be leader of the free world, well, none of them resonate with me. The closest would be Obama, only because he has said he will end the war. He's the only one who said that."

Before I went to visit him, I asked the colonel to fill out a questionnaire that included his most important issues, top down. Iraq was first. "We have been paying incredible amounts of money for no apparent purpose or gain. We have no reserve forces to respond to threats or national emergencies." Afghanistan was second, with the reason being an academic soldier's efficient "ibid." Special interests in government and politics were third. The parties, Chamberlain argued, had been bought and paid for. Presidential candidates are selected by these interests. Energy policy was fourth, and the economy was fifth, including "the ever-growing national debt being bought up by our close personal friends, the Chinese."

Despite the absence of a Republican candidate he cared to connect with, Chamberlain followed the presidential campaign closely.

He watched polling results as over time the Iraq War began to slip down the list of priorities as the economy worsened. The presidential candidates of both parties followed that change too. What had been a national conversation about the war became a national conversation about foreclosure, bank failure, a faltering stock market, disappearing jobs, people losing their savings, and great uncertainty about the future. He was bothered by how rapidly the focus changed and believed that on the campaign trail it was a clear sign of a lack of leadership.

"I guess what I see is nobody seems to have character or strong beliefs of their own. They all believe what they think people want to hear. So if 58 percent are now concerned about the economy, that's what they are concerned about. And it's not to say they shouldn't be concerned about what the people are concerned about, but that's not leadership, that's followership. You don't see leaders anymore. You don't see any men or women of vision stepping forward in our country to run for president. It gets back to something we were talking about. What is our focus as a nation? We don't have one. Are any of the three candidates currently still in contention providing any kind of focus? No. They are not. So we just kind of exist, and we tolerate it. The electorate doesn't care."

It's a point Chamberlain touched on much earlier in the conversation when we were talking about soldiers. When his grandfather's generation saw the nation under attack at Pearl Harbor, it sent young men by the thousands to enlistment centers. They lined up around the block, eager to join their nation in fighting back and protecting the homeland. But after 9/11 most people apparently thought it was enough to buy a flag or a bumper sticker. There was no great rush toward military enlistment, no public outpouring or national sacrifice beyond an expression of grief and some symbolic gestures. "We don't have any sense of nationhood, I don't believe, where we say, 'Here's where we are going. Here is our vision. Here's the future of our country.' Our education is appalling. Our medical care is won-

derful if you've got the money. Our inner cities are absolutely incredible. They're combat zones and we've given them up."

The colonel was heating up.

"We have the highest incarceration rate per capita in the world.
More Americans are in prison per capita than any country in the world.
Does that mean that's because we're stricter enforcers of the law? No,
it means we've got more crime. You and I have been in places in the
world where they don't even have running water. Or they didn't have
any food to eat. And yet our vision is that we have just given up on the
poor. Homelessness in this country is tragic. How many veterans are
out there and why? The military is disfranchised. We have no voice
and no vote. We have no connectivity with the system any more, now
that the draft is gone."

We are self-centered, Chamberlain said, so local issues like potholes are very important. National issues like war, the economy, how
we use our resources, are not. "It's kind of like we are this amorphous
mass that has 300 million parts to it, and there is no cohesion. . . .
The sole purpose of Congress is to balance the power between the
judiciary, the executive, and the legislative, but we've got no balanced
account. All the power went to the executive. Congress has rubber-
stamped everything George Bush has done for seven years. And a lot
of what he has done was not right for the country. But the electorate
didn't care enough to do anything about it."

Chamberlain inevitably reached a point where he developed a
comparison between a failing United States and the collapse of the
Roman Empire. Modern soldiers who attend three colleges and pick
up a few graduate degrees often spend a lot of time reading military
history, much of which leads them, as all roads did in ancient times,
to Rome and its decline. "How many people in Congress now have
served? Damn few," he said. "Go back to Rome. You had to do twenty
years in the army, even though you were in the senatorial class, before
you could serve in the Senate. And what that meant originally was

that Rome engaged only in wars that Rome could win. They were judicious in their war pride, and they were successful. Later on they watered that down because it was inconvenient. The senators didn't want their children spending twenty years in the army before they moved into the Senate. That's when Rome fell. They started engaging in all kinds of wars and conflicts they couldn't win. That's because the people making the decisions had never served. They didn't know what it was like to be down in the trenches and to go face-to-face with somebody in combat. We're in the exact same position in this country today. We're making decisions about war in a very dangerous world, and the decisions are being made by people who have never been there. War is what they see on TV or in the movies.

"Now, we're not going to pass a law requiring that kind of service in this country, but we have to do something. It's going to get more dangerous as we get bogged down in excursions that have absolutely nothing to do with our safety. The simple concept of the military is to provide security for the state. You only go to war, not when your national interests are threatened, but when your national survival is threatened." World War II was the last time that happened, in Chamberlain's view. That may explain why Korea, Vietnam, and now Iraq have been such difficult experiences for the military. They were projections of force against real or perceived ideological enemies, not wars to protect the homeland from threat.

He believes that what the United States faced in Iraq was an insurgency. Chamberlain is deeply versed in how American soldiers have fought insurgencies in the past. In the Philippines and in the wars against Native Americans, the tactic was the same, and not a tactic any U.S. commander-in-chief would embrace today.

"You have to go in and kill everyone. That's how you defeat an insurgency. That's the only way it will work. It's immoral, and it's not something we would want to do, but we learned that in the Indian Wars and in the war in the Philippines." That would mean embracing what General Philip Sheridan said about Native Americans, but applying it to the Iraqis: "The only good Iraqis I ever saw were dead."

As the war and the presidential campaign ground on, Chamberlain became more positive about the options Obama offered and less and less impressed by what he heard from the Republicans. On the eve of the vote he had shifted into a "I hope Obama wins" mode, along with legions of other military men, Republicans, and independents who stayed focused on Iraq as their central campaign issue.

A month before the election, Chamberlain told me in a long note, he went to Fort Riley, Kansas, to say farewell to his old battalion as it headed off for its fourth tour of duty in Iraq. If you could dig deeply enough into how Chamberlain thinks, at the center of it all would be this loyal connection to his battalion, to the men who served under him. He and his friends in the Eighteenth Infantry Association (his unit) still buy phone cards to send to the battalion so soldiers can make calls home. "I wept when the troops passed in front of me," he said. "There's not a lot of combat experience in that group, which concerns me. It's a sign we cannot keep good soldiers in the ranks for repeated combat tours in spite of hefty financial incentives being tossed their way. Blood for money only goes so far." A week later he went to the VA hospital to be fitted for hearing aids (there's nothing like an infantry career to wreck your auditory nerves), and as he was stepping into an elevator he met a young Hispanic soldier who was quadriplegic. His father was with him. The father leaned over and kissed him on the forehead. "The young man also apparently had brain damage, because you could see in his eyes that he didn't know where he was or what was happening to him. He had an abject fear in his eyes which I had only seen before in combat. I left that elevator in tears, and I damn this war every minute of every day. That kid is alive through the miracles of modern science, but he is already dead. We shouldn't ask that of them for a war that has no meaning and no value. What does this nation gain that is worth this cost? Nothing."

The colonel remembers the day he came home from the war in Kuwait after eight months of carrying the weight of fifteen hundred soldiers as their commander. He got off the plane and stood in front of his wife, his rifle over his shoulder, and looked at his children. His two-year-old son Billy was reaching for him. The colonel said he could not stop weeping. One of Chamberlain's young infantry captains, Malcolm Shorter, came over and took his son from his wife. He suggested a trade, the rifle for the baby.

"And Malcolm gave me my youngest son and took my rifle. What a symbolic moment that was for me. I traded my rifle for my son." War touches families as much as it touches soldiers, he said. His wife Sherry was the volunteer who went with the chaplain to talk to the widows of the two men who were killed under Chamberlain's command. "Did she have to do that? No, but that was her valor. The rest of the nation doesn't understand. The army is at war now. The Marines are at war now. But the nation is not. It's not sharing the tragedy."

But as the election approached, the nation was sharing the anger about the war. Almost seven in every ten people were opposed, and about as many thought it was a bad idea from the beginning. There can be no doubt about the role the war played early in the campaign, when it was almost everyone's top issue. It gave the Democrats, particularly Obama, the topic they needed to rally their base and set the Republicans in a defensive mode.

But in a development that seems somehow in lockstep with Chamberlain's thought that the nation is not really connected to the conflict, to its soldiers, to its losses, Iraq later dropped far down on the list of issues people were citing as reason for voting. In the days before the election, only 7 percent said the war was the central issue. A different set of concerns had become priorities as the nation's focus shifted to an economy that was beginning to slide and would only be sliding down a steeper slope as November neared.

5

PRIMARY CALCULUS

LOOKING AT THE primary campaign schedule from very early in the process, one assumption seemed safe: Senator Hillary Clinton would be the big winner on February 5, 2008, Super Duper Tuesday, with twenty-four primaries and caucuses. This would end the game once and for all, allowing her to ascend to what many viewed as her rightful place at the top of the Democratic ticket.

Clinton would be able to claim she was winning all the "big" states—like New York, Massachusetts, and California—that Democrats often turn to when they are looking later for Election Day salvation. This would give her that "proven vote-getter" mantle people look for in primary contests. How else could it turn out?

Unexpectedly. The reason would not be apparent to anyone without an obsessive's interest in the tortured modern history of the Democratic party. Assumptions about her inevitability aside, Clinton was marching proudly down a path full of perils that seemed tailor-made to undermine her campaign.

Almost since the 2004 presidential election, Clinton had been sitting safely on an assumption that she would be the party's nominee in 2008. To that end she had been raising money and lining up all the institutional support she could get within the party. Unlike the general election, primary elections always draw the most committed of the party faithful. To be sure, intense battles erupted over the nomination in previous elections, but Clinton seemed to have everything on her side early in the process.

There are no more loyal Democrats or Republicans than those who show up in relatively small numbers early in the process to help select delegates for political conventions, and Clinton—before Barack Obama even announced his interest—was assumed to be the candidate of the party faithful. After all, she was Hillary Clinton, D-Bill. And despite President Bill's getting trapped between the faux Victorian morality of the spiteful House Republicans and his own silly concupiscence, he was still an immensely popular Democrat. And Hillary had the "first woman" component that plays so well with a big bloc of women voters, a brass ring for women Democrats if ever there was one.

It all made sense. Every four years for the past few election cycles, the rush to be a part of Super Tuesday became a piece of every election's narrative. It would go something like this: "The state of X has decided to join twelve other states in holding their presidential primary elections on February X, in an attempt to make certain it retains its influence in the nominating process." The fear was that waiting until April, May, or June might mean missing the political boat. Later, when you wanted to ask for an important favor, the White House wouldn't return the call. Also, the army of reporters and TV correspondents that descends in advance of any primary and leaves money, ozone, and a lingering taste of bile in its wake might not show up. That's a lot of hotel room rent gone away, not to mention tabs for bars, batteries, beauty treatments, internet service, and everything else modern media run on. All of this rushing spawned yet another fear: that state X would get lost in the Super Tuesday mosh, losing any influence it might have gained by moving its Election Day forward.

The 2008 campaign presented perhaps the most ridiculous of these scenarios, for not only did Super Tuesday become a Super Duper Tuesday of twenty-four state primaries, but Michigan and Florida tried to up the ante by shifting to *pre*-Super Duper Tuesday status and were removed from the game by the referees at the Democratic National Committee for being determinedly offside. The concern was apparent. Anyone who tried to bump New Hampshire and Iowa from their cherished first places (Iowa is a caucus and New Hampshire is an election, so they can both be firsts) would risk having those legislatures shift dates even earlier. In this game of chicken in 2008, there was even talk of pre-Christmas primaries in 2007 should anyone try to bump those firsts. Iowa was January 3 and New Hampshire January 8. When Michigan shifted to January 15 and Florida to January 31, breaking the February 5 taboo, both became campaign-trail persona non grata for the Democrats. (Despite an abundance of rhetoric, in the end delegates from those states were seated at the convention, had a half vote each, and made no difference.) The candidates agreed not to campaign there, but when it was clear that Clinton would win Michigan and Florida, she became the loud advocate for counting the heads of the displaced delegates from Motor City to Miami Beach. (Obama's name was not even on the Michigan ballot, and he did not campaign there or in Florida, adhering to the party's dictate.) This did not work for the New York senator.

Why the rush? It has been assumed for a long time that muscling a whole gaggle of states into something like a national primary would complete the messy business early. It would provide the blessing of regional advertising and media budgets, a shortened season, and lower expenses. A candidate—Clinton in the 2008 scenario—would thus grab the nomination earlier in the season and have a lot more time to raise money and agitate toward the general election campaign. Even interpreting "beginning" fluidly, the Democrats had begun angling two years before anyone was going to vote.

But this strategy only served the purpose of the media and party regulars, who wanted everything to be over as soon as possible and to follow a safely predictable course. That would clear the field of the Bidens, the Obamas, the Dodds, the Edwardses, and open the gates for general-election fund-raising. This approach was good for the media too, because it's cheaper once there are no longer twenty-three candidates to spread across two parties. You don't have to pay attention to the people who were losers from the day they first announced their candidacy, and no one can complain you're being unfair. One Democratic candidate is ideal for the media. An extended primary contest, though it draws attention and sells advertising, is hard on already tortured newsroom budgets.

What gets lost in the push to decide on a candidate in an allotted time frame is what's at the heart of the democratic process: the right of individual voters to consider and select the candidate of their choice. Primaries and caucuses exist because the old way of a few powerful white men deciding who would run didn't work. I am always suspicious when I hear people say, "Will this never end?" if only for the thought that Clinton would have been the automatic nominee without the primaries. The choice instead should be made by voters, however messy the process might be. It seemed sadly disfranchising for all those people who had the bad luck to live in a state with a late primary date—Pennsylvania's in April, for example.

The cacophony of the campaign process overwhelmed even these evolving schemes to cut the process short. In 2008 nothing happened the way people at the top thought it would.

As it turned out, the thought that Super Duper Tuesday would make it all clear was all wrong. As the primary process played out, it was as though the New York senator's forces had dropped in from a different planet and were talking about a different contest. They kept pointing to the numbers of people who had cast a vote for Clinton, not even a solid measure in the general election, as the nation learned in 2000 when popular-vote winner Al Gore had watched George W. Bush, with the Supreme Court on board amid recount shenanigans, "win" Florida's electoral votes and the White House with them. In retrospect, Clinton kept hitting that voter-numbers point because it was all she had. Primary presidential politics lives in an unusual world where the big issues that motivate most voters—the war, the economy, education, health care, jobs—take a back seat to party loyalties and strategy. Yes, there are debates, and the candidates get aggressive with one another. But they are debates in which, strangely, beyond the tough talk, everyone essentially agrees. None of the Democrats wished to expand the war in Iraq, for example. So it became a debate about how quickly to end it and which Democrats could be blamed for supporting it at the outset. No one wanted fewer jobs. Everyone wants health care of some sort. Schools should be better. Who can be against that? Essentially the candidates parade themselves in front of the voters like the swimsuit competition in the old Miss America contest. With the exception of Senator Joe Biden of Delaware, everyone was playing it safe. Biden was not because outrageousness had somehow become part of his métier. No one ever knew what he was going to say, but people would get over it. He didn't mean to say Obama was the first "clean" black presidential candidate, it just came out that way.

In the primary campaigns the candidates continue to talk about the same issues that are reflected in the endless varieties of polls of likely voters. But there also can be bumps. Obama's bump was his battle to contain the damage caused by his preacher. Clinton recalling racing to avoid bullets (which never happened) in the Balkans was her bump. Perhaps one of the greatest bumps in modern campaigning history was Bill Clinton's effort in his first campaign to contain what became known as a bimbo eruption, briefly enlivening what had been a campaign based on economics.

Primaries are most certainly a different game, a big contest cut into small slices, each demanding its own special attention. From the very beginning of his presidential bid, Barack Obama surrounded himself with people who were good at that game, which meant the real agenda wasn't always what was reported in the media. They knew that in winning the nomination, a number collected in Idaho was just as good as a number collected in New Jersey, New York, or Pennsylvania. They knew that coming in second might have looked bad for the one day when the whole contest was measured in a huge headline, but that even a loser could walk away with a good bunch of delegates to carry into the larger war.

You could easily view Obama's stunning Iowa caucus upset as a result that he was loved there. He may well have been. People behind the scenes know it was because Obama had enough people, enough cars, enough money, enough coordination, and enough phone banks to flood caucus meetings with his supporters.

With that kind of knowledge in your head, watching Clinton win an "upset" in the New Hampshire primary was a little disappointing for the Obama campaign, particularly after the Iowa victory. But it wasn't fatal, especially when you measured it in terms of delegate math. For John Edwards it was fatal. He finished too far down the list and won just four delegates. The Obama people had their plan, and they knew where they had to go to get their numbers. Obama strategist David Axelrod told me he knew after Iowa that Obama would win the nomination, but that he was all the more certain after Super Duper Tuesday. They exited that big day with a hundred-delegate edge over Clinton, by their count, with no place left for her to pick up head count that would not also add to Obama's total.

How could that be when all the headlines were pointing to Clinton's revival in New Hampshire and new life was flowing into her campaign in the form of cash? One important answer to that question is that in 2008 media too sometimes seemed like they had dropped

in from another planet. Too many people were paying too much attention to raw voting numbers and not enough attention to what they
meant. The unintended consequence of reform was playing out, and
you could see it clearly in the numbers.

"Clinton, McCain Rebound, Reshape Primary Picture," was
a good headline for the Wednesday morning after the New Hampshire primary, but misleading for the Democrats. Clinton and Obama
would walk away with the same number of delegates at the end of the
day—nine—which was what it was all about in the first place. She
got the headlines with 39 percent of the vote. He got nine delegates
with 36 percent of the vote. Although not as compelling to say, "It's
a tie," that was the real result. It became even more interesting when
all the numbers were crunched later and Obama, the "loser," got
twelve delegates from New Hampshire to Clinton's nine. That was a
result of the proportional awarding of delegates, down to the voting
district level.

New Hampshire was a brief look at what would happen around
the nation as the primary season played out. Clinton could come out
of Pennsylvania in April, for example, with 54 percent of the primary
vote and 85 delegates, but Obama was right behind her with 45 percent and 73 delegates, and he was already closing on the 2,118 he
needed. But the media continued to insist on using the wrong measure of victory, getting tangled up in the parsing of racial voting. Clinton's backers would argue that they had won primaries in states with
bigger populations. They would become enmeshed in nets of speculation about what candidate X would have to do to "win" the state.
Meanwhile, candidate X—Obama—was using a different measure.
"I'm coming out of here with 45 percent of the delegates. Not bad for
a loser." It's a calm, knowing way to survive a brutal process.

Obama's people realized that one bite less than half a big pizza
is still a lot of pizza. All of that scampering around in caucus states,
where Obama had a strong advantage because his ground game was

amped from day one and full of spunky young volunteers and paid staff, brought big returns. People are always talking about "ground games" in elections. In Obama's case, because of his immense army of volunteers and his vault of money, the campaign could round up the people it needed for caucuses and get them to their meetings on time and with the right message. "Round up" is not hyperbole. In some states, volunteers actually drove around to pick up voters and carry them to polls or caucus sites.

The Clinton campaign tried to diminish that performance by arguing Obama was good only at winning caucuses. The Obama answer could well have been, "Well, yes, we sure are!" Once again, the process doesn't care where the delegates come from, just so they come.

And so it ground on. Clinton's forces were able to crow about the people's will and a victory within grasp. All the time the Obama team sat with its calculator, calculating. Their delegate counter, Jon Carson, had identified every potential delegate pickup from Super Duper Tuesday onward. The campaign aimed to go get them no matter where they were. On television it seemed as though the process was perilous for Obama, with Clinton picking up delegates here and there, and of course the party's super delegates—a collection of luminaries inserted into the process to make certain the Democrats didn't lose control of it—lined up on her side. As the battle neared an end with no one left in the field but Obama and Clinton, Obama was gaining victories in North Carolina and Oregon, places where the Clinton campaign could no longer afford to compete. Even as the Illinois senator moved toward the magic number in May, Clinton was still trying. She beat him 219 delegates to 189 delegates in the month's worth of primaries before it was all over, but it didn't matter. The super delegates were sliding into the Obama camp, casting off the old Clinton loyalties they had embraced back when it looked like she was going to win no matter what. On June 4 it was over. Obama crossed the delegate threshold, and nothing remained for Clinton to get. It was quite brilliant, a true measure of what you can do when you have tens of thousands of volunteers, hundreds of millions of dollars in contributions, and a cool candidate surrounded by people who know exactly how the system works.

You can't watch this process reel out on the Democratic side without asking, "How did this happen?" On the Republican side, it's a very different story. You win the primary, you get all the delegates. John McCain managed to seal the nomination long before it was clear that Obama would be the Democratic candidate. He needed a little more than eleven hundred delegates, which he won early. Everyone else in that contest faded away handily. The Republicans play the game differently, mainly because in the modern era they have resisted attempts at convention and primary-election reform. After Barry Goldwater and Nelson Rockefeller had their big GOP dustup in 1964, the Republicans considered reforming. Instead their Republican Election Reform Commission focused on what the Republicans might to do make their convention more appealing to a TV audience (I am not kidding). Subsequent attempts at reform occurred in the 1970s too, particularly when the Democrats were pumping up their efforts, but they never produced results.

Not the case for Democrats. The fear of God had been pushed on them by a disaster. Before it, big political powers in state capitals— governors, party leaders, and lawmakers, with their big-city counterparts—had decided who would run for president and made sure it went that way. Perhaps William Marcy "Boss" Tweed of New York's legendary, festering Tammany Hall expressed it best. He didn't care who did the electing, he said, as long as he did the nominating. You didn't have to win any primary elections.

On the other side of the disaster was a long and complicated series of reforms, like safety regulations that flow in the wake of a major workplace calamity. It took the Democrats decades to grasp the decline of party power and the growing power of voters, and of course it took a blow on the head with a club to make it sink in. These reforms brought the party to a place where a very smart staff with a very smart candidate could look at a nominal front-runner and find a legitimate way to push her aside.

The disaster that changed everything was Chicago, 1968.

Understanding how Clinton slipped from the anointed nominee to second place becomes all the more surprising when you realize it happened because of Chicago, and it happened because of reforms years earlier that flowed from that train wreck of an event.

The Democratic National Convention in Chicago that year was a mess. It selected Vice President Hubert H. Humphrey as its presidential nominee after Eugene McCarthy, the peace candidate, had drawn anti-war support everywhere. Robert F. Kennedy, who had won the California primary election, had been murdered earlier in the summer. The most liberal part of an increasingly liberal party had moved from the fringe toward the center of the party through the peace movement. The streets were filled with police officers and anti-war protesters, and when they came together, it was violent, bloody, and, worse for the party's interests, broadcast on national TV. (Most of the audience sided with the police.) What ensued became known as Bloody Wednesday. The Democrats were humiliated in November and determined to reform their nominating process by emphasizing primary elections. The pathway that Barack Obama would follow in 2008, then, was blazed by the reforms spawned by that hideous convention.

Not much is more ephemeral than the details of political reform. Generally it involves extended droning in hearings, and infighting, and hard negotiations before anything really happens, which was particularly true as the Democrats tried to fix themselves in the wake of 1968. Shifting power away from those who are used to it is difficult. But for the Democrats, it was like vacationing in the Balkans just before World War I. They were trying to shift power away from the institutional party and into the hands of its rank-and-file members. All the party's many competing factions showed up for the struggle.

U.S. Presidential Primaries and the Caucus-Convention System: A Sourcebook, by the presidential scholar James W. Davis, published twelve years ago, is the bible of primary campaign history. Davis knows his political history, making it worth the book's expensive price tag in trying to understand how an all but unknown Chicago politician, an African American at that, could so clearly master a system and ride it into the White House. The simple explanation is that the Democrats wanted to fix things.

How Humphrey became the Democratic standard-bearer in 1968 is a function of what happens when political insiders gather alone to dictate an outcome. The voters in 1968 sent loud and clear messages. Senator Eugene McCarthy of Minnesota, almost unknown, had nearly upset President Lyndon Johnson in the New Hampshire primary (this was before the days when it was all about delegates; instead it was all about perceptions). It also looked as though McCarthy would defeat Johnson in the Wisconsin primary. That was said to have led Johnson to announce he would not seek his party's nomination for another term and would not accept a draft.

What caused the greatest suspicion and anger within the party was Humphrey's nomination then, even though he had not entered a single primary election. McCarthy's backers may have seen it coming. Earlier in the summer, Iowa Democratic governor Harold Hughes and a commission took a close look at the nominating process. "The Hughes Commission reported a disheartening picture of unfair practices," Davis writes. Twenty states had either inadequate or no regulations for delegate selection. Proxy voting by party leaders was rampant. In some cases they cast more votes than were available. No one posted times and dates for precinct caucuses, where the delegate process began. Delegate candidates would run with no sign they were connected to any candidate. The commission found scant "fidelity" to the principles deemed so important to democracy. When the Hughes report was presented at the 1968 convention, it drew some gestures but nothing central to the nominating process. The genuine process of reform didn't begin until 1969, with something called the McGovern-Fraser Commission. Among its many suggestions was the one that would turn out to be most valuable to the Obama campaign: proportional representation in allocating delegates.

Adopted in 1972, proportional representation meant that a candidate who got 25 percent of the vote in a state primary would get 25 percent of the delegates. It also meant that the Democrats were about to try something new: democracy! A similar rule would apply to caucuses, and in both cases a candidate would have to break a 20 percent threshold before gathering support. Then, in a slap at the leadership of the party, the commission did what a lot of commissions do: it said there could be no ex officio delegates. No proxy voting. No slots for governors. No slate making. The reformers had squeezed all the fun and clout out of the game played by the party leaders.

Because reform never ends and sometimes shows up in disguise, more commissions followed, most of them flowing from conditions the party leadership disliked. And a condition the party leadership disliked most of all was President Jimmy Carter and his army of outsiders from Georgia, who marched into the White House in 1977 with their own agenda that did not include consulting the party on much of anything. Ronald Reagan, who carried forty-four states, crushed Carter like a bug in his reelection bid. That came after Ted Kennedy mounted a serious challenge with lots of party backing aimed at knocking Carter off the ticket. They failed, but an idea flowed from the defeat that would once again play to Obama's advantage.

Angered that the party leadership had been losing influence even as voter behavior played a greater role in choosing candidates, another Democratic commission concluded that the primary process needed something called super delegates. They would be unpledged to any particular candidate and would make up some 14 percent of the delegates at the convention. In short, a measure of clout returned to the nominating process. It wasn't the same kind of smoke-filled-room scenario that obtained before 1968, but it brought the power-brokers back into the game in a big way. It meant that no one would win a Democratic nomination without the backing of the institutional party. No more Jimmy Carters could turn up their noses at the political process as embraced by party leaders. It also meant no unhappy floor fights at the convention. Between these two reforms—proportional awarding of delegates and the creation of the super delegates—the party redefined the role of the nominating convention. Instead of deciding anything, it simply affirmed. The super delegates were like chaperones who would keep an eye out for hanky panky and pour ice water on it before it had a chance to blossom into true love. That made all the difference in the world. It meant they could decide any close convention contest by climbing on the likely winner's side of the seesaw.

More reforms followed as the Democrats wrestled with factions and problems that plagued them through the 1970s and 1980s. Rules on proportional representation were relaxed a bit. It was decided that women would play a more substantial role everywhere, from the county to the national levels. Also, Jesse Jackson and Gary Hart raised hell in 1984 after Walter Mondale lost the general election, arguing that the super delegate process was unfair (it had given Mondale the nomination) and that the threshold for winning delegates in caucuses, then 20 percent, was too high. Unintended consequences ruled the day as the party responded to the recommendations of the Jackson-Hart Fairness Commission. The Democrats agreed to cut the threshold to 15 percent, a nominal victory, but added even more characters to the pool of super delegates because they didn't wish to look as though Jackson or other special interests were pushing them around.

These changes set the agenda that Obama's campaign would use to shatter the assumptions about Clinton's anointment. They went delegate hunting and found what they needed. To Davis's eternal credit, he may have seen it all coming.

Analyzing the consequences of all these reforms, Davis and other political scientists said they seemed to create a situation in which a virtual unknown with a compelling speaking style might come from nowhere and win a party's nomination—and perhaps the election, even though there would be no sign the candidate had any background in running government.

"The reformed delegate selection process has opened the door to the nomination of untested candidates who may be skilled at the art of campaigning for high office, but who do not understand how to operate the levers of power," Davis wrote. The problem with that assessment is that those who were experienced at government also proved disastrous in handling the levers of power. Jimmy Carter, a president who became much more compelling after he left office than when he was in it, comes to mind. But not as much as George W. Bush, the Texas governor surrounded by an array of deeply experienced characters who presided over foreign and domestic policy disasters that just kept coming. They gave experience a bad name.

Obama and his team understood this when he launched his campaign, which was what the message of change was all about. When Clinton amended her tone during the long primary season, shifting from emphasizing her experience to claiming the mantle of change, Obama and his staff knew they had the advantage. That would be happening again in the general election.

But what Obama needed most and first was command of the primary-election process, which turned out to be an unintended gift from the party's tortured past, an old and ugly piece of Chicago history that created the pathway to a new era. He was the inexperienced candidate with a gift for campaigning that the political scientists were concerned about just a few years earlier. The great irony at the center of his campaign was that his lack of experience, which should have been a disadvantage, had become an asset.

Axelrod said his only real worry when Obama discussed his plans before they dove into the primary campaign was whether the senator was simply too normal to run for president. "The effort that it takes requires an almost pathological drive," said Axelrod, who was a reporter long before he was a political consultant, and who has seen that candidate pathology at work. But being so normal, he told Obama, "You're going to have to find your drive somewhere else."

"You know, being Barack Obama is a pretty good gig," the senator told Axelrod. "I don't need this job to validate myself. I do feel strongly, though, what you could do if you got it. And I think once I am in, my natural competitiveness would compensate for my lack of pathology."

"And that," Axelrod said, "is exactly what happened."

Everything that had to break Obama's way eventually broke Obama's way. It took a while for the Clintonians to get the message, which came in the form of mounting debt, growing numbers for Obama, and a sense that the Chicagoans had gamed a reformed primary system almost perfectly.

6

THE STAGE IS SET

THE PRIMARY SEASON ended with a whimper, not the bang the media anticipated as they slogged their way through the longest run-up ever to a presidential nomination. By June, Barack Obama had collected enough elected delegates and more than enough party luminary super delegates to claim the nomination, leaving Hillary Clinton's forces broke, bleeding, angry, and eager to push an agenda that might well have wrecked the party's November chances. Winning the nomination had so much meaning to so many people. Blacks had, for the first time, a candidate with a good chance to win the presidency. Teeming millions of whites, many of them first-time activists and young people who had signed on to Obama's campaign with small contributions that helped make him the greatest political fund-raiser in history, were delighting in the flush of victory. In Mudville, meanwhile, there was no joy. Senator Clinton, so likely, so inevitable, so certain only a year before, was through. Everyone who viewed 2008 as "The Woman's Year to Win the White House" now had to find a way to accept that it was not, that it was something no one had anticipated.

To their credit and eventually benefit, the Obama people realized there would be much bitterness early on. They not only reached

out but stretched and stretched to get the candidate and her supporters—who were passionate, many in number, and threatening to
defect—back in the game. There were hints at a vote for McCain, just
to protest. On the Hillary side, rumblings sounded that it would only
be fair if she were added to the ticket, given her performance, the
argument being, that way you would have everything the party had
to offer in one place. She deserves it. She "won" it. But she had not
won anything.

Wisely, the Obama people announced that she was under serious consideration. What else could they do? They needed to buy a
little time for negotiation with the Clintons. What they did not leak
was that adding her to the ticket would be like releasing a wolverine
in your house in the form of her husband, who exhibited just enough
pouting and arrogance during the primary campaign to become
freshly unlikable. No one doubted that Hillary was up to the job. But
Obama was certainly not interested in bringing a co-president on
board. Vice presidents don't have a lot to do beyond being there in
the event something very bad happens and breaking ties in the Senate. It might not seem that way given the role Dick Cheney played
as George W. Bush's vice president, but Cheney was exceptional in
ways the President of the United States was not. And the thought
of admittedly brilliant but undeniably flawed Bill Clinton unleashed
in government again after all those years, even as a spouse (a role in
which he had performed badly before) was simply too much. Obama
would opt for a better running mate after a decent interval of paying
tribute to this important, threatening loser. She would get her own
night at the Denver convention, a traditional Democratic perk for
those who came close. Bill could be there too. (And of course Obama
would bring her into the heart of his administration as secretary of
state later.)

Obama's team had known he would win the nomination since
February 5, Super Duper Tuesday, when their delegate advantage

became clear. Even the buffeting that came with the discovery in March that Obama's pastor at Trinity United Church of Christ in Chicago, Jeremiah Wright, was a loose grenade didn't hurt them for long. That debacle, which centered on black church rhetoric that is common to many who have visited black churches (but not common to those who have not), was tamped down very effectively. "The government gives them the drugs, builds bigger prisons, passes a three-strike law and then wants us to sing 'God Bless America.' No, no, no, God damn America," Wright had said in a 2003 sermon. "God damn America for treating our citizens as less than human. God damn America for as long as she acts like she is God and she is supreme." America's own behavior was the cause of the 9/11 attack, he said. Because Trinity sells video clips of all the reverend's sermons, it was a simple matter for ABC News to buy the sermons, then scour them for the reverend's frequent hyperboles, which it did.

Reverend Wright is not the first pastor to suggest that government was behind the scourge of drugs in the black community, that government was a force of evil, that it represented the devil, that it invented AIDS to kill young black men, and an extended string of other criticisms that are common in black churches. It is difficult for middle-class whites who attend, say, a Christian church where the same service is repeated each week and the sermons are a little less gritty to understand the fluidity of the black church. It evolved to help an aggrieved body of people find some temporal peace in their passionate, direct connection with God. Itemizing the slights and offenses of society, which includes government, has always been a part of that process. It's like the blues, but holy. Wright, however, may well be the first to see his preacherly hyperboles become national political talking points because of their dissemination on YouTube and the internet. Wright's sermons and the commentary they spawned seemed to be everywhere. For a while it was as though almost everyone forgot that churches of all kinds in America are wellsprings for a stunning array of ridiculous pronouncements. God does not hear the prayers of Jews, we have been told. AIDS is punishment for gay behavior, we have been told. God sent Katrina to punish New Orleans for its gay pride parade. Hitler's Holocaust was inspired by Roman Catholicism. These are all church-spawned outrages, the last pair from McCain supporter Reverend James Hagee. Hagee has apologized for many of his comments, particularly those that hint that the Roman Catholic church is actually godless and the biblical great whore of Babylon. He has acknowledged on his Katrina comments that no one can know God's thoughts, but argued he was misunderstood in many ways by people who don't really understand scripture as he does. He has some 99 million broadcast listeners all over the world. McCain slipped away from Hagee's endorsement when it became an issue as the Wright story was heating up for Obama. It was already a hard year for Republicans to keep Catholics in the camp. They just didn't need the whore of Babylon problem. Why all the fury settled on Obama and Trinity United Church of Christ when the whole field of religious nose-poking is so ripe for a determined punching remains a mystery. At least Reverend Wright had logic on his side—not debatable in his formulation is the maltreatment of black people by government and institutions over time.

In retrospect, it's very clear that most of the small explosions that sent shrapnel and concussions across the political process during the primary season would not have happened without willing media and an aggressive internet audience eager to grab anything it could find. It was a reflection that the old definition of news, something that actually happened today that didn't happen yesterday, was gone. In most of media, with big newspapers being an exception, nothing is researched in depth anymore, rather merely reported. Then a new process steps in either to whittle the allegation down or add more fuel. Words take on an unusual weight in this process. What someone said at some point carries the same gravitas as something someone did. The difference of course is immense. Saying "I could just kill you" in a big battle with a lover is not news, but actually plugging the bastard no-good with a .44, now there's a headline! (And maybe a blues song!) For days the report that there was tape of Michelle Obama using the word "whitey" bubbled and squeaked on the internet, like it might have some great and defining significance if she had used the phrase. She had not, she announced, but the rumor rumbled on anyway.

Here is how the process works. Someone says something or posts something on the internet, perhaps on a blog or on a partisan website. Then other partisans use the internet to fuel the fires of commentary. The claim then breaks into mainstream media, either in the form of a link or as a story about the allegation surfacing in a corner of the blogosphere (perhaps even with disclaimers). Then it moves more deeply into the mainstream, where it is digested, dissected, and served up in dozens of different ways. Examples would be a heavily researched *New York Times* article on the claim versus a Keith Olbermann or Chris Matthews broadside on MSNBC. Fox News would get drawn in. Maybe Bill O'Reilly too. Or even that frustrating, engaging, and always interesting king of hyperbole, Rush Limbaugh! Maybe much later the "never happened" part comes out. The libel at the heart of whatever it was is truly ephemeral. Then someone walks in with a shiny new Christmas ornament of a libel or slander and everyone is distracted, drops the old subject, and rushes way over there for something brand-new.

What is missing from this picture is any weighing that doesn't involve lots of people with their thumbs on the scale because of their interest in keeping "the story" alive. What Reverend Wright had to say may well have been offensive to many people, but I would suggest not as offensive as finding out the man you have been confessing to for a decade is a child molester. Now *that* is offensive. Most people, I would suggest, keep pulpit talk in context, though they believe and are inspired by what they hear.

Complicating the scenario, the media ship—and not just the newspaper media ship—is taking on water, which means all hands are desperate to do whatever they can to advance their own interests and pump some buoyancy into their brand. A couple of seconds of Reverend Wright screaming and waving his arms is good for a couple of hours of shouting, a key component of modern cable TV political coverage. That CNN had decided it was fielding the "best political team on television" (and announcing it so often you wanted to reach through the screen to strangle Wolf Blitzer) didn't help, because it didn't want to get scooped on such a juicy story by MSNBC, the other best political team on television.

David Axelrod was Obama's key adviser on the Wright problem, and he concluded that this decision would have to come from Obama alone. Wright had been the preacher when Barack and Michelle were married. He baptized the girls. He was often described as Obama's spiritual adviser, the man who awakened Obama's Christian faith two decades ago. That the two shared an undeniable closeness when showing up at Trinity, an important political church in the community and a frequent place to visit for curious white outsiders, was an advantage. Now it was not. Obama did what he has done before, exiting the situation smoothly but clearly. No matter what your connection to Obama, it can be cut if you step over any number of lines. But first he delivered a defining address on race in Philadelphia likely to set the measure for dealing with these kinds of problems for many future campaigns.

"For the men and women of Reverend Wright's generation, the memories of humiliation and doubt and fear have not gone away; nor has the anger and the bitterness of those years. That anger may not get expressed in public, in front of white co-workers or white friends. But it does find voice in the barbershop or around the kitchen table. At times that anger is exploited by politicians, to gin up votes along racial lines, or to make up for a politician's own failings," Obama said.

"And occasionally it finds voice in the church on Sunday morning, in the pulpit and in the pews. The fact that so many people are surprised to hear that anger in some of Reverend Wright's sermons simply reminds us of the old truism that the most segregated hour in American life occurs on Sunday morning. That anger is not always productive; indeed, all too often it distracts attention from solving real problems; it keeps us from squarely facing our own complicity in our condition, and prevents the African-American community from forging the alliances it needs to bring about real change. But the anger is real; it is powerful; and to simply wish it away, to condemn it without understanding its roots, only serves to widen the chasm of misunderstanding that exists between the races."

However controversial, Obama said, Wright was an important part of his life, a part he could not and would not deny. Did he hear the heated rhetoric at Trinity? Yes. Did he agree with it? No. He noted that it is not unusual for people in church to disagree with a pastor's sermon. The so-called race speech was a masterwork Obama wrote himself. It is full of passion and honesty, a man of great rhetorical skill describing perhaps the most complicated problem in American history, the role race plays in modern life.

But it did not end the furor over Wright, who only made matters more complicated by not shutting up. He said in a National Press Club appearance that Obama was distancing himself from his old pastor for political reasons. Later a Catholic priest who is popular in the Chicago black community spoke at Trinity and mocked Clinton's teary New Hampshire moment, a small measure of humanity believed by some to have converted the state to her cause in the primaries. That was enough for Obama. He and his wife met with Wright's successor pastor at Trinity (Wright had retired by then), and it was agreed that it would be best for Trinity to fall back into relative quiet, which could only happen if Obama quit the church. He cut that tie and moved on, solving the problem for the moment and defusing it for the general election campaign too.

The Wright controversy, which seems such a distant campaign-trail marker now, gave everyone a close look at one cool character in action. This was the persona Obama would exhibit all the way through the primaries, all the way through the three "debates" of the general election campaign, and all the way to the November election. A small number of people have always hated Obama for their own reasons. But they can't hate him for being inconsistent. We may never have had a more consistent candidate for the presidency. Axelrod said Obama never has to act because he is always himself, and that may have been what was coming through from the February 2007 opening of the campaign right through to Election Day.

An unusual hiatus lives between the end of the primaries and the party conventions that no candidate has ever seemed to handle with much aplomb. From having all your buttons flipped "on" to having all your buttons flipped "off" for a while is a jarring, unpleasant transition. It drives reporters crazy too. Clearly everyone on the Democratic side needed a break. McCain and his team had been on break for many weeks because of the nature of the Republican "winner takes all" primaries, where he picked up the nomination on March 4. So there was a lull. The next important thing would be completing the tickets. Who would be Obama's vice president? Who would be McCain's?

Always astute about technology, the Obama campaign decided to turn the announcement into even more of a splash than a vice-presidential announcement typically would be by shipping the word out to supporters and contributors first by cell-phone alert. To be a true Obama supporter, you had to have the cell-phone connection. There were millions upon millions of them. At every Obama rally all over the nation, the first campaign character an audience met was a young person who came out holding up a cell phone and giving people a number to text message. When you plugged that number in and sent the text message, a whole Obama digital world opened to you. Mostly that world was about very clever personal appeals for money and street support, an unusual development because it worked so well. But in the selection of a vice president, it was about the announcement itself.

The Obama people were going to end-run the media, where that kind of news would typically be presented, and go directly to their audience. It was bold. It depended on secrecy and no leaks. All you had to do was text "VP" to 62262 and you would be in. It worked, sort of. There was a lot of speculation that Joe Biden would be the vice-presidential choice, including a *Los Angeles Times* story saying he was the man and Larry King's report on CNN the night before, based on some John King sources and on the fact that a police car had shown up at Biden's Delaware house in the middle of the night. But there was no confirmation. That came at 2:44 a.m., August 23, in the text message to the cell-phone-connected Obama fanatics. It was very simple: "Barack has chosen Joe Biden to be our VP nominee." A news conference was scheduled for 3 p.m. "Spread the word." It might seem like a small thing until you stand back and look at it as a tiny part of a vast network of messages among the like-minded who had signed on as Obama backers. How many of them watch Larry King is a question. How many of them watch their cell phones is not. On Election Day those people would be energized as never before. There were roughly 13 million, a huge network of potential free campaign workers and dependable contributors. Cutting them in and making them feel special in the Biden selection only helped fuel those passions. The Larry King scoop was one of those old media developments that matter in this era only to reporters. People are unlikely to remember who had that story first. But they are not likely to forget that cell-phone text message in the middle of the night. The formal Biden announcement was made in Springfield that afternoon. The convention began on Monday and ran for four days.

What exactly is the point of the modern political convention? It no longer plays any decisive role in the selection of presidential candidates, a process that shifted into the hands of the voters with the reforms the Democrats embraced in 1972. It's essentially a huge television show, but even that part doesn't get as much attention as it did in the days when Chet Huntley and David Brinkley explained the process to a waiting, eager nation. The party still cobbles together rules and a platform, but it would be hard to find anyone who could summarize what was in any of the Democratic platforms over the past four presidential races.

For Obama, the Denver convention was a chance to showcase his family on his own terms, his message and his running mate all in one place, with some assurance that a big TV audience would see at least some of it. It was at the Democratic Convention in Boston in 2004 that Obama introduced himself to America and planted the seeds of his own presidency. In Denver the convention had its unforgettable moments. "We need a president who cares more about Barney Smith than Smith Barney," said a warehouse worker from Indiana named Barney Smith in a little cameo of "average voter" speeches. The Democrats crammed some 81,000 people into Mile High Stadium for Obama's nomination acceptance address. That was impressive. Running mate Joe Biden did not go on and on and did not say any-thing that got him, Obama, or anyone else in big trouble. He bobbled a few phrases in his speech and laughed them off. His image, that of the husband, father, and grandfather, a man whose life included its tragedies and triumphs, was showcased at every opportunity.

The convention provided a spectacular backdrop for cable TV and media coverage, though it must have left a lot of newsroom budget watchers at newspapers scratching their heads and asking, "Why did we send ten people?" Habit and history dictate cover-age as much as the distant chance news might happen. Not so long ago managing editors would show up and command their troops as though they were heading into battle. No longer; instead it is a scheduled event for newspapers, where great effort is taken to make sure nothing spontaneous happens. It is a different matter for TV. The networks cut way back, suffering their own version of the same money shortages that have plagued newspapers. The cable channels, particularly CNN and MSNBC, went damn near crazy. CNN opted for the same tiered collections of bloviators, partisans, and former well-knowns who gabbed their way deep into the night during the primary season. One team would exhaust a time frame and then another team would be dragged into camera view. CNN tried mightily to make certain all sides were represented, with Wolf Blitzer cast in the role of emcee and balance referee. It was like a Greek chorus that had not been well rehearsed. At MSNBC, Chris Matthews, who had been Tip O'Neill's flack back when the speaker ruled the day in the U.S. House, and Keith Olbermann, who wears his sense of outrage on his lip, delivered a downsized version. Rachel Maddow, engaging and beyond witty for TV, was the cleanup batter and welcome relief. Key speeches received little prime-time coverage on the networks, but the days of gavel-to-gavel broadcast coverage, complete with speeches from future luminaries, shifted over to network websites.

All of it seemed aimed at underlining the profound nature of the change that had swept over news media, which had shifted from something that told you what was going on only a few years ago to something that told you all about how it felt during the 2008 campaign. For traditionalists, this is not a happy change and does not bode well for the value side of journalism, already under heavy fire because it has lost its golden-goose status. That call to simply and clearly report what was happening would be sorely missed as the campaign played out. What was required when John McCain announced his ticket mate a little while after the Democratic TV show ended in Denver was a cool head that would ask just one important question: Why is he doing this? That's not what happened. Why John McCain turned to Sarah Palin, the Alaska governor of two years, remains a question that will tease political scientists for years.

Consider the playing ground. McCain had been aggressively challenging Obama on the basis of his lack of experience for months. At seventy-two years old and with a record full of serious health problems, he had to know that one of the first questions anyone would ask about his vice-presidential choice would be: "Is this person ready to be president?" It was clear from early on that, despite her support from conservative commentators eager to have anything fresh and new arrive in the McCain campaign, there was no way Sarah Palin was ready to become president. Neither was she ready to become vice president or a national candidate for a major political party. She seemed full of spirit. She looked good. She had a bold-looking, outdoorsy husband and an interesting family that included a special-needs baby. It all looked very American. (A pregnant teenaged daughter drew some tsk tsk's from the bluenoses, but anyone who has raised children in modern America knows how common that is.) Her record included some bumpy spots as governor and before that as mayor of Wasilla, a small town with a big mall.

None of that was the real problem. The real problem was that the McCain campaign knew from the outset that it had to keep the Alaska governor on a short leash. The woman was explosively controversial, on everything from claiming foreign policy expertise that came with being able to see across the Bering Strait into Russia to her noting that there was a lot she could do as vice president to fix up the U.S. Senate, a thought that was frightening for the lack of knowledge it revealed about what a vice president does. To be sure, Obama kept Joe Biden on a short leash too, but no one could ever tell that because he never became the lead campaign story. He did what good vice-presidential candidates have always done—went to the places the candidate had no time for, shook the right hands, smiled and supported the candidate's agenda, and stayed well out of trouble.

But Palin had one prime-time TV interview that was an embarrassment and stayed an embarrassment for days. She had the great blessing and great misfortune to be almost as good looking as TV star Tina Fey, who managed to create a parody Palin that was both hilarious and vicious. Satire is now an integral part of modern campaign coverage (witness the role of *The Daily Show*, a news program satire, and *The Colbert Report*, a satire of a right-wing TV show). But this went beyond simple satire. The Fey parodies were key internet events, shared millions upon millions of times, a process that dragged the offense well beyond its *Saturday Night Live* initiation. And because Fey, with lots of makeup help, looked almost like a cookie-cutter version of Palin, the shows seemed far more damaging than one of *SNL*'s most legendary satires, Chevy Chase's depiction of a bumbling Gerald Ford, stuffed dead dog beside his desk. One might chuckle recalling the Chase performance upon seeing Ford in that era. With Fey, it was like seeing Palin with her personality dialed up to about fourteen.

The Palin candidacy had two other problems, with the first being insurmountable and the most serious. No matter how compelling, the vice-presidential candidate cannot be the central story for more than a few days, generally just after the selection is announced. Sarah Palin became the big draw in so many ways. The big rallies the McCain campaign was dismissing when they were for Obama became big McCain rallies when Sarah Palin was on stage. That created a misleading impression about what was going on. Very few people invert the order on the ballot. They vote for president, not for vice president. But there was no way McCain could pump the kind of energy from a crowd that Palin could draw just by walking on stage. While it is true that support for her diminished as time passed, the people who stuck with her simply love her (to this day) and believe she is the party's salvation. On everything from the sanctity of the lives of unborn babies to tax policy, they found a soul mate in Sarah Palin. But that was supposed to be McCain's role.

The second problem with her candidacy was that the story ran away with its subject long before anyone got to know who Sarah Palin was. People who knew nothing of her record had heard she was being investigated by the legislature for one of those seamy personnel things so common in state capitals. People knew she could field-dress a moose. The political enemies she made (they *all* make enemies) emerged. Then there were the Fey parody episodes. No one has cast the measure yet, but there should be a point at which it becomes apparent, based on the subject matter in parody, that a candidacy isn't going to work. For some people it became difficult to discern which Palin was Palin, the Fey-Palin parody or the governor herself, who sometimes seemed like a parody. The "there you go again, say it ain't so Joe" moment in her single debate with Biden was a case in point. Going on *Saturday Night Live* and hamming it up may have shown she was a good sport but was ultimately a foolish political move. All it did was shine klieg lights on what a ripe target she was for parody with her blinking, winking ways and "you betchas."

McCain, who loves to gamble, had obviously laid a bet on the thought the campaign could control the Sarah Palin image and that she would help with that, but he was as wrong as he could be. The Republicans buffed the Palins up with wardrobe changes (even that became an issue, as though the family had violated some unspoken Farm and Fleet Flannel Shirt Loyalty Oath by going to Neiman Marcus and Nordstrom at the party's expense) and makeup and some tutoring in being public personae, but the family always seemed to be one stretch of ice away from plunging into cold waters. The Lower 48 simply could not be ready for that kind of political presence, complete with moose hunting, stories about shooting wolves from helicopters, and drill, drill, drilling for oil, that obviously sells so well in Alaska. Or it could simply have been a very bad attempt at the Hail Mary pass the McCain campaign needed to pull itself up in the rankings. Either way it clearly did not work. Her ratings slipped as Election Day approached.

The people at the center of the Obama campaign had a good laugh at the Palin selection, though the initial reaction included waves of polling-fueled fear in the Washington arm of the campaign. She did give the campaign a bump when it needed one. Axelrod's counsel was to wait her out, that the initial blush would be gone in a couple of weeks when people got a much closer look at who Palin was. "Remember the whole month or six weeks up to the Palin selection they were running a strategy that said, 'John McCain is experienced. . . . He's the one who will make decisions that always put the country first.' And all of a sudden, he picks Palin, who is completely inexperienced, puts her a heartbeat away from the presidency, and plainly wasn't making a decision that put the country first. And they sort of blew up their own strategy and decided to play the game on our court, which was change. That was one of the fun moments in the campaign because, you know, you knew what they were doing."

Then there was the Republican National Convention in Minneapolis–St. Paul in September. Again it is hard to say what these events are about. What is not hard to say is that it was off track from its very first day, which turned out not to be its actual first day but technically its second day. The first day was canceled because of weather several hundreds of miles away, which was a most revealing decision.

There may be no better measure of the damage the Bush administration inflicted on Republican fortunes than McCain's decision to delay the opening of the Republican Convention until everyone got to see whether Gustav, kicking up waves out in the Gulf of Mexico, would revisit the locus of the Bush administration's great Katrina debacle, New Orleans, and the Gulf Coast. The delay could in no way appear to be anything more than a gesture, and an empty gesture at that if Gustav had actually been the killer everyone feared. Assume for a minute that Gustav was going to be Katrina II. To postpone the convention for a day to see what would happen works, but then what? Postpone it forever while the nation tried to figure out how to help the Gulf Coast? Postpone it just long enough for the Bush administration to get its chastened Department of Homeland Security on the scene for photo ops and assurances that this time everything would be handled by the book? The truth lurking behind the questions is revealing. The convention is a TV show. Without questioning the sincerity of McCain or Palin, the strategic reality for the GOP was that another huge hurricane would become the only story TV would take an interest in. The convention, had it continued in the face of the storm, would have been pushed so far to the back of the stove, it wouldn't even be near a burner. That would mean the lasting memory of TV politics for the summer would be of the Obama and Biden families all clotted up on that stage with eighty thousand cheering Democrats all around them and red, white, and blue confetti cascading down on everyone even as prime-time TV ended its day with the Obama anointment. The Republicans weren't having that. They got some compassion credibility by calling it off for a day.

As the storm weakened and it became clear Gustav would not be Debacle II, the convention opened. All the big contenders were there: Mitt Romney, Rudy Giuliani, Mike Huckabee, and even Fred Thompson, the former senator and movie star who went from possible party savior to "not interested" in record time. The best speech came from McCain, who has the most compelling story in the modern annals of Republican politics.

"I fell in love with my country when I was a prisoner in someone else's. . . . I loved it for its decency; for its faith in the wisdom, justice and goodness of its people. I loved it because it was not just a place, but an idea, a cause worth fighting for. I was never the same again. I wasn't my own man anymore. I was my country's," he said, reflecting on his days as a prisoner of war in Vietnam. He has told this story many times before, but it never fails to touch anyone who hears it.

The next best speech at the convention came from Palin, who was perfectly in rhythm with what the party wanted to hear and in lockstep with her mission. Her job was to try to recast Barack Obama in a different role that emphasized his lack of experience, his anti-patriotic attitude toward the wars in Iraq and Afghanistan, and strangely, the gift of his rhetoric as a disadvantage, not an asset. She needed to jab the media a couple of times. Hunter that she is, she aimed and took her shots well.

"Before I became governor of the great state of Alaska, I was mayor of my hometown. And since our opponents in this presidential election seem to look down on that experience, let me explain to them what the job involves. I guess a small-town mayor is sort of like a 'community organizer,' except that you have actual responsibilities. I might add that in small towns, we don't quite know what to make of a candidate who lavishes praise on working people when they are listening, and then talks about how bitterly they cling to their religion and guns when those people aren't listening. We tend to prefer candidates who don't talk about us one way in Scranton and another way in San Francisco," Palin said.

"As for my running mate, you can be certain that wherever he goes, and whoever is listening, John McCain is the same man. I'm not a member of the permanent political establishment. And I've learned quickly, these past few days, that if you're not a member in good standing of the Washington elite, then some in the media consider a candidate unqualified for that reason alone.

"But here's a little news flash for all those reporters and commentators: I'm not going to Washington to seek their good opinion—I'm going to Washington to serve the people of this country. Americans expect us to go to Washington for the right reasons, and not just to mingle with the right people."

The response to both speeches was thunderous, a surprise because the Republicans had held their convention in a much smaller hall than the one the Democrats used. The event closed with a balloon drop that was so well executed it buried in balloons lots of people who were still on the convention floor.

The minute the Republican Convention ended, the process shifted into a different world, no longer the world of bold partisan activists who define the Democratic and the Republican party but the world of the electorate, where people are a lot less passionate about their politics and a lot more focused on what is actually happening in their lives. A candidate might be able to incite the fire-breathing loyalists with tough talk in either party because that's what they want to hear. Outside, a different conversation was underway, one that would define the outcome of the election.

It was as though the world that described politics when the process began almost two years before had somehow been transformed by outside forces. The war in Iraq, defining for both candidates at the beginning, had become much quieter. At home, it was as though a lot of people could stand in the street and watch as their most precious financial asset, their house, melted into the ground. When the letter carrier brought the quarterly 401(k) report, everyone knew what was happening. That money put aside for retirement was disappearing, with everyone sharing in the loss. Everything that had seemed so certain only sixteen months ago was cracking, crumbling, evaporating. How long would it last? How deep would it go? How much would we lose?

Coming out of those conventions, less than one in five people thought the country was on the right track. To the Republicans, that was seven years of George Bush coming home, the piper at his side looking for payment. To the Democrats, it meant their mantra of change had been perfect from the beginning. A couple of factors would determine how this election would play out. One was money, which the Democrats had in great abundance. The second was message. Obama's had been clear from the beginning.

Now all they needed was the voters.

7

THE STORIES THEY TELL

THE CAMPAIGN was in full force as I headed out to visit with some of the "likely voters" who always show up in polling news stories. I had been talking with some of them since the campaign had begun and was also paying close attention to polling results, but I wanted to find out more about individuals' decisions. In the country or bustling city, far away or close to home, there was a vast array of opinion about the election, what direction America should take, and even what the real issues were. True believers are like children on the way to the ocean for a vacation: the closer they are to the end of the ride, the more excited they get. As fall approached, it seemed like Barack Obama was surfing a few yards ahead of a wave of support from people upset about George Bush, particularly the independent voters (a large slice of the electorate). Call it momentum, call it whatever you will, it was building and was powerful.

John McCain seemed to be in trouble and without much time left. The strong conservatives at the heart of the Republican party were unimpressed. McCain had abandoned the argument that he had the experience to be president and had now embraced Obama's theme of change. That's a hard sell for someone who has been a fixture in

Republican politics for decades. The selection of Governor Sarah Palin of Alaska as McCain's running mate provided momentum and heated up the conservative party base, but just as Obama adviser David Axelrod had predicted, it began to soften as the TV satires took their toll and Palin poured water on the fire with her campaign-trail performance.

The debates were over. Obama supporters believed he won, McCain supporters believed McCain won, and in the vice-presidential contest, the same applied. As always in the absence of a big mistake, it depended on whom you backed. Some people were beginning to make their final decision, others had decided way back in the primary season, and still others had been informed by a lifetime of interest in politics.

The Democrats were feeling confident, the independents were breaking left, and for the many believers on the conservative right, the nation was on the verge of making a huge and disastrous mistake.

MARTIN P. GERAGHTY

In his Evanston backyard Martin Patrick Geraghty was grilling two of the biggest porterhouse steaks I have ever seen. He decided this would be better than going to a restaurant and trying to shout above the noise. He served the steaks with a little salad and the manly, starchy, processed default side dish, toaster-ovened Tater Tots, to set the stage for a three-hour talk about politics.

I knew I wanted to talk to Geraghty because he is first of all a staunch and consistent conservative who thinks and speaks clearly about his beliefs. I have known him for thirty years, and though we have disagreed on just about everything in that time, he remains a respected source of thought on conservatism. This is not an easy thing in Evanston, Illinois, one of the most liberal towns in America and a place where Democrats get elected to almost everything. The joke about Evanston, home to Northwestern University, is that its election returns are always late because its citizens think the referendum questions deserve essay answers. It is one of those places where people will not take "yes" for an answer, preferring to continue the discussion in a quest for consensus. As he flipped his steaks, Geraghty noted that eventually he will probably have to depart Evanston for a more politically congenial place. "Look around," he said. "There are no McCain-Palin signs here."

Geraghty is a successful man in a tough business, putting together commercial leasing packages in downtown Chicago, its suburbs, and around the country. A faithful follower of everything political, he is an occasional guest on Chicago radio and television programs, eloquently defending his positions. He shouts well too, an asset in modern media. When I set out to write this book, I knew my tendency might be to gravitate toward the emerging liberal majority in looking at this election—it's easy to reach, eager to talk, and filled with anger about the Bush years. I believed Geraghty would help me balance it with his insight. I was not wrong.

If you knew only about Geraghty's childhood, you would make the mistake most people do when they think about Chicago (in the 1950s and later) under the Mayors Daley, that this guy was one of those neighborhood Democrats to the core. But getting to know him is a lesson in understanding where conservative political values come from and how important they are to the people who hold them. This is the heart and soul of modern Republicanism, even though Geraghty thinks of himself as conservative first. He does not call himself a Republican, drifting in and out of the party depending on what options are available. He has voted for Democrats when the alternatives were not acceptable. This time around he was not comfortable with the options.

It's surprising Geraghty votes Republican at all, given his deep roots in a Chicago ward on Addison Street, the traditional heart of North Side Democratic power, but that's what makes the story riveting. "I was baptized a Democrat," Geraghty says. "When I was born, it was assumed that I would always be a practicing Catholic and a good Democrat. I can remember when I was a little kid, we lived in a three-flat with a basement apartment below us, and the kid from the basement apartment was my age and his mother was divorced, which was pretty unusual in those days. One day I learned she was going to hell. And the reason I knew she was going to hell was that she was going to vote in 1952 for Dwight Eisenhower. It wasn't because she was divorced. It was because she was a Republican. That's why she was going to hell."

Geraghty's dad worked for the Democrats but was never on the party or city payroll. "He knew there was St. Francis of Assisi, St. Francis de Sales, and Franklin Roosevelt. We all knew that Franklin Roosevelt was a secular saint who had made all the difference in the world. Roosevelt was this revered human being in our house, and you could not say anything bad about him." Geraghty's mother and father had both come from Ireland, where they had lived some thirty-five miles apart but never met. They collided at a Fourth of July picnic in Chicago in 1925 and were married in 1938. Pat Geraghty worked in a variety of jobs, one of them being fish-cutting, where he became a fish fileter so highly skilled and quick that his co-workers were eager to be on his cutting team. Geraghty was born at the very end of World War II. He has a brother, now a retired Chicago cop, and a sister, who is a B.V.M. nun.

Not much for reminiscing, Geraghty says his brother and sister are the repositories of all childhood memories. Geraghty does recall one of the first black men—the mailman—he met, but he doesn't remember him primarily as a black man. He remembers they became good friends when he was young: "My mom would let me walk a few doors with him to deliver mail. He would hold my hand when we went up the steps and talk with me. I loved him. He was just this guy who was always there, part of the neighborhood scenery. To this day I can't tell you whether his name was Kilpatrick or Kirkpatrick, but he was what I aspired to be, this black guy. I think I never really knew that he was black."

Geraghty's father had an eighth-grade education but never stopped reading. The neighborhood kids would visit on Sundays, when his father would first read the comics to the children, then read them the editorial pages. "Think of that," Geraghty said, "he would read the editorial pages to us kids." Geraghty advanced beyond his father's education, first attending St. Andrew Elementary School, then St. Jude Minor Seminary with the Claretian order in Momence, Illinois.

Initially he wanted to be a missionary priest. While many young Catholic men followed the same course in that era, not many sought to become missionaries. Being a parish priest in Chicago, in Geraghty's mind, just wasn't enough of a challenge. Working with poor people in Central or South America, now that was a test. The largest number of young men left seminaries after realizing how engaging and friendly women could be. Geraghty didn't quit because of women, though he took a healthy interest in them later. (He is the father of eight children, of whom six survive. One was stillborn, and one died after eight days.) It was the vow of obedience that bothered him. His objective was to save souls in foreign lands, but the vow of obedience could just as well mean he would end up teaching religion at some high school in New Jersey if that is what the order wanted him to do. He could not imagine being that obedient, so he quit and attended college and then graduate school. At Loyola University in Chicago he earned a bachelor's degree in political science. At the University of

Missouri he earned a master's in political science with a specialty in Latin American affairs in 1969.

Geraghty remembers voting for the first time in the 1967 mayoral primary election in Chicago for Mayor Richard J. Daley, who was midway through his long reign as party boss and city leader. Then everything changed. Geraghty, living up to Roman Catholic and Democratic expectations, was about to make a major life adjustment, and it wasn't in his religion. He was about to risk hellfire by becoming a Republican.

At first, he recalled, it was all about getting work out of college. The Illinois legislature offered a handful of internships for good students, and Geraghty had always been a good student. Interns were assigned to work for either Democrats or Republicans. Geraghty ended up working on the Republican side for Senate president pro tempore W. Russell Arrington. Jim Edgar, who went on to become an Illinois governor, worked alongside Geraghty and became a friend. Arrington was a visionary lawmaker, a hard-nosed, cigar-chomping, insurance-executive conservative before anyone thought of distinguishing between "conservative" and "compassionate conservative."

Geraghty began to think of himself in the Senate as working for the good guys, with the Democrats not necessarily being the bad guys, just not the good guys. As time passed a handful of issues arose, with school choice rising to the top for Geraghty at the time. Later, sanctity-of-life issues became important as abortion moved to center stage. A product of Catholic schools, Geraghty believed finding the best school for a child was one of the most important parental responsibilities. Democrats opposed school choice. Welfare spending bothered him too, but he saw the value in short-term help for people in trouble. Gradually he began to view it as capitalism versus anti-capitalism. Even though his father had been a Democrat, he had worked hard for every penny he brought home. When Geraghty's

internship ended, he joined the Republican staff. Now he was helping write legislation and developing his own views about how to be a
conservative and a Republican. He considered taxes a problem, with
Democrats wanting higher levies.

But working in Springfield wasn't so much about philosophy. It
was tough, gritty work on difficult legislation that touched on almost
every aspect of life. "It convinced me that taxes were a bad thing,
and that the idea in running any government agency was not to find
enough money to do what everybody wants to do, but to cut back on
what people want to do and respect the right of the public to keep its
own damn money." It was a hard lesson for the Republicans who were
defeated in the backlash after Illinois instituted an income tax under
Republican governor Richard Ogilvie. Arrington left the Senate after
a debilitating stroke, and though Geraghty could have kept working
there, he didn't like the senators who stayed behind. Having arrived
in Springfield as a naive intern, he left a committed conservative.

Geraghty had his own brief stint at public office in Evanston as
a councilman, where he tried to push for spending cuts in the city
budget, only to be challenged by a city manager who announced that
the first "Geraghty cut" would be to eliminate the nursing mothers
program. "Hell, I was married to a nursing mother at the time," Geraghty protests. But the city staff's handling of the issue made Geraghty seem the enemy of nursing mothers, at least in the minds of
the softhearted folks who showed up to protest. Once a Republican
bastion, Evanston was in a period of rapid change that would leave it
solidly Democratic. Geraghty's civic career ended.

Although he worked in real estate in downtown Chicago, Geraghty remained a political animal. At Arthur Rubloff & Company,
he convinced the executives that they should have their own political
action committee to support like-minded politicians. "I kind of made
a name for myself. I don't think, as I recall, that was my intention.
But the boys on executive row liked the idea that this punk kid was

willing to suggest such an idea on behalf of good people, which is my definition of Republicans ... or, at least conservatives." From there he began his own business, but his drive for politics didn't diminish.

Recalling the story of his stillborn child, Geraghty spoke with passion about the value of human life. He held the boy, mourned him, counted his tiny toes, and noted the soft hair on the backs of his fingers. Because of that, Geraghty could never think of him as anything but a fully formed human being. His commitment to life, he says, stretches from conception to death. While conceding that the state has the right to execute criminals, Geraghty believes the state should not exercise that right. Confronted by someone with a weapon, he says, he would fight to save his own life.

The issue closest to Geraghty's heart is education and whether anyone will ever understand how to transform the collapsing hulk of the public school system. His solution is school choice, which he describes as the great civil rights issue of the modern era. "For generations, the wealthy have been voting with their feet in search of schools where their kids can succeed. The poor (usually 'the blacks') have watched generations of their kids die of mal-education." His thoughts on this subject are controversial. While he sees the status quo in urban education as a system designed primarily to employ and indeed enrich large numbers of middle-class black and white teachers and administrators, he believes the Democrats, who control the majority of urban public education, are happy to "endure" the side effects of this system: bad schools with no hope of producing a generation of well-educated blacks who would naturally turn into Republican voters, or at least enough of them to wreck the math that keeps sending Democrats to office.

It takes fast-forwarding to bring Geraghty into the current election cycle. What you speed past is a debate about the real meaning of Chechnya and Islamic fundamentalism; whether we didn't actually create Osama bin Laden back when we supported the

mujahideen against the Soviet army in Afghanistan; the greatness of
Newt Gingrich's Contract with America and the inside-the-Beltway
virus that made so many of Gingrich's radicals into pork-barrel specialists before you even knew it; Ronald Reagan's competence and
George W. Bush's tragic lack of it; how Bill Clinton managed to get
away with the public embarrassment of a blow job in the Oval Office when Republicans can't get away with anything; the lack of good
choices in the Republican presidential primaries (he voted for Mitt
Romney but would have loved a chance to vote for Gingrich); and
many other subjects. His mind is as fast as a pinball machine, with
bounces in as many directions.

When we first talked he was uncertain about what he was going
to do in November, so late in the campaign I dropped him a note
and asked for an update. I suspect many conservatives were wrestling
with the same issues—a candidate they didn't love running against a
candidate whom no one knew much about.

"It's hard to be Marty Geraghty these days," he wrote. "It's mid-
October and Obama is cruising while McCain refuses to fight back."
He was never excited about John McCain (making him one of a great
many likely Republican voters unenthusiastic about McCain's nomination). Geraghty saw McCain as the Bob Dole of 2008, a man who
won the nomination because the party thought they owed it to him.
Geraghty was angry that McCain would not "take the gloves off" and
"cite chapter and verse just how unworthy a candidate Obama is." He
was deeply worried about Obama's candidacy.

"With the confluence of McCain's ineptitude and the crashing
economy, we are about to elect a Manchurian candidate whose plans
go far beyond a mere tack to the left. This is a guy with ambitions of
his own and a roster of allies to convert our very free enterprise system into one that seeks retribution on the rich (merely for being rich).
After four years of Obama, America will be a second-rate country
unable to regain its stature as the greatest nation in history, self-hating

and self-disarmed so badly that we will be neither willing nor able to stand against the forces that want us to die.

"The media loved McCain when he was the least conservative Republican in the race. He thought they would continue to offer him the kid glove treatment denied his opponents then. What a fool! As soon as he became the more conservative candidate, the left-wing media did to him what they had just done to Hillary."

Geraghty believed Obama was not presenting his true plans for the nation because it would have been electoral suicide. So Geraghty filled in the campaign-trail blanks. In his view, Obama wanted to reduce the size of the military, reduce or perhaps end missile defense plans, nationalize the medical system, pull out of Iraq despite the consequences, make the nation far greener than it was (with no drilling, no nuclear energy, no clean coal, "no warmth, no industry"), allow unlimited abortion, allow gay marriage (perhaps by some other name), and prosecute those who disagreed with him about gay marriage and abortion on hate-speech charges.

"We have never had a candidate so unknown to anyone. In the last thirty years you could look up Kerry or Reagan or Dole or Gore and find out what each of them was doing five or ten or twenty years earlier. Even if you read both of Obama's autobiographies, you get almost no real information about what he did during the '90s." And this lack of knowledge was complicated in the campaign, Geraghty argued, by a mainstream media that wasn't willing to ask tough questions about Obama. The reason for that? The media already knew that the answers would damage Obama's campaign.

He viewed the selection of Sarah Palin as McCain's running mate as a good sign. What she didn't know about international relations, she could learn, Geraghty thought. Then he touched on something that might have been at the heart of Palin's support in a part of the Republican party that had long felt abandoned: "Our governing class has become very insulated from the rest of America, and she'll bring them back if she's in the White House, especially if she has several years to learn the ropes (but not get entangled in them) as vice president. There's a kind of Beltway-speak that fills the airwaves today. For a while it appeared Gingrich's boys in 1994 would choose not to learn it, but most of his guys were co-opted by it. A number of true believers term-limited themselves out of D.C. before they could have enough effect."

According to Geraghty, Biden was a blowhard who voted wrong on the First Gulf War and then lied about his reasons for voting for the Iraq War. He believed Biden and Obama wanted to "surrender to the savagery of radical Islam in Iraq. They seem to believe we will be less likely to go to war if we can be so badly disarmed that we lack the ability to go to war. Thus, very much of Obama's budget cutting will come, as did Clinton's, from reducing the size of our military."

His worries about Obama ran deep.

"Never before have I felt this way about a candidate. I detested Clinton, Gore, and Kerry, but each was a reasonably conventional Beltway liberal with no burning agenda in his soul. . . . The more I read about Obama, the more I am convinced he is imbued with this notion of white responsibility for the oppression of America's blacks and committed to redressing this evil, no matter the consequences. If I believed in intercessory prayer, I'd pray that I'll be proved wrong. But unless McCain manages to rise up and speak the truth about this guy, we are in for a long, dark night of oppression from our government and savagery from our international enemies."

BRIAN VACHON

The view in Brian Vachon's backyard takes in a healthy Vermont hillside a mile or so outside of Montpelier and a couple of outbuildings,

one of which contains two brown-eyed "pets" that Vachon bought
for a daughter years earlier and then never had the nerve to exile. It's
not that they seem out of place, it's just that you don't expect a man
with such an esteemed background in writing, business, and politics
to own two goats.

At first this seems like an unlikely place for a conversation about
presidential politics. On an October day Vachon was sitting on his
patio, shirtless because he had been told it's good for his health to sit
in the sun for a little each day to help his mood and build Vitamin D.
Despite the chill in the air, it made perfect sense in Vermont, a place
that seems to have been meticulously built by craftsmen of a different age, determined to make a point about small-town democracies
as they constructed backdrops for Norman Rockwell paintings and
Currier & Ives set pieces. Going outdoors and breathing deep, it's
good here.

It hasn't snowed yet, so the place doesn't look quite like a Christmas card, but you can imagine down in front of the small, pristine
state capitol building in town exactly how it would look with fat
snowflakes falling. Even the thought of it makes you want to find a
Christmas-tree-shaped sugar cookie with green sprinkles on top and
a cup of hot cocoa.

Barack Obama almost owned this territory during the primaries,
a state filled with liberal people who viewed the eight years of President Bush as an abomination that had to be pushed from the stage.
And what better way to do that than to vote for an African-American
Democrat talking about the need to give government back to the people? That was important rhetoric in Vermont, where civic mindedness
is as endemic as red-maple leaves signaling a lovely seasonal change
on a fall afternoon. They still have town meetings where everything
is decided. They vote in numbers higher than in most other places:
Vermont is one of ten states where some 65 percent of the voting-age

population went to the polls in 2004, well above the national figure. (Minnesota was highest with just about 80 percent. Hawaii was lowest with just over 50 percent.) That's not to say that it's perfect, and especially not to say it has always been liberal and Democratic. But in this election, Vermont was in the vanguard of places for Obama.

Vermont is independent to its very roots. Vermont voters show no shyness in voting for either party. They sent Bernie Saunders, a socialist (running as an independent), to Congress and then to the Senate in 2006. He was outspoken about everything. "The major issue of this campaign is pretty simple," he said on his website. "George W. Bush has been the worst president in our lifetimes and perhaps the worst president in the history of our country. What this campaign will determine is whether we continue four more years of Bush's disastrous policies, or begin the process of moving this country in a very different direction." And yet Vermonters elected a Republican governor. As party labels continue to melt away, Vermont may be an augury of what America will look like in a distant political future, a place where politics is about individuals who are well known by the voters. It is not unusual to walk down the street in Montpelier and run into the governor, not surrounded by a brace of beefy state troopers but just strolling, maybe for a coffee. Most of America isn't this way, but on a brilliant autumn afternoon Vermont seems like a comfortable, engaging place and a fine role model.

Vachon is a good character to take the measure of Vermont. Like so much of Vermont's current population, he is an outsider. Raised in New York and employed as a writer all over the place before coming to Vermont, Vachon moved there in the 1970s to be editor of *Vermont Life* magazine. His background included work at *Psychology Today*, *Newsweek*, the *New York Daily News*, and *Saturday Review*, and he was also a public relations supervisor for years at a big insurance company. While he has a lot to brag about, he doesn't. At twenty-seven he was named editor of a magazine for girls called *Charley*. He was a senior editor at *Saturday Review* by the time he was thirty. He was at the top of his game. All of that landed him in California, which he despised because it was all about pot for younger people in that era, and he learned he was all about alcohol. The seasons never changed, it was always delightful, and when he came back east to write a story, he ended up weeping. "I was crying. Just standing there and crying and wondering, 'What am I crying about?'" When he saw the *Vermont Life* job advertised, he became one of two hundred people who applied, and he was offered the job. He took a large pay cut, moved to Vermont, and immersed himself in state history, geography, and politics for a decade. Then he became vice president for communications at National Life Group, a job he held for twenty-five years. Three years into it, he went to his boss, announced he was an alcoholic, and said he needed to go into recovery, which the company supported. He retired and now counsels young people on the writing of essays for college applications. Governors in both parties have named him to a variety of commissions and boards. Education is one of his passions.

"Vermont is a state that in its first 150 years had never elected a Democrat. I mean, they didn't even bother running here. And then a guy named Phillip C. Hoff came in during John Kennedy's presidency, and it was the first Democratic governor the state had ever had. Then the demographics of the place began shifting. People like me started moving in, and people who were native Vermonters started to be outnumbered. Then the younger people started coming. Now we are probably the safest Obama state in the nation. That's remarkable, because fifty years ago they would still not be sure who Obama was in Vermont. I don't think Vermont is essentially racist, although it is the whitest state in the country. But I think the whole notion of electing a liberal Democrat would have been so unheard of half a century ago, and now the whole notion of voting for John McCain is equally unheard of."

Vachon has no problem describing himself as liberal and explaining where that came from. But he is scrupulously independent about his politics, making him an example of one of the most important components in the Obama network, which would require the support of an army of all kinds of independents if it was to grab the electoral votes it needed to beat John McCain. With Election Day just a few weeks off, 36 percent of Americans told Gallup they were Democrats, and 28 percent said they were Republicans. It was the best showing for Democrats since the 1980s but left a huge pool of independent voters, a group potentially as big as the Democrats. A conversation with Vachon showed why it was wrong to think these people were not ideological. Instead they represented a big change in how people thought of themselves and their politics. The idea of being in a party was becoming passé, but the idea of being ideological was not. It's just that the ideologies of the parties, now vague after the political turmoil on all sides since the Vietnam War and the heavy watering-down of the 1980s and 1990s, didn't fit anymore.

"It's not that I'm not connected," Vachon pointed out, "but when someone says, 'I'm a Democrat' or 'I'm a Republican,' I say, 'Okay, but why?' Why would you affiliate yourself with a party? If I were a Democrat, I would probably vote more for Democrats than Republicans. Jim Douglas, our [Republican] governor, is a personal friend of mine. Of course I would vote for him. I don't understand party lines. I don't understand them at all." Read a little about Douglas and you get a sense of exactly how independent Vermont is. He has been a fixture in state government and politics there for decades. In many of the state offices to which he was elected, he had the nomination of both parties. It's hard to imagine something like that happening in Illinois, Pennsylvania, or New York, but it's routine here.

All over the United States are people like Vachon and his fellow Vermont independents. You never really know how they are going to vote, but they have made it clear they aren't buying into any tradi-

tional political models. Conditions seem to define how they feel about
candidates and parties. After eight difficult years that have yielded
frustration, two wars not yet won or ended, the worst economic crisis
in decades, and an overwhelming sense that the country is on the
wrong track, they were the people drawn quite clearly to the message
of change that was the mantra of the Obama campaign.

People who carry no party affiliation may be the most genuinely
ideological voters of all. In fact they may not even vote in an election if they don't feel moved, either by the personality of a candidate
and what he or she is saying, or by the ambient conditions in the nation that have always motivated people toward the polls. Any analysis
of the question "Why didn't people vote?" includes the reality that
many nonvoters don't like the choices they face. Change those conditions by offering a compelling candidate with a clear message, and
people tend to get up and vote. Whatever this phenomenon reflects, it
does not reflect the status quo. Vachon and his like-minded independents were not voting because they felt they should but because they
felt they must, given the conditions. And they were leaning toward
Obama because he was, most of all, not the standard political choice.
A candidate has to touch something deep inside Vachon, something
that has been there since his childhood, to draw his support.

One of his defining political moments came when he was attending high school in Manhattan. Most of his classmates were African
American and Puerto Rican, so though he didn't have the best voice,
he landed one of the lead roles, that of Woody the tobacco farmer, in
the school play, *Finian's Rainbow*. He was seventeen and had already
faced several challenges in his life. His father was John Vachon, a legendary photographer for *Look* magazine, the Works Progress Administration, and the United Nations. Brian remembers a talented man but
a serious drinker. His mother, a liberal activist who adored Eleanor
Roosevelt, had been in and out of mental institutions all of her son's
life. On opening night she was hospitalized once again. He focused

on his role, did well, and, along with the rest of the actors, came out for a bow. Standing in front applauding was Eleanor Roosevelt. "God, my mom would be so thrilled with that," Vachon thought.

He recalled going downtown in Manhattan with his mother to buy a shirt, but when they got to the store they ran into a picket line. "We don't cross picket lines," she told him, and he never has, even as a member of the Vermont Board of Education. "That would be like throwing a book away for me," he said. "I guess my liberal roots are a lot deeper that most. And yet I have to say that a lot of my favorite politicians are of the Republican mold."

But there wasn't much to draw him to the Republican side as the 2008 campaign began to play out. "My overwhelming, driving feeling as it started was that I was so sickened by what this administration did, that unless there was just a Republican who dazzled my socks off, I was naturally going to be looking at the Democrats," Vachon said. "I was very attracted to Joe Biden. I liked Dennis Kucinich a lot. I hated Hillary Clinton for personal reasons that had little to do with politics, but I just don't like her much as a human being. Obama was intriguing, but I didn't know anything about him. John Edwards— I am embarrassed to admit how much I liked him. He looked ten years younger than he was. I always wanted to look ten years younger than I was. He was very articulate. I knew he was full of shit because he was a multi-millionaire. He fell into it. But I was okay with him being a millionaire and being full of shit. I forgave him because I really thought his instincts sounded pretty extraordinary."

He liked Biden, and it was an old affection. Biden's problem with plagiarism back in the 1980s didn't bother him a bit, Vachon said, "because God knows I haven't written an original word since I was twenty-seven. So I like him, and I think he is bright and has real feelings. When it became obvious that it was going to become Hillary and Obama, I didn't have to wake up at night and wonder which way I was going to go. The more I kept looking for Obama's faults or issues, I really couldn't find any. And to this day I can't find any. Plus, I am so much in love with his wife, I can't stand it.

"I met McCain a couple of times. He's pretty affable, and I kind of like him—and then I started disliking him more and more and more. And ultimately I ended up despising McCain and adoring Obama. I am there." He searched. He could not find a single thing about McCain he could be drawn to. The Sarah Palin selection only sealed that conclusion.

"If you are going to be stupid, you might as well be as stupid as a human being can get. I loved it. It was glorious. [My wife] Nancy and I watched it on *Saturday Night Live*—the Tina Fey imitation—I was on the floor holding my side. I almost wished Sarah could win it so we could have this for ten more years or so. And then a funny thing happened with the last debate. I realized I didn't care anymore. I'm not going to be swayed. Not only am I not going to be swayed, nobody's going to be swayed. Here, on October 9, in my humble opinion, there is not an undecided person in the United States."

Vachon guessed there were perhaps as many as 25 million racists in the United States who would never admit it and would not vote for a black man. "But there are 25 million young people who are going to be voting for the first time in their lives, and that's the other side."

It was getting dark, so we went inside to look at some unpublished pictures of a character his father loved and Vachon loves too. In a stunning black-and-white photograph was a young Pete Seeger with his banjo. That led to a story that, in the context of the election, might have been as revealing as anything we shared that afternoon. Vachon noted that he and his wife had gone to a Pete Seeger concert just a few weeks earlier. He was telling some young women he tutored about going to the concert, and they thought he was talking about *Bob* Seger. "Suddenly, I realized they had no idea."

The concert by the then eighty-nine-year-old folk singer, whom Vachon first saw at Carnegie Hall with the Weavers when Vachon was fifteen, was apparently remarkable. Seeger started out like a creaky old guy, and then the years just melted away and he was back in form. "It was wonderful," Vachon said. On the way out he was telling the story of the young girls who didn't know who Seeger was to one of his friends, and one of four young women in front of him turned, saying, "I apologize." "I said, 'For what?' and she said, 'For my generation.' And I said that was something she didn't have to carry on her beautiful young shoulders. I told her, 'We're counting on you now to pull this thing off,' and she said, 'We will.'"

"They will," Vachon said. "They will make this happen. And if they sleep late that day, I move to Canada and we deserve what we get."

BIRCH BURGHARDT

Giving people are hard to find. Some people just send money. Some people send their concerns or their wishes for the best. Some people send their prayers. Birch Burghardt does all of that, but she also sends herself, making her unusual in the firmament of givers. Whether it is supporting after-school programs for disadvantaged children or tackling the biggest of all challenges, teaching in Chicago public schools, somehow she has been there. And if, for the moment, she is not there, she is thinking about being there, about how people can elevate themselves. There are people like this all over the North Shore of Chicago, folks who could sit comfortably back, send a check now and then, and feel just fine about it. But they don't. The place buzzes with do-gooders, many of whom actually do good instead of just talking about it.

Burghardt lives in a couple of places, one of them Evanston and one of them an island off Seattle, where she and her husband Galen have constructed a dream house for themselves and their children,

Galen Jr. and Sarah. A strong singer and lover of folk music, she is frequently seen in the company of her daughter, a tall blonde like herself with blue eyes and the gift of a strong alto. They are a very musical family, and an interesting political family. Birch is not a member of any political party but has her thoughts about politics. Galen may well be Republican, but it's not something he flaunts. The sense is that they have figured out how to keep diverse political views while having a close relationship. In the world of diplomacy, this would be called existing in a spirit of mutual respect and cooperation. They seem to get along very well.

I asked her to watch the Republican National Convention in Minneapolis and tell me what she thought of it. Because there is no television at the dream house (perhaps one reason it *is* a dream house), Burghardt watched the convention speeches on her laptop. I believed she would be particularly astute at this assignment because, first of all, she is fair-minded, and second, she is very smart, with a master's degree in economics from Georgetown and a doctorate in education from Northwestern.

She has a fascinating background. Burghardt was born in New Haven, Connecticut. Her penchant for improving schools might have come from her own first-rate experience: she went to public schools in Farmington, then shifted to Oxford School, a girl's day school in Hartford, for junior high school, and then went to Miss Porter's boarding school for high school. She studied at Kirkland College, a new women's college associated with Hamilton in upstate New York, and at Georgetown and Northwestern for advanced degrees.

She spent her childhood in such a strong Republican family that she was sent to school wearing a gold elephant pin that said "GOP" on it, or an "I Like Ike" button. This changed in the 1970s and 1980s when her family abandoned the Republican party and became activist Democrats in the wake of the Nixon administration and Watergate. They were inspired by Jimmy Carter.

It's hard to tell from Burghardt's position on issues which way she will vote. Her priority is "sharing our wealth with the world through generosity," which makes her sound like a Democrat. But she also believes outsourcing can be a good way to give impoverished people a chance to "climb the ladder out of poverty," which she feels strongly about, arguing it is "both morally and strategically wrong not to do so." She wants the next president to be careful about balancing the Supreme Court and not being so partisan when filling its vacancies. She wants serious action on the environment, believing the nation can't turn back the clock but that it must make a commitment "to reduce our negative impact on the environment from now on." Having taught school in Chicago, Burghardt knows the "immensity of the challenges faced by the schools," so federal funding efforts are crucial. Then she pops up with an issue that sounds classically conservative to me—"balance the budget"—but adds she would support tax increases to do so, which sounds Democratic again. She does not like the fact that the Chinese hold so much of America's debt.

Put it all together and you end up with a voter who looks a lot like many independent voters across the country: concerned about social issues like education and improving living conditions around the world, a little conservative on budget questions, and an advocate for public schools. It's healthy that her positions are unpredictable, because most people probably don't fit very handily into the boxes created for them. Some conservatives and gun-owning liberals, for example, deeply oppose the death penalty. Some libertarians feel pot-smoking is just fine, and some Democrats support strong enforcement against all drugs. People are just not that easy to categorize.

Simple descriptions are not broad enough for people like Burghardt. Because of her background as an economist, she has an inherent distrust of big government and what it can do. At the same time she liked the description "compassionate conservative" when it popped up in Republican circles in 2000, because it sent the message that you could be conservative and also care about the well-being of your fellow man. "It really made me think that people do care," she said. "They want there to be goodness. They want there to be kindness. They want there to be relationship and caring. They want to help people who need help, but they are still conservative." She hastened to point out that she believed President Bush was disingenuous and had never voted for him.

When I first approached her, Burghardt was "leaning" toward Obama but had some affection for John McCain, given his record and the way he handled himself. She seemed slightly concerned that Obama was riding on his popularity and eloquence and not offering much substance. She was not impressed with his speech at the Democratic National Convention, concluding he was just telling everyone what they wanted to hear.

By the time the Republican National Convention rolled around, with its faux start because of Hurricane Gustav, she had been following both sides of the contest closely and was eager to see what the Republicans had to say. My sense was that even though I thought of her as liberal, she could be swayed by a good argument to do an about-face. Her comments on the convention indicated that was most likely true up to a point—with the point being the arrival of Alaska governor Sarah Palin.

"I thought that at the beginning, McCain and Fred Thompson were incredibly eloquent," Burghardt said. "And they said what was most important. The most compelling thing about McCain, I think, is that he has in the past been really open and he's been really productive, often working across the aisle. He has that experience of being a prisoner of war and being very loyal to the United States. I think that is compelling. Whether it is important or not, I don't know. When I watched those speeches, I just kind of went, 'Huh, maybe I'd vote for McCain. Too bad I don't agree with him on some points.' So, anyway, I thought he was extremely compelling and impressive."

Young Galen was out on the island with his mother when McCain announced the Sarah Palin pick, "hammering away on his computer and going, 'Whoopee! He chose Sarah Palin! I really wanted him to choose her.' And I knew nothing about her except that Galen would say, 'She's a real reform candidate. She's been really colorful in Alaska.' And I thought, 'Huh, I'm interested. What am I going to see?' So, when she gave her speech, I hated it. She was so sarcastic. I thought she was playing herself up as a great person, really spunky and neat, right? But not really a person of substance so much as a person of punch and power. And then this nastiness came out, I was very sad . . . then Giuliani's speech, same thing. I thought he was unpleasant. . . . I mean, he smiles and it looks very strange. So anyway, I thought, 'Okay good. I don't have to vote for McCain.'"

As the convention progressed, she became convinced that the Republicans were still working on the party base very late in the game. All of the speeches seemed aimed at convincing the party faithful they had nominated the right candidate, even though McCain's conservative credentials were hardly sterling. The more she learned about Palin, the more concerned she became that the Alaska governor was unprincipled. Palin's problem with the so-called Bridge to Nowhere got Burghardt's attention. The Alaska governor claimed she had canceled the project, a pet project of Alaska senator Ted Stevens, but that happened only after she first supported the construction project, then canceled it, and used the money on other highway construction.

"There's that," Burghardt said. "I mean, the *New York Times* has biases, but they probably don't report falsehoods. Then there's the trooper story, which just makes me think, 'I want a slime ball like that as president?' Inexperienced and a slime ball. An emotional slime ball. Oh God!"

The conversation with Burghardt continued for some time, but it never moved beyond the point of picking a candidate. A couple of months from Election Day, she still didn't know enough about what Obama would do, though she was impressed with his presence, coolness, and rhetoric. She wondered what that had to do with being president. McCain presented her with a deal breaker by choosing Sarah Palin as his running mate. Burghardt is not a vulgar woman, so when "bitch" slipped out, she grew a little pink and apologized. It was a fetching gesture, but not a good sign for the McCain-Palin ticket.

After making her decision, Burghardt didn't just send money or offer lip service, she gave herself to the Obama campaign. That led her to one of those great stories about what a person does on Election Day, but that story comes later.

E. MICHAEL McCANN

Few citizens are more familiar with what happens when people slip off the legal track and into criminal behavior than E. Michael McCann. Until his retirement a few years ago, McCann, now seventy-two, had been the nation's longest-serving prosecutor as the district attorney of Milwaukee County. He still looks like a prosecutor, with the demeanor of someone you wouldn't want to cross. He had a reputation for being rumpled at the courthouse, and you get a sense that at least part of this image was cultivated because he didn't want anyone to think he was putting on airs. He lives in Milwaukee, a couple of blocks from the Brewers' ballpark, in a house where he and his wife, Barbara, a former newspaper reporter, raised their two children. He decided to live modestly years earlier when he realized that a county prosecutor might need to be able to walk away from a job for a variety of reasons. He also did not want the weight of a big mortgage affecting his decisions. So for E. Michael McCann rumpled is good, the way it was good for Peter Falk when he played Lieutenant Columbo on television.

There's nothing rumpled about the way McCann thinks. Beginning each day at Mass, he ponders the ritual's meaning and applies the lessons of an ancient religion to modern life. It's a consoling discipline for a man who has spent many years dealing with the consequences of what can go wrong. He has prosecuted crooked cops and corrupt public officials, street criminals, and violent people who commit senseless crimes. He has won homicide charges against a company that had misread Pap smear tests, a mistake that led to two women dying of cervical cancer. No one had done that before.

Pulled into the center of the Jeffrey Dahmer case, McCann still worries that many people could have been taken from the streets by a serial killer, murdered, and not missed. Dahmer was arrested in the summer of 1991 after many brushes with the authorities and ultimately indicted in fifteen of the seventeen murders he was charged with. In a search of his Milwaukee home, police had found an abundance of evidence, including human remains in his refrigerator and freezer. Dahmer's murders had involved torture, sexual abuse, and mutilations; in addition, he had consumed some of the remains of his victims. Since no doubt existed about the murders, McCann instead argued that Dahmer was not insane but a criminal with bizarre tastes and interests who took steps to cover his trail, exhibiting behaviors that were rational and well planned. In McCann's view, Dahmer had known exactly what he was doing. He was convicted and sentenced to fifteen life terms, only to be murdered in prison in 1994.

Even though McCann is not a hardened man in the way some cops and prosecutors become stonelike, he was not shocked by the Dahmer murders. "I mean, there are guys like John Wayne Gacy who had done thirty-four. We had a serial killer in Milwaukee, but the biggest surprise was that we didn't know he was there, that he could slay that many people in the city and no one knew it because there were no bodies. . . .

"I believe when a person is insane he should not be held accountable for what he did. I did not believe, nor did anyone who worked with Dahmer believe, that he was insane. He drank blood. He ate parts of bodies. Somehow you think this is insane. But that's not what insanity is. The test is, how do you function? Dahmer was holding a job. No one who worked with him thought he was insane. None of his family members thought he was insane. People who lived in his building did not think he was insane. He was not insane. He had bizarre tastes. The things he did were not normal. Necrophilia is not normal. But bizarre tastes and repeated criminality do not add up to insanity."

In nearly four decades on the job McCann has watched his city, his county, his state, and his nation change in ways no one could have imagined. He was special prosecutor in 2002 in a Wisconsin corruption case so serious that it forced the state Senate's majority leader from office, after which he was sentenced to prison in a plea agreement. Other politicians were also swept up in the investigation in one of those classic pay-to-play scandals too common in state capitols across the nation.

From this long history in public office, McCann reaps a gravitas that gives him some authority on the question of presidential choices, with perhaps his greatest qualification being that he left office with a reputation for complete incorruptibility, the straightest boy scout who ever held office. He didn't like it that his nation had been misled into a war. He didn't like the fact that, even after it was clear Iraq was the wrong place, the wrong time, and the wrong war, the nation reelected President Bush. He has absolutely no time for dishonesty in public office, an attitude that stretches from the lowliest public servant up to the Oval Office. Perhaps the greatest quote of his long career is, "If I were a vindictive man, you would know it," from an interview with a Milwaukee paper just before he retired.

McCann doesn't hate the people he has prosecuted. He has spent a good deal of time pondering the connection between economic decline and the increase in crime. He knows that a few minutes' drive from his modest home, where he delights in taking walks, the streets are not safe at night. He has watched the city and county he loves struggle with economic changes that have forced thousands of people out of work and closed the doors of opportunity to many young men and women. He knows that it's likely that if women who are at the bottom of the economic ladder lose their marginal jobs, prostitution, drug abuse, frustration, and perhaps child abuse may follow. He sees the connection between the way things are and how they affect people. Milwaukee remains a delightful town, but McCann knows the city and the statistics it creates. He knows there are deep problems.

"We wound up with the highest rate of black incarceration. We have the largest number of blacks living in our county, but would you believe Wisconsin has the lowest rate of African-American high school graduation? It has the second-highest or third-highest rate of white graduation. Milwaukee has the third-lowest graduation rate of the fifty largest metropolitan city school systems. Memphis and Cleveland were worse. As a black young man, if you don't get out of high school, this is the entrée to a trip to prison," McCann says. "I saw it happen. I was elected in 1968 and took office in 1969. Milwaukee was once referred to as the machine shop of the world. I saw that decline coming. Now it's gone. It probably peaked at around a hundred thousand jobs. Now Siemens has a couple of hundred guys and the rest is a shopping center. American Motors—thousands of jobs gone. Square D, gone. You can go through the list. We have lost tens of thousands of jobs. If you were a high school dropout then who could work hard, you could have damn good pay. These were good-paying jobs. They are gone now. You can flip hamburgers, but what your dad did, that's gone."

There were consequences. When McCann took over as district attorney, he and his staff pursued 30 to 40 homicides a year. In 1989 the crack-cocaine epidemic that was wrecking neighborhoods in American cities arrived in Milwaukee and the homicide rate climbed to an annual 87. In 1990 it was 116, and in 1991, 160. "Violence.

Gang struggles. Who is going to control the streets? Just once, in 2004, we dropped down to 88 homicides. But after 1990 we were never less than 100."

After a lifetime of watching violent crime, McCann has thoughts about how to limit your chances of being murdered: Stay away from bars where men tend to be armed. Don't take a night job at a gas station or convenience store where there is cash. Don't use or deal with drugs in any way. Don't get involved in the movement of drugs. Don't sit in bars. Don't honk your horn at anyone. Don't get angry at anyone. If you are a young black man and you become involved in a love triangle, use drugs, hang out in the wrong bars, or get into a gang, the chance you will be murdered increases dramatically. It's remarkable that this vastly experienced white man is so well acquainted with the calculus of survival in the city. But that's one reason why McCann is such a good person to talk with about politics.

There was nothing abstract about what McCann was talking about—he was not suggesting what "might" happen. He was reporting, not guessing. It took an hour for our conversation to shift to politics, and even then McCann was the kind of man you want to sit back and listen to. He's a Democrat but isn't happy with what has happened in politics, particularly the bitterness and partisanship that have become part of the daily workload of the modern politician, even in state legislatures. The days when opponents would meet in civil discourse and emerge with a compromise are gone, even in Wisconsin, which, along with Minnesota, was once legendary for its ability to work things out.

"I suspect people want a change," he said. "And for me, Barack Obama is change. This guy embraces the concept. I'm not a fool. I believe there's an ideological and substantive blank with this guy. I know I am pouring my expectations into that blank and partly exporting my expectations of what that tabula rasa will prove to be. I may be wrong, but I know what Clinton is, and I want change. I'm hoping. I spent a year at Harvard in the law school. You don't become editor of the *Law Review* at Harvard unless you are an extremely hardworking, intelligent guy. I know I could be surprised on the downside. . . . And I'm sure the Clintons have been hoping for an October surprise, that a child will emerge somewhere or something. [We talked at the height of the primary season.] Or that a woman will come forward and say, 'He beat me mercilessly.' Jeremiah Wright [the controversial preacher] was like a gift from heaven."

It's not that McCann didn't have sympathy for Hillary Clinton. He believed her husband deserved a whack with a stick for his awful behavior with White House intern Monica Lewinsky. He believed the former president humiliated himself and the nation. "You know, this is a very intelligent, bright, quick woman. It was utterly disgraceful for him to do that to this woman. So I am sympathetic to her. But I really just don't like her."

As Election Day approached, McCann returned to a subject that had never been far from his mind as a politician (he ran generally unopposed for district attorney every two years): the corrupting influence of money in politics. Heading into what would become a billion-dollar presidential race, he worried that Obama would be dragged into the same swamp that seems to capture anyone running for public office—the command to raise and spend as much money as possible. To be sure, he noted, Obama had constructed a broad base of financial support that included many small donors, but he tapped the big money too. What would that mean?

"It's out of control," he said. His own investigations of political corruption led him to conclude that we have created a system of legalized extortion, a campaign financing process that's still dominated by special-interest groups who have found open pathways around campaign finance laws. "Obama is very much the product of big money, or he's going to be," the retired prosecutor said. "I just hope somebody can break through it and put the public interest before the election."

ANN MARIE BANFIELD

I was eating a bagel outside of Manchester, New Hampshire, on a Friday morning in October when a news story in a local paper captured my attention. I was in New Hampshire looking for a bright Republican sign, any good news for the Republicans, and I wasn't finding it. Sometimes a voice pops up in your head that tells you to pursue things, and this was one of those moments. The name Ann Marie Banfield surfaced in a political story. As it turned out, that was a good thing, because she helped me understand with clarity why John McCain was in trouble. It was about a month after McCain announced that Alaska governor Sarah Palin would be his running mate. It seemed like either a bold or desperate move. She had no experience, which made her an unusual choice for a man who had claimed that Barack Obama, a rookie senator and product of Chicago politics, was not experienced enough to be president of the United States. Should McCain win the election, he might not be able to finish his term because of health or other issues that come with age.

This issue became central in the attack on the Palin decision—that she was too inexperienced to be vice president to a somewhat fragile commander-in-chief. She had been mayor of a tiny town and completed two years as governor of a state filled with stunning vistas, wildlife, and oil but no people to speak of. Palin was certainly an unknown to most Americans, and Alaska's population of 683,478 and its unusual demographics didn't make it a handy bellwether of anything. But coming to the national stage with no accepted narrative is a dangerous thing for a politician because inevitably the media create one for you.

But what media? There was a time when a candidate could cuddle up to, say, a *New York Times Sunday Magazine* writer, provide all the access necessary, and watch a wonderful, defining profile play out in full color. Or perhaps with some luck one of the softer TV magazine shows (not *60 Minutes*) might provide some sympathetic time, given a good narrative, to help get the word out. Rounds of meetings with "local" press could work too. With a collection of overworked and underexperienced local reporters angling to get somewhere better, "local" media might be the quickest way to a set of positive clips that could be packaged and dispensed to even more local media.

All of that is gone now. What you get instead is, first, bilge from a wildly partisan blogosphere that seems primed and happy to spray stinky essences on everyone. Left, right, or center, there's always someone ready to despise you on the internet. The internet broadside would be followed by a frisk from Jon Stewart on *The Daily Show*, the go-to spot for political news for the thirty-four-and-under demographic, and very popular with a lot of thirty-four-and-overs too. There you would be cast as an idiot character in a satire aimed at emphasizing whatever stupid things you might have done in your career, however unrelated. Then Stephen Colbert, the other half of the most sophisticated political hour on late-night television, in his role as faux right-wing gasbag, might seem to embrace you just enough to extend the foolishness. One or two rounds of that and your public image is formed without your help. The attempt to get it back, in Sarah Palin's case an interview with Katie Couric on CBS, was a rolling disaster. What Palin did know, she didn't express very well, and what she didn't know, well, that didn't stop her from speaking, a fatal mistake in a TV interview that will be edited for airing later. NBC stepped up with its Tina Fey contribution, that hilariously vicious *Saturday Night Live* parody of almost every aspect of Palin's affect.

It didn't help Palin that some of the Republican establishment, including a few of its pundits, were inadvertently harsh during the Republican convention in comments that were accidentally (it was said) broadcast. Other conservative writers urged her to quit before it was too late.

No matter what you thought about Palin, it was clear that the well was poisoned within a few days of her arrival. In a calmer world, Palin might have had a better chance at explaining herself and her vision. But media don't present that world anymore. It could just be that running down this flaming media tunnel and coming out the other end is one of the new tests of presidential abilities. Barack Obama certainly proved he could do it. Not Sarah Palin. The media assault was so effective that the Obama campaign never had to say much about the Palin choice. Obama himself made it clear that Palin's family was out of bounds when media began churning after they discovered a pregnant teen daughter. One unfortunate thing led to another—the clothing debacle, the state trooper allegations, the "she banned books, no she didn't" tangent. All of it got in the way of presenting any clear picture of Sarah Palin and her potential.

So I had a sense as the campaign was playing out that we would never really get much of a chance to see what Palin was bringing to the ticket because the focus was on damage control and keeping her away from spontaneous moments. That's why the article I saw in the Manchester newspaper attracted me. It was about "Team Sarah," a web-based organization that was beginning to blossom in conservative areas of the country thanks to funding from the Susan B. Anthony Fund, which supports efforts to end legal abortion in the United States. If you visit its website, you find this: "With this donation, I want to join the fight with Susan B. Anthony List in the fight to end abortion in America and advance pro-life women in politics like Sarah Palin." The article announced a rally and referred me to Ann Marie Banfield.

One of the blockades in the quest for political understanding is the mistrust between conservative America and most of the mainstream media. For once I was happy that I could tell Banfield, who lives in Bedford, New Hampshire, with her husband and three children, that I was in no way affiliated with the media, I was just writing a book and needed her help. I sent her a questionnaire about her political history, which she agreed to complete. We talked a bit on the phone, and then I sent her some questions about Sarah Palin. I wanted an unvarnished picture of Palin's impact on the campaign. Fortunately for me, Banfield, born in the 1960s but a Republican from the moment she was old enough to vote in the 1980s, turned out to be the perfect person to explain what was going on.

I decided I wanted to let her tell the story in her own words without any filtering, because somewhere in the chronology of the 2008 presidential campaign Sarah Palin's supporters need to have their say. Her responses were revealing, not only for what they said about Palin but for what they said about true conservatives in the party and how they felt about the election.

She wrote: "One reporter at a Sarah Palin event asked me if I was essentially voting for McCain-Palin because there was a woman on the ticket. My answer was no. If Sarah Palin were a man, I would still support the ticket. It's what she embodies. It's what she stands for that attracts people like me. Many Republicans like me see a lot of Republican politicians embrace too many liberal ideals, especially on the social side. Sarah Palin seems to support not only fiscal conservative ideals, but social as well. She is the whole package. I think this is what creates the problems and divisions in the party. Her addition to the ticket definitely brought me on board. The fact that she is a woman is very much welcomed by me, but if she were a woman who didn't stand for conservative ideals, I wouldn't be supporting her. As a woman, she will bring some unique qualities, which could prove to be an asset. She has done more to call attention to the unique and special value of Down's syndrome children than anyone in my generation. Just showing this country the value and dignity of these special people has been a huge gift to this nation. We need more people to be in the public eye valuing all human life, and she certainly respects that."

I could not understand why John McCain was having such big problems with his own party and even bigger problems with independent voters. McCain was nothing if not an independent character, especially during the last decade or so of his career. Banfield saw it differently.

"Many Republicans like myself see McCain as a moderate Republican. Not something we tend to appreciate in a candidate. However, the addition of Palin helps bridge the gap, but maybe not for everyone. The Bush presidency has been a disappointment for many in this country. We are supposed to be the party of fiscal restraint and less government. Many of us saw our government expand and watched the out-of-control spending. These ideals are not what true conservatives believe in, and in fact this is more of what liberals have stood for, for a long time. So the fact that there is a backlash in this country is no surprise. What many have not figured out yet is they are angry about an eight-year presidency that looks to me more liberal than conservative. Democrats are capitalizing on this, and it's hard for Republicans to counter their arguments because they have no record to point to.

"In the Palin-Biden debate, what could Sarah Palin point to as a success of the past eight years? The surge? Many do not like this war, and even though the surge seems to be working, that is not going to resonate with voters. They cannot point to fiscal restraint and they can't point to less government. They were successful in the area of tax cuts. Unfortunately they missed out on the opportunity to cut spending so we wouldn't have a huge national debt. . . . I think the main problem is it's hard for a Republican to run when you have to run against the record of the Republican leaving office, especially when that Republican, again, looks too liberal."

I read Banfield's comments three times before I concluded that I had finally found someone who could explain John McCain's problems in his own party. The fact that she was in New Hampshire, a state that has shifted from rock-solid Republican to much more Democratic in the past few years, seemed to make her all that more relevant. What she was saying made perfect sense. The believers at the heart of the Republican party wanted someone who clearly reflected the values that defined them. In her own case, Banfield, a Roman Catholic raised in Calumet City, Illinois, said she had five political priorities going into this election: First, pro-life—"Without life, you have no freedom," she said. Second, family issues—"The family is the foundation of this country." Third, fiscal restraint (out-of-control spending devalues the dollar, creating economic problems). Fourth, low taxes—"Just makes sense." And finally, foreign policy, "a return to a policy of non-interventionism."

No wonder she felt a little lost in her own party. Beyond the media noise, it was clear why Palin was a good addition to the Republican ticket. She spoke to the believers, to the people who were waiting for a sign from John McCain that he knew who they were and what they wanted. Her critics may have decided to measure her against the "presidential readiness" standard, but that really wasn't the issue among those drawn to her candidacy.

A great and unfortunate irony was at work for John McCain in the Palin chapter of his campaign. She was exactly what a disconnected part of the Republican party needed to feel that it was back in the game again. But her addition added even more distance between the McCain campaign and the independent voters he would need to mount a serious challenge to the Democratic front-runner.

VERONICA CARROLL

Veronica Carroll has a sad story to tell about growing up in a tough time in a tough part of North Philadelphia in a world that became so violent she was basically sent away, out to Levittown to live with a comfortable white family in an arrangement set up through a church. She is fifty now, tall and comfortable and easy to look at and listen to. All these years after she left her home, after her alcoholic father died (and she blamed herself as a little girl because she got the jar of alcohol down from the shelf that he drank on the night he passed away), after the mother she loved died, after jobs and dreams seemed to evaporate around her, it would be understandable if she embraced a deep bitterness. She does not.

She remains quite remarkably committed to the possibilities presented by American politics. They were drummed into her as a child, and they never left. The neighborhood, the city, the state, the nation—they all have the capacity to change, to address and solve problems. Maybe not overnight, but in good time.

This election presented a set of options that Carroll would have viewed as impossible only a few years ago. That a woman and a black man could have been in serious contention for the Democratic presidential nomination was astounding, Carroll said, a measure of the nation's progress.

Barack Obama and Hillary Clinton were battling it out when I first met Veronica Carroll in Wilmington, Delaware, near her home. She was watching the contest closely. She had been out of work for months, the victim of a cutback at the insurance company where she worked. At this point we had no idea that she would be joined by millions of other people forced out of work by the time the election rolled around. The collapse was so serious that it rearranged the issues the public was most concerned about on the eve of the election. The economy overwhelmed everything else.

Carroll doesn't fit handily into any category. Media struggle to place people into the boxes created by polling results. She might fit only in the sense that she was a Democrat and very upset with President Bush. But everything else about her background—from her upbringing in a family that is still active in Philadelphia politics to her stint as a model in Europe, from her job in insurance to her current pursuit of a master's degree in pastoral counseling—sets her apart.

The experience of living with another family was so important to her that she uses "my mom" to describe both her mother and the white woman who played such an important role during her teenage years. She had three brothers and two sisters in her own family, but she still calls the now grown youngsters from the Levittown family "brother and sister." It makes it both confusing and interesting to talk to her. Most people have only the delights and difficulties of life with one family, but Carroll's were multiplied by two, meaning she could tell stories from two different worlds.

Veronica Carroll was beautiful by anyone's standards, with one of those Angela Davis afros that defined black beauty in the 1970s. It was not easy shifting between a white world in suburbia and her black world back home in Philadelphia. What may have helped the two worlds connect was the high level of political activism in both families. It also helped that she moved from a black Democratic family to a white Democratic family. It might have been a lot more difficult if she were leaving North Philly, with its tough street politics and social causes, and moving in with a suburban Republican.

Her North Philadelphia home had important rules. As soon as you were of age, she said, you had to register to vote. "And I had to either work or go to school or do both. To my mother, not voting was a dishonor for the thousands who had risked their safety, and for some, their lives, for others to have the right to vote. Those words, her words, are fresh to me today: 'Don't let their blood be in vain. Get off your butt and vote. If you don't, then shut up.'" Veronica's mother carried the same message into the streets for her voter registration and get-out-the-vote drives. She was the Democratic block captain in her neighborhood. People would come to her with their problems, and she would do what she could to help. She battled against drugs and violence in the community and was tireless in her efforts to make the neighborhood safe and comfortable for her children and their friends.

If that sounds like the description of the modern suburban mom, think for a moment about where Carroll was growing up. North Philadelphia in the late 1960s and early 1970s was beyond hard. There were riots in the wake of Dr. Martin Luther King, Jr.'s murder. Drugs were mutating from problematic to menacing, unleashing waves of gang violence in the neighborhood. Frank Rizzo was a tough mayor, and the police department was not shy about leaning hard on people in the black community. Carroll and her friends found themselves dodging bullets on the way to school.

That is why she and a young black man ended up living with the Levittown family, George and Kitty Taraba and their children Eddie and Elaine. It was a move into a different world, safer but confusing for a young black woman. In the summer of 1968 Veronica visited the Tarabas for two weeks. "Elaine has a picture of me. I looked like I was petrified. I had never been away from my family for that long. I thought my mother had given me away because she didn't want to deal with my crying." Veronica shut down after her father's death, rarely talking, worrying everyone. It would take years for her to grasp the awareness that she was not the cause of his drinking problem and not the cause of his death.

To this day, when you ask her to tell the story of her life, she begins, "In February of 1968 I lost my father. He was forty-two and he died from cirrhosis of the liver brought on by acute alcoholism. We were living in North Philadelphia, considered the ghetto. My mother was thirty-eight years old when she found herself a widow. I was ten."

The initial two-week visit to the Taraba home led to holiday visits, and Veronica said she began thinking of them as a second mother and father. In 1972, when it was time for Veronica to go to high school, she moved to Levittown full time, both for safety and for education.

She went to Neshaminy High School in Levittown—safe, demand-ing, and not at all like schools in North Philadelphia.

Even though the transitions from North Philadelphia to Levit-town were difficult, Carroll talks with great affection about her second family. Her "second" mother, Kitty, "fought for every known cause to man. She is a phenomenal woman, very open before being very open was cool. She took a risk taking two black children into her home. It interrupted the patterns in their own lives. They already had two children to raise, and now there were going to be two more. Things were going to have to be shared."

Carroll learned some unpleasant lessons about racism too. It was cool in the 1970s to be able to hang out with an attractive young black woman, but it was not cool enough to get her a date to her senior prom. That was no great loss, she said, "because if I went to one more damn party and did the bop shoo bop, I was going to shoot myself." She became student council president, "first woman, first black, just to make a point." But what she remembers most about that part of her life was that she didn't want to be in North Philadelphia because "that part reminded me of struggle and pain," and she didn't want to be in Levittown because the novelty of being the black person had worn off. She graduated and went to Temple University to study mu-sic. It didn't take long for her to rebel. She was attending a religion conference where a favorite professor told her, "If it's hard to serve God, you need to question that. If your religion makes it hard to serve God, you have to question your religion."

She walked out of that conference, never went back to school, and hopped on a plane for Paris, where she intended to become a model. That was Easter Sunday, 1979. She ended up modeling for a time in Germany, then eventually made her way home. The money she sent home was spread all around her family. She eventually went back to school, first at Wesley College and then Neumann College. She spent some time working in the insurance industry and was licensed to sell securities. That led her deeper into the insurance business and eventually to the last job she held, as a senior manager.

She was working for a company called Elder Health when I contacted her at the beginning of the presidential campaign. Then Elder Health reduced staff and she lost that position. She had been looking for work for two years now and went back to school in the meantime to earn a master's degree in pastoral counseling.

"The political climate in our country is exciting to me now," she said. "When I was in Greece, on the front page of the local paper were Obama and Clinton, and you know, that was amazing. Europe is watching us, because the outcome of this election could lend hope to a lot of wannabe Obamas and a lot of wannabe Clintons." She doesn't hate President Bush, but noted, "I wish we had a sharper knife in the drawer, if you know what I mean. Secretly I have my candidate, but I could be compelled to vote for either Hillary or Obama. I'll do anything to keep a Republican out of office. I would vote for my dog!"

She was hoping early in the contest that Clinton would get a "spin doctor" to help her become more serious about her role and about what needs to be done. At that point she was hoping Obama would surround himself with people who had deep experience in foreign affairs. "I believe in Obama. I don't believe that hope is one of these nebulous, atmospheric conditions that produces nothing. There is a scripture that says 'patience develops hope, and hope is not ashamed.' I love this man's audacity."

She wanted some honesty from the campaign: "I want someone to tell us we are in a recession. That would be okay. I don't want someone to tell us we will be out of Iraq in sixty days, because that would not be true."

I went back to Carroll in the fall to see whether her circumstances or her thoughts on the election had changed. She replied with a note that summarized her hopes, her troubles, and her optimism. I asked her if her thoughts on Obama had changed. She said they had grown stronger.

"I have watched him mature during these campaigns, and I'm impressed. In addition to the issues that affect me and many more Americans since we last spoke, I'm particularly keen on Senator Obama's ability to not appear 'rattled.' I think he's shrewd, calculating, and focused. None of which are necessarily negative character traits and if used wisely, they are essential for the next president of this country. I think he has his 'finger on the pulse' of this rapidly changing global community and understands that we cannot do business as usual. Is it a gamble? Absolutely! Do I believe we have another viable option in the Republican nominee? No. In fact the Republicans have pissed me off to the highest degree of 'pissed-ivity.' I am insulted that they would select an inexperienced woman vice-presidential candidate for the sole purpose of securing the 'uncommitted and Hilary-ites.' To me, this shows their utter lack of commitment to the American people and the insincerity of their position. As I write, they have endeared themselves to their base and ignored the remote possibility that they could even try for my vote. And another thing (am I venting?), their present attacks are not only appealing to an already paranoid segment of our population but there is growing danger of inciting a mob mentality as confirmed by the crowd's comments of 'terrorist,' 'kill him,' and 'traitor.' Obama gets my vote if no more than to say to the Republicans, 'take that.'"

She had no luck in searching for work. Her savings were depleted, along with most of her investments. Her reaction to this condition, which might lead most people to despair, was a testament to Carroll's ability to transform disaster into another kind of opportunity. "I'm reluctantly appreciative of this experience. A year ago, my salary classified me as upper middle class. Today, I am classified as close to the poverty line. I am fifty-one, unemployed, I have no health coverage or insurance, and my house is threatened. Am I the poster child for this election or what? I have watched my investments and savings tank to the point of disbelief and ponder how a lifetime of effort can be annihilated in such a short period. Yet my present circumstances only confirm what Epictetus, the stoic, taught and what I believe—'We have the power to choose how we respond.' So, I've flipped the script on the 'classifications.' I am unemployed, but I am free to pursue opportunities that I may not have seen or thought possible with my attention diverted by work. I am free to assist those that are living in circumstances that are indeed worse than mine, Habitat for Humanity, feeding the homeless, etc., and I am free to devote more time to the ministry. And though I sometimes wake up with tear-stained cheeks and stand on wobbly legs of faith, there is a noticeable increase of volume from the still small voice, that mantra, 'All and me will be okay.'

"The economy? Everything is cyclical. But the stakes are higher this time because we are no longer an insular economy—we sneeze and other nations get pneumonia. We will come out of this, but I believe that the road will be long and governments will change how they do business with us and themselves. There is danger because our need for cash sets us up for more potential economic prostitution with nations that have other motives for us."

She sent along a newspaper clip of a Robert F. Kennedy quote from 1968: "Things are moving so quickly in race relations that a Negro could be president in the next forty years. Prejudice exists and probably will continue to, but we have tried to make progress, and we are making progress. We are not going to accept the status quo."

8

GOLDMINE.COM:
MONEY AND VOTES

LONG BEFORE anyone paid close attention, Barack Obama was opening his rallies, cell phone raised high, asking supporters to text a simple number on their own phones. Later, when Obama became such a phenomenon that his rallies resembled rock concerts, he would send a staff member out to make the pitch before anything else happened. It always worked. Hundreds, perhaps thousands, of excited supporters would text the number.

Before they knew it, the texters had arrived at the Obama campaign's inner sanctum, a digital dwelling place that helped perform a modern political miracle: shouts morphed into volunteers and votes, head counts translated into money.

Primitive attempts at this technique had been made before. John Kerry had dabbled a little with it in 2004 with the help of technology-savvy Silicon Valley imports. Howard Dean offered what might be called "Dem-tech! (Version 1.01)," using technology to identify his supporters and pick up some money in a revealing digital/political experiment. But Barack Obama incorporated modern technology into his campaign so well that he eventually had millions of digital followers, which opened the doorway to the most successful fund-raising effort in political history. It was powerful enough to push the perceived front-runner, Hillary Clinton, to the sidelines in the primaries, and strong enough to send a tsunami of campaign money into the battle with John McCain and the Republicans in the general election.

No one could begin to compete with it. As the election approached, the Obama campaign had successfully constructed a new model for modern presidential campaigning. With future development it will shatter the old ways of raising money and reaching potential voters. In 2008 it managed to transform an entire cohort of supporters into a self-selecting, connected, active, contributing, and volunteering mass that far exceeded anything accomplished in previous campaigns. Two components together—technology and outreach to young people—are keys to understanding the campaign's strategy and how it played out.

These two factors gave the Obama campaign the power to reach out and scoop up tens of millions of dollars in small contributions, not with vague mailings that anticipated small returns but with specific solicitations to people the campaign knew it could tap because it had two important pieces of information: a record of previous contributions and a credit card number. The volunteer effort gave Obama millions of ground troopers, people who would donate their time, their cars, whatever they could, just to play a small part in a large campaign.

The effort didn't stop at volunteers and fund-raising. Obama's staff understood the various recent changes in the way people communicate, giving them an opportunity to tap or create a new version of social networking for political purposes. A communications hierarchy built on trust and connections instead of hype and traditional advertising pitches presented immense potential for a campaign. Traditional mass mailings to young people did little good because the people in this group may not have an address of their own and may consign mass mailings to recycling bins without a second thought. But no matter where they lived, almost all young persons had a cell phone in tow, and so did their parents. Cell-phone users are notoriously difficult for landline-based polling companies to reach. But it wouldn't be difficult to reach them if instead of trying to call them you found a way to make them call you, which is why all Obama rallies began with a cell-phone solicitation. It eliminated randomness from the formula, telling the campaign, "Yes, I want to hear from you," and also encouraged the potential voter to participate.

Better, the social networks were the preferred digital gathering places of countless millions of college-age young people, one of the most valuable untapped political markets. The students were in instantaneous contact with one another, eager to volunteer and so committed to Obama's campaign that they would form a key slice of the core of its support at the polls.

How did a candidate who started out with little more than a well-received speech at the 2004 Democratic National Convention in Boston build a campaign able to raise nearly $800 million in contributions, pull people who had never considered voting into the process, and walk off on Election Day a couple of years later with an electoral college landslide?

It wasn't just about technology, because no matter what happens in the digital world, it still can't create something from nothing. Obama's campaign was a masterpiece of strategy, street smarts, and organization. But technology became one of Obama's most powerful weapons, made all the more effective because his opponents in the primary and general elections all but ignored its potential until late in the game.

I bought into it early on. I sent the magic text on my iPhone in April at a rally in Pennsylvania, then contributed some money to both Hillary Clinton's and Obama's campaign (more over time to

Obama), at first just to see what would happen. I quickly became digital friends with the Obama people. Barely a couple of days passed without a "plouffe-o-gram" (my description of campaign manager David Plouffe's pleadings) or thoughts from the candidate himself. I filed it all in my computer under the heading "Beggingbarack."

The Pennsylvania primary had barely ended before an email with an embedded video arrived in the inbox on my laptop and also my phone (the Obama people made certain they could reach people at three levels—on home computers, on PDAs, and on cell phones), addressed to "Charles." Obama had lost in Pennsylvania and was changing the focus to Indiana:

"People are paying attention to what happens in Indiana this week. They know how far we've traveled together, but they want to know whether we can close this race, secure the nomination, and finally bring about the change our country so desperately needs.

"We can bring jobs back to communities across America, reduce the price of gas, and put an end to the war in Iraq—and it all begins in Indiana. In the next eight days. I hope you'll join us. Barack."

Obama was asking me to volunteer to travel to Indiana to help with door-knocking and soliciting support in an array of public places. I had gone earlier to Iowa to encourage Democrats to use absentee ballots. (That was also before Obama secured the nomination, so it was not literally in support of his campaign. But my three fellow volunteers and I all knew it was, and so did the astute Iowa Democrats we visited.) I had no interest in going to Indiana. That didn't stop the messages. In all, I received seventy-two messages from Obama between April and November, most asking either for a few bucks or for some time to make phone calls. (They would provide the names and numbers at their social networking website, called MyBarackObama.com.) Because I live in Evanston, Illinois, some of them asked if I could go to Wisconsin or Michigan to knock on doors or volunteer for get-out-the-vote (GOTV) programs on Election Day.

Another important component to the Obama technology drive was that it allowed the campaign to make news on its own terms—from key speeches, to responses to campaign-trail slights, to Joe Biden as vice-presidential candidate, it reported the kind of campaign-trail proposals most media outlets ignore. Direct from Obama headquarters, his staff created an end run around the media, with its interpretation and its penchant for focusing on momentarily explosive embarrassments. For the people who texted those numbers to the campaign, the connection to the candidate was direct. That had not happened before.

Hillary Clinton became my digital buddy too. Actually the message came in Bill's name:

"Dear Charles, Here's the most important thing you need to know about this race: it's neck-and-neck. Only 130 delegates separate Hillary from Senator Obama—and that's not counting Florida and Michigan. The difference in popular vote is less than 1 percent, and millions of voters have yet to make their voices heard. This election should be about their choice. But now we're hearing people—elected officials, party members, and Obama campaign surrogates—call for Hillary to pull out. With the race this close, it sure doesn't make sense to me that she'd leave now—does it make sense to you?"

It continued, with Bill Clinton arguing that it was time to show the media that his wife was still viable by helping her reach her goal of $3 million in contributions by March 30. At this stage of the contest, the super delegates, who had been on her side at the outset, were beginning to feel the earth move as Obama built support. Hillary was almost out of money and looking at a fight with a man who was setting funding records every day.

The problem with the Clinton effort was that it never reached the level of sophistication that defined Obama's digital campaign. Sure, she invited people on the internet to help her choose her campaign theme song. (A terrible choice, it turned out—"You and I," by the

Canadian Celine Dion. "You and I were meant to fly, higher than the clouds," she sings in a firmly Canadian alto. A remarkable cliché of a song, it takes time to lumber down the runway before it becomes airborne. Not everything an internet audience chooses reflects wisdom.) Sure, Clinton had a contest to see whether a supporter might win the chance to come over to the Clintons' to eat popcorn and watch the Super Bowl.

But Clinton never constructed the presence that came to define Obama on the internet early in the game, when YouTube renditions of "Yes, We Can"—written by will.i.am of the Black Eyed Peas, based on an Obama speech, and performed by himself and other attractive entertainers (with sixteen million views by November)—were spreading across the nation. She tried a bit. In the wake of "Yes, We Can" was a "Hillary" song, but it looked dated, like a collection of well-scrubbed folks following an inspirational script, the kind of thing you might get in church. It was tragically not cool. The internet is ruthless in separating cool from kitsch.

Obama's digital presence was almost inspired, always built on either a real or a perceived slight or visionary call to make history. It was not overproduced. Some of it looked like it came from someone's basement, giving it an authentic feel. Highly produced television presentations don't look authentic on the internet, whereas home videos of how to play songs on a guitar can draw hundreds of thousands of viewers. Sometimes all it took was not the typical pretty talking head to make a point. Clinton's messages had a sound of desperation to them. On May 22, for example, she reached out and used an impending decision by the Democrats on whether to count the votes of Michigan and Florida voters as a chance to ask for money. It was clear by that point in the campaign that many of the super delegates were shifting to Obama. Her message read:

"On May 31, we'll hear the decision from the DNC's Rules and Bylaws Committee on whether they'll seat the delegates from Michigan

and Florida. And while we wait to hear their ruling, you and I must keep fighting together to win every last vote in the final three races. Let's fight to the finish—make a contribution today.

"Our recent string of victories in Kentucky, West Virginia, Indiana, and Pennsylvania showed that we have what it takes to win in November, and our campaign is moving full-speed ahead toward the final contests."

Clinton was essentially running on fumes. Obama needed just a few delegates to win the nomination. In the same time period Obama's campaign email built on a *fait accompli* sense that the nomination was almost in hand and it was time to move along. Jon Carson, the campaign's delegate counter and voter outreach expert, asked supporters to participate in a survey:

"Thanks to you, Barack Obama is within reach of the Democratic nomination. We've learned a lot together over the past sixteen months, but we're preparing for a journey more demanding than any challenge we've faced. Yet in this challenge we also have an opportunity to run the broadest, most effective grassroots presidential campaign in American history. Thank you in advance for your participation in this important survey. You and people like you in communities across the country are the heart of this campaign. Thank you, Jon."

The survey sought advice on what worked and what didn't during the primaries. It also asked, as all messages from Obama and his senior staff asked, for money. Not a lot, just a few bucks on a credit card to help keep the campaign properly fueled. For believers, a few bucks is not a lot of money. Multiply it by perhaps a few million and you can immediately see how Obama was able to roll up $30, $40, $50 million a month in small contributions.

His opponents were obviously worried about his success. Someone (no one knows who) tried to undercut it by leaking a fake story on the internet under Maureen Dowd's *New York Times* byline, which charged that many of the small donations were coming from foreign nations, Saudi Arabia being one of them. This myth fed into the "Obama's a Muslim" fear that persisted until Election Day despite rigorous proof otherwise. The story had a brief lifespan. Snopes.com (a popular website for checking out rumors) pursued it and quoted Dowd as saying she was a columnist, not a reporter, who never wrote about fund-raising, and in particular had not written the story being spread around under her name. The story, Snopes.com concluded, was false. Another effective Obama campaign use of technology was the construction of a website that did nothing but debunk rumors about Obama. It was updated as warranted and let no offense pass without a determined response.

A larger message was being sent from the Obama campaign to its followers, perhaps more important than any message other candidates were sending. From the beginning Obama had been telling people that the campaign would respond to their suggestions, ask for their help, and appreciate every penny and every minute it could get. This reaching out seemed to separate Obama from everyone else during the primary season, and particularly during the general election campaign. A day did not go by in the last few months of the campaign without some notice or appeal from Obama, delivered directly to the email inboxes, cell phones, and PDAs of supporters.

During that time I received exactly one piece of direct mail from McCain asking for a contribution, which came by snail mail. That surprised me. The Republicans entered the 2008 election with a solid reputation for succeeding at almost every aspect of presidential campaigning, but they had clearly missed technology this time around. I assumed the McCain campaign got my name from the Republican party, and I had always assumed the Republican party got my name from the National Rifle Association, of which I had been a member for a few years. Why else would they be sending me smiling pictures of Mr. and Mrs. George W. Bush at Christmas? It could be that my Democratic leanings were so apparent that the Republicans removed me from their list. But I still have an Illinois firearm owner's identification card, and the odd piece of NRA junk mail occasionally floats my way, so maybe they were just incompetent or too far behind the technology curve.

While examining the impact of technology on these campaigns, it struck me that I was watching a sophisticated, up-to-the-moment campaign on the Obama side while Clinton's and McCain's campaigns seemed to rely on old political formulas. Clinton was tapping the old Democratic money when the campaign began—where else would that money go, given the assumption she was about to be president? And McCain was struggling because people were angry about Bush. And even traditional Republican fat cats had been pinched by campaign finance reform, which limited direct contributions to candidates to $2,300. Still, people could have poured bundles of bucks into interest groups or the parties themselves.

It took me a while to realize what was actually happening. When it finally did, light bulbs seemed to twinkle all over the place. Just as the Obama campaign understood that it could play the primary election system to pull the carpet out from under Hillary Clinton, it also realized that campaign finance reform created a great opportunity instead of the expected limitation. And much of it was happening because of technology.

Snippets of technology news littered the 2008 campaign trail as devotees scrambled to note the embrace of this program, that operating system, this network, that community. Subjectivism is the Achilles' heel of technology writing. Everyone pays tribute only to the woman he loves, rarely standing back to show where she fits in the crowd. The *Atlantic* finally reported at length on how the Obama campaign effectively incorporated technology into its daily campaign strategies in "The Amazing Money Machine" by Joshua Green in June 2008. Green observed that the Obama people had tapped Silicon Valley early in the process. Inside the Clinton camp there was agitation to do the same, but those in charge decided not to. The Clinton effort was structured more for a mid-1990s campaign and based on the assumption of an inevitable win that simply was not supportable. The networks Obama tapped most effectively didn't even exist when Bill Clinton was president.

Many people made good money in technology by recruiting a pool of experts in the fields of networking, community, and, coincidentally, financing. Although the great technology explosion had imploded, there was still plenty of money on the table and expertise of a particular kind in Silicon Valley. These characters were not interested in perfecting something already invented; they wanted to take risks to invent something brand new. And nothing was riskier in the world of politics in 2005–2006 than this new senator from Illinois who might run for president. But California already loved the Clintons—could there be a new heartthrob?

As it turned out, relatively *old* California loved the Clintons: the show-biz people, the real estate barons, and old money ("old money" meaning 1990s money). The big new money—Silicon Valley money—wasn't even money yet when Bill Clinton ran his last campaign. And this new technology money wasn't concerned about lack of experience. Instead it liked buzz, substance, and novelty. And Barack Obama was that perfect trifecta. He was simply too cool to be overlooked.

The Northern California venture capitalist Mark Gorenberg, Joshua Green reported, was central to the Obama Silicon Valley connection. Gorenberg found himself becoming more political as President Bush's administration became more aggressive about Iraq and displayed breathtaking incompetence on the home front. Political finance, which hadn't changed in years, puzzled Gorenberg, because everyone followed the same formula: endless cocktail parties to entertain rich people who have bought access either to living-room face time (i.e., big dollars) or out-in-the-yard face time (i.e., moderately big dollars). Campaign finance reform shattered that model. It did, however, present an opportunity for people known as "bundlers" to expand the number of campaign donors. While you could no longer give $200,000 yourself, you might be able to line up a thousand contributions of $2,000 each, given your contact list. Gorenberg pursued that thought to become John Kerry's biggest fund-raiser in 2004. He tried again on some congressional campaigns in 2006, where it also worked, helping the Democrats win the House.

Just before he announced running in 2007, Obama connected with a group that might be called the Silicon Brain Trust, and as a result added Gorenberg to his national finance committee. That led Obama to an entrepreneur named Steve Spinner, who would become a big bundler fund-raiser for Obama, and, because of his knowledge of the industry, a talent scout. Joe Rospars, one of the early fund-raisers with Howard Dean, signed on. So did Chris Hughes, co-founder of Facebook. Out of this combination came MyBarackObama.com. It lends new meaning to the phrase "one-stop shopping," because you are the product at the center, not Barack Obama. Anyone familiar with MySpace or Facebook will understand the concept. Once an Obama supporter has identified himself on the site, he can review and join thousands of groups, look for events, contact voters, and of course contribute. Like all good community websites, it presents the illusion that you are actually in control, even while you are being solicited and drawn into a network to perform specific tasks.

This creates a community of inestimable value for a politician. The website's community aspect helps create trust among its members and fosters a connection with the candidate that a user might have with a good friend. In old politics—1990s politics—there was no real way to do that. The conversation is constant and can be sparked by anything from campaign-trail developments to national events to debate performances. Whether the Clinton and McCain campaigns overlooked the potential of this technology or just didn't understand it, each paid a high price by not using it. MyBarackObama.com was at the heart of Obama's funding, and just as important, at the heart of reaching out to voters most candidates had ignored—people between the ages of eighteen and twenty-five.

By incorporating this type of technology into politics, a new class of financiers—people much more like the electorate than the traditional elite fund-raisers, and fairly new to politics—bought into the system. A month before the election the *Los Angeles Times* wrote an article about Martha Murphy, a grandmother from Syracuse, New York, who was inspired by Obama's keynote address at the 2004 convention in Boston. She began contributing small amounts whenever the Obama campaign asked or whenever something happened on the campaign trail that bothered her. She did that 104 times between the primary and general elections, a total of $2,475.34 in contributions. The campaign estimated it had about 2.5 million contributors, a vast increase over anyone else in presidential campaign history. The average contribution as the election approached was $84. Yes, Obama got his share of big money from attorneys and other professionals, but more than a third of the $458 million he had raised by the end of the summer had come from contributions of $200 or less. This fact drove the Republicans crazy. Since campaigns aren't required to identify contributors who give less than $200, there was no way to see where that money came from. The development even flummoxed the Federal Election Commission and the finance websites that list contributions. Because the records list only contributions of more than $200, the "system" missed thousands of contributors in assembling its records for campaign contributions. There was no doubt, though, about the impact.

In August Obama raised $62 million, a record that had everyone taking deep breaths and wondering where it might end. The answer came a month later when September's total reached $150 million, $66 million of which came in donations of $200 or less. McCain was able to collect just $9.9 million in September. The Obama campaign claimed it added more than 600,000 contributors who gave less than $200 each in September.

The contributions that showed up on the radar (via the final reports submitted to the Federal Election Commission) provided a clear picture of what had happened. By Election Day Obama had reported total receipts of $775,855,737, of which $662,084,911 came in individual contributions. McCain reported receipts of $339,826,076, of which individual contributions comprised $205,9400,472. Obama spent $760,389,695 on his successful campaign. McCain spent $373,920,686.

The candidates, in other words, presented history's first billion-dollar presidential campaign, with Obama in position to spend roughly two dollars for every dollar spent by McCain. That meant television advertising almost at will, paid campaign staff wherever the Obama campaign wanted it, a network of volunteers unparalleled in history, and no concern about the senator's decision to refuse public financing for his campaign. It could also ultimately mean the end of public financing in presidential politics. If a candidate is able to create his own public financing system by tapping millions of supporters for small contributions, why accept the limits that come with public money?

For McCain, it meant waking up every morning to see a huge wave on the horizon headed directly toward him. It wasn't a question of valiantly trying to ride out a perfect storm. It was coming, and it was about to crush him in so many ways that the post-election Republican party would look like the Gulf Coast in the days after Katrina. McCain complained that no one knew where Obama's money came from. His party filed lawsuits. That "spunky underdog" talk began to emerge, the default setting when the skies become so heavy with clouds that you can think only of rain and see no other way out of the storm. For John McCain, it was about to get worse. The jolliness that arrived with Sarah Palin's selection had dissipated. Finger-pointing had broken out in the McCain campaign as aides and advisers tried to spread the blame, then ran for cover. That's how it looked in October, no matter what the polls said, no matter what the campaign reported. I'm certain McCain knew. Sarah Palin knew it. Obama and his campaign knew it too.

It was a good time for me to check on some people who were part of the perfect storm wave. I called Angela Inzano and invited her to my house for an interview. A cautious young student at Loyola, she asked if she could bring her boyfriend, Nick Giannini, who goes to Marquette University in Milwaukee. They are both Obama volunteers on their campuses and well connected to Democratic politics. I said yes immediately, recognizing the opportunity to get perspective from two different places.

Angela is from Perry, Ohio, and Nick is from Berkeley, Illinois. She has two half-brothers, he has three sisters. Both come from middle-class families, his more conservative than hers. When I met with them, she was twenty-one and Nick was twenty. They both came to the Obama effort through Democratic party activism. At Loyola, an active campus for Obama, Angela rose through the party ranks to become president of the Loyola College Democrats. As Election Day approached, college students at Loyola and throughout the country were expressing strong preference for Obama. They also stepped up for volunteer work, including the grueling but essential demands of phone-bank efforts, where endless lists of likely voters are contacted by campaigns eager to nail down votes.

Earlier presidential contests had also seen predictions that students and young people would play a decisive role—predictions that usually failed to materialize. This time around the younger generation showed up in great numbers to participate not only in voting but also in campaigning. I wondered whether that had to do with the times we are living in—with the war, environment, and economy being important issues among young people—or with the compelling message of change sent by Obama.

"For a long time politicians didn't pay attention to you," Angela said. "They didn't have to because young people don't vote, so why pay attention? I think Barack Obama has been the first candidate in a long time to take a chance on students and really to put that as a priority. I mean, he has High School Students for Obama, College Students for Obama, this whole infrastructure that the other campaigns really didn't have. And I think that by taking a chance on us and listening, I think that helps. You listen to us and then we start to pay attention and be more passionate about it. I think it also helps that he is younger and that a lot of people—especially a lot of people at our age—are already beginning to get disillusioned, so it helps that he's kind of this whole change movement."

The Obama campaign reached out to students in a way they could understand. Any time Angela needed an Obama campaign speaker on campus, the campaign would send one over. Everything a student might want to know about Obama's positions and proposals was easily accessible on his website. And the MyBarackObama.com website opened the doorway to the kind of community building that has become a *sine qua non* in communication among young people, an audience not interested in candidates or surrogates speaking at them from a podium a football field away. Put the right video on You-Tube and this audience gets it immediately. Obama's announcement in Springfield, his race speech in Philadelphia, his global address in Berlin, his nomination acceptance in the Mile High Stadium in Denver, his victory address in Grant Park in Chicago—they could be accessed instantly and therefore in the hands of young people long before being digested and interpreted by news announcers and columnists. Pre-chewed news is unappealing for young people when the raw material is only a click away on their cell phones and laptops.

At Marquette University in Milwaukee, the Obama campaign had installed a paid field organizer to handle the Marquette campus as well as the Milwaukee campus of the University of Wisconsin. This was not just a gesture. Student activism ran at fever pitch in Wisconsin on a gamut of issues stretching far beyond politics. A Democrat ignores the potential of college voters at his own risk, especially in a state where Republicans seem to hold sway the minute you leave a couple of liberal bastions like Milwaukee and the state capital, Madison.

"We have weekly meetings of the College Democrats, and then afterward people stay around for a while to do call sheets to make sure everyone is signed up and ready to vote," Nick said. "We've registered a very large percentage of our campus, and so my only concern with students turning out in the Milwaukee area is the lines, because there have been, especially since the Obama campaign, a couple of events to get students to go to City Hall and vote early. The big concern is that people show up and then have to wait in line for an hour, and they don't want to. There's going to be a lot of stuff going on to make sure people stay in line."

The Obama people are good at that, Angela noted. In Iowa they organized pizza parties for eighteen-year-old high school students (and earlier pizza parties for students who would be eighteen on Iowa caucus day), and after stuffing them full of soda and pepperoni, the campaign provided transportation to the caucus meeting places so they could show their support for Obama. This level of thought and organization allowed Obama to claim a huge victory in the Iowa caucus. Obama's win proved not only to white America but to black America too (more important at that point because of African-American loyalty to the Clintons) that white voters would support a strong black candidate without hesitation.

Some interesting campaign calculus was at work on campus too. Angela voted in Ohio by absentee ballot because it was clear that Obama was abundantly safe in Illinois and particularly safe in the North Side Chicago neighborhood where Loyola has its campus. Nick, on the other hand, voted in Wisconsin, where it can get dicey for a Democratic presidential candidate if everything doesn't swing in the right direction. This object lesson is something most people never think about: how sometimes one vote is more valuable than another, particularly if it's in a precinct where a race is tight. Both Nick and Angela spent time explaining absentee ballots and voter registration to students. Wisconsin has same-day voter registration, though Illinois doesn't.

Angela and Nick both did fieldwork for Obama in Iowa, where they learned some of the sad facts about race and politics that might not be apparent unless you actually walk around and ask people what they're going to do. From the beginning of the primary season, race had been the elephant in the room. Lots of pundits assumed that racism, bubbling beneath the surface but not apparent, would cost Obama many votes in primaries and also in the general election should he win the nomination. True to its nature as the dangerous third rail, no one talked much about this in the open. My own experiments in Pennsylvania had found surprising support for Obama in places I didn't expect to find it. But another aspect was at work that I had not noticed, nor had many other observers of the contest: the one person who realized that race would not be an issue in the campaign was Obama. From day one he had managed to balance the promise that a black candidacy held for the nation with the claim that he was running as an American, not as a black person. Before his campaign, Jesse Jackson's two presidential runs seemed aimed chiefly at gathering black votes; while important to Democrats, there weren't enough of them to elect a black president. Some have argued for years that Jackson's attempts weren't about winning the presidency but about sealing his position as leader of the most important bloc of voting Democrats. Obama never fell into this trap, not in his Illinois State Senate contests, not in his U.S. Senate campaign, and particularly not in his race for the White House.

That's not to say Nick and Angela found an America eager to embrace a black candidate.

"I went to a lot of areas in Dubuque, and there were some where you would walk away from the houses with a sense that people are not going to support him because he is black. It was really disheartening," Nick said. "You would just finish the day—it was a cold and rainy day—with so many responses like that, it just was frustrating. I mean, there are college students who don't support Obama, but it's not racial. . . . I don't think race has ever come up actually among my friends."

"When I was canvassing in Iowa," Angela recounted, "I went up to one house and this older gentleman opened the door. We were talking a little bit about values and everything, and he looked at me and said, 'Is that the colored fellow?' And I didn't know what to say because I was, like, 'Do I really want to correct him?' I just don't want to get into that. And I said, 'Yes,' and he responded, 'Yeah. I'm going to vote for him.' I said, 'Okay, see you later!' So I feel like even people who come from that, where it's acceptable to call somebody that, say, 'Yeah, I'm going to vote for him.'"

Both of these students developed their Obama pitches in the face of these experiences. I asked them to pitch me to see how much thought had gone into the effort. "Well, first I would say that he's really running on a platform of reform and change," Angela said. "We all know that the last eight years have been in a certain direction that most people don't want our country to go in. And then I would ask what issues are important to you. And then I would go from there. I don't want to just start running off a list of issue stances because some things are more important to other people. So let's say I was talking to a woman who had college-age students, and she said, 'Well, once they are out of college, they're not on my health insurance anymore because they are not in school.' And I would say, 'Well, Obama has a plan to extend the amount of time that children can be on their parents' health insurance beyond where it is now.' I would usually start with a broader theme and then narrow it down."

"At the end, I just kind of learned that an interesting difference between Obama—and even in the primaries in Iowa especially—is that his message has stayed consistent," Nick said. "You go to the house, you introduce yourself, and you say, 'We were interested in what issues you are concerned about most, education, health care, whatever.' And you have kind of a set of talking points from the campaign, and you close by noting that this has been Obama's position since the beginning."

So how much impact could two college students have in a presidential campaign? That's not the point. It's what they represented. The Obama campaign had been training its kids in Obama campaign camps for months. It had been inviting volunteers of all ages into every stage of the process. Toni Gilpin was the Obama field coordinator in Evanston, where I live and where, from the day Obama announced his candidacy, the place was ready to anoint him king or whatever he wanted, the support was that strong. There was simply no point in sending people door-to-door in Evanston to convert people who were already chirping away in the choir. But the Obama campaign created a need in a lot of people to participate, and Gilpin and her volunteer staff in Evanston were eager to find a way to tap it.

This is why we all ended up in the Democratic headquarters in Clinton, Iowa, squeezed in between a bug-killing company and a wholesale carpet place in a positively wretched strip mall, as Election Day approached. We listened to an Obama fieldworker apologize because, counter to what had been promised, there would be no delicious, nutritious meal for those of us who had spent the day rushing from house to house, but we could go to the deli downtown and buy ourselves a sandwich and some chips and a Diet Coke. Not everything ran smoothly in the Obama campaign.

Three new friends and I had rocketed across Illinois in my Jetta for door-to-door efforts. I got involved in this because of that text message I sent back in April in Pennsylvania. As with most of the interesting developments in my life, I just wanted to see what would happen. Gilpin's Obama radar had picked me out based on my zip code and a host of other details I had included on my MyBarack Obama.com website contribution form. She knew I was an Evanston Democrat, and she knew I had already stepped up to contribute a little, which meant I was in the game. So her email effort, she knew, would not be wasted. About fifty other people in Evanston had been gathered into the same group and set off to Iowa for volunteer work.

They may not have arranged the promised meal, but they sure had Democratic registration lists. If you registered or voted as a Democrat in Clinton, Iowa, the party knew where you lived and unleashed the gaggle of us the way an army sends out rifle squads. We knew exactly where we were going and exactly what we were supposed to do. In my career as a reporter I had made many cold calls to people, looking for information for stories. People are not generally happy to see a reporter at the door. But people, at least Democrats in Clinton, Iowa, were most welcoming when the Illinois volunteers showed up. They shared coffee, Kool-Aid, cookies, and, more important, plenty of conversations about how angry people were at President Bush, the war, the economy, Katrina, and the whole litany of eight years of trouble.

Weeks later I talked to Toni Gilpin about the Illinois volunteers. By the time of the presidential election, they were moving in busloads to Iowa, Wisconsin, and Michigan, everywhere the party needed help. Obama and his team had made a vast investment in technology and outreach early on, and as the day of the big battle approached, it was paying off. In Evanston alone, Gilpin said, some six hundred people had volunteered for campaign work.

This was happening all over the country in the weeks before the election. It was as though the forces unleashed over the past year were combining as planned. The technology was flawless. The money was flowing. Bodies were on the move. With the election not many weeks off, the wave was growing, even in some very unlikely places.

9

NORTH CAROLINA:
BECOMING BLUE ENOUGH

SHARING COFFEE in Maria Smithson's kitchen in Charlotte, North Carolina, the thought settles as she talks about politics that you would not want to run against her. She is political to her core, a lifelong, determined Democrat. Yet she's so devoted to raising her daughters, Molly Adele, Chloe Anne, and Nora Grace, that she has passed up chances to run for office. She and her husband of sixteen years, John Hayden Smithson, have constructed one of those rare partnerships around a home life centered on children. They work hard at it, and it shows when they gather to watch TV together, study, or feed roasted rosemary-lemon chicken, mashed potatoes, and green beans followed by ice cream to a guest. But politics is never far beneath the surface. Maria Smithson does what she believes she should, whether it's leading the homeowners' association in her neighborhood or jumping in to manage an all but hopeless congressional campaign—which is what she was doing, just because the Democratic party had asked— as Barack Obama was pursuing the White House.

In a busy life, time is usually not wasted. That may be because Maria Smithson's experiences with cancer over the years—her own, her father's, and a friend's—taught her a lesson about making the hours count. She knows that look. You can see it in the eyes of someone who is afraid, she says, waiting to find out whether cancer will take a piece of a life or all of it. Matched with her eloquence, this awareness gives her gravitas, a sense that she has thought hard about life and the choices you make.

So much of what we see in political campaigns is superficial—a snippet of a quote, a sound bite on the evening news, a passing reference on a website—that it's unusual to have the luxury of talking about politics with someone for days. What comes through in these conversations with Maria and John Smithson is that politics is layered. There may be a decision capping it all—"I am for Obama" or "I am for McCain"—but that conclusion isn't reached in an instant. It has roots. People come at it from different directions. Their lives may have led them to the private decision they make in the voting booth, but they don't think about politics all the time.

Maria Smithson is different. It seems that she actually does think about politics most of the time. She would likely rise to manage whatever involves her. She has such well-developed multi-tasking skills that, even as she talks about the congressional contest, the Obama race, and what's going on at home, she is at work on an outline for a book about effective ways to keep teenagers safe, particularly on the road. Her more aggressive side comes out when she talks about running political campaigns. She is definitely the politician in the family.

That part of the conversation is a visit to the inside of the head of a born campaign manager. People who don't know how campaigns play out, for example, might shun the idea of negative campaigning. Smithson understands it as strategy. Sometimes you have to go on the attack because that may be an underdog's only avenue. Outsiders who have never run political campaigns or who have never run for office can complain about the evils of "going negative." They want campaigns to be only about an individual running on ideas, on strengths, on character. It's a noble idea, but sometimes that's not enough.

From the inside, it's a different conversation. You back the candidate you believe in and, within legal limits of course, you do what you can to get that person elected. Negative campaigning can be a part of that process. Sometimes you run against someone whose behavior is so glaring, whose incompetence so determined, that you have to point it out. And sometimes it's all you have. It has been that way in American politics since early in the nineteenth century when campaigns became truly populist events aimed at the masses. Andrew Jackson was moved to tears when his opponents described his mother as a "common prostitute" brought to America by British troops. That was just before they labeled his wife an adulteress and suggested that people who behaved this way should not head a Christian nation. It has always been tough, and it's not about to change.

Smithson would do well at aggressive campaigning, I suspect. If you were running against her candidate, before you knew it all your secrets would be exposed, and people would be shaking their heads while she stood watching in the background. I don't want to imply at all that she is mean-spirited. She is not. She is delightful. But she would consider an attack campaign in terms of its effectiveness as strategy.

Like a general, what Smithson wants most of all when she is involved in politics is an effective strategy. That makes her a particularly valuable reviewer of the Obama-Clinton and later the Obama-McCain contests in North Carolina, a crucial state in the 2008 primary and general elections. She knows that when a negative strategy appears, it's a sign that a campaign has reached a barricade it cannot cross with words, money, media, or personality. When Clinton or McCain began drilling down on Obama's association with ancient radicals who happened to play on the same Chicago political field he played on, it signaled their level of desperation to find anything to cut into Obama's advantage. The later this happens in a campaign, the more revealing the message: with the real ammunition gone, you have decided to start throwing furniture and food at the enemy.

Smithson may be one of the most politically experienced thirty-nine-year-olds I have met. When you ask her, "How is the Hillary-Obama battle going in North Carolina?" the reply fills up three pages—a detailed response from someone who arrived in North Carolina just a few years earlier.

Winning is important to Maria Smithson, even when she loses, which she would have a taste of in 2008.

I had come to Smithson's house because, months before anyone knew how this presidential campaign would play out, I thought North Carolina would be crucial. I also knew that even though she had no direct role in the campaign, Maria Smithson would be watching it the way a hawk in the treetop watches squirrels. She would miss nothing.

Talking with her husband John was an unexpected benefit. He is not overtly political but very smart. His career is like a chronicle of what has happened in the economy from late Ronald Reagan right through the second Bush term. It also presents a timeline in political development as he moved from the conservatism of Ronald Reagan to the magnetic liberalism of Barack Obama. He is as much of a businessman as ever, focused on local, national, and global economies because that's where his job carries him. But now he has added social policy and education to his portfolio, both classic liberal causes.

North Carolina's strategic importance is a story of demographics and transformation in one of the nation's most rapidly changing states. It's interesting that the Smithsons would settle here after starting to build their family in Oregon, because North Carolina is one of those locations in the South that have been drawing people from around the country for years. There is no better place to understand why the continuing clichés about the American South are outdated and deserve to be abandoned.

What's happened on the bright side of the American economy over the past decade has happened here, even as the aged pillars of North Carolina's success—textile manufacturing, old money, and to-bacco farming—disappear. This is where worn-out thoughts about race and its role in the South come to die too. That's not to say that race is no longer a factor in politics; it's simply no longer as important as it once was, particularly in close races. The state has its history, with the state chapter of the Sons of the Confederate Veterans hav-ing met here to decry the unfairness of Abraham Lincoln and the brutalities of his war generals, and to argue about restrictions on the public display of the Confederate flag. Its more radical members view Lincoln as a war criminal.

You can still go to stock car rallies, see Confederate flags, and find people who say "nigger" and talk about how the country is going straight to holy hell. It makes for good documentary footage but gen-erally reflects only what is in front of the camera. The vast majority of people in North Carolina have never been and aren't like that. Self-proclaimed rednecks will tell you they worry about Obama's Muslim religion, how he would be sworn in on the Koran instead of a Bible, how he took off his flag lapel button and won't salute or say the pledge of allegiance. When you point out that none of that is true, it has no impact. It's what they've chosen to believe. They also believe seces-sion would be good, would get the country back to the way things were in an imagined, perfect America they and their ancestors likely never experienced. This exists on the very small stage of Southern ra-cial behavior, but the days when some Confederate credentials were mandatory for local office holders in the South have long passed.

North Carolina is now one of the most progressive states in the nation. It's also closely divided along political lines that seem to be defined by culture. City professionals tend to be Democratic. Suburban and rural dwellers and downtown businesspeople tend to be conservative Republicans. A deep religious strain can still be found in the state. Democrats do well in state offices, Republicans do well in federal elections. North Carolina's population has boomed, climbing by some three million over the past few decades.

The Smithsons' town, Charlotte, is the birthplace and headquarters of big banks like Bank of America and Wachovia, and a welcoming home to many high-tech headquarters. It's very accommodating, having elected both a liberal black mayor (Harvey Gantt) and a conservative white woman mayor (Sue Myrick, who is now in Congress). Charlotte hosts an immense amount of regional pride. In 2010 it's scheduled to open a NASCAR museum.

These large, new institutions, companies, and banks have brought new people to North Carolina. The state built a robust and noteworthy system of colleges and universities and some of the best private schools in the nation to help serve its new population. Many of these newcomers will probably be going back to college again and again as jobs and attitudes shift over the years. Relatively cheap real estate in the highlands has also been a magnetic draw for retirees. Craftsmen and artisans in particular find it a welcoming, supportive state. All these characteristics add up to an expanding population and a set of demographics different from those that defined North Carolina for much of its history. North Carolina's politics are changing too.

In 2008 this would become apparent only when the election was over. But on the eve of the decision it looked as though North Carolina was ready for a shift. It had been a solidly red presidential state for years. George W. Bush did well there in his two contests, winning by a wide margin over Al Gore in 2000 and John Kerry in 2004. Even the presence of John Edwards, the state's former one-term senator, as John Kerry's vice-presidential running mate did not pull North Carolina into the Democratic column in 2004. But the Bush presidency has not been good for North Carolina or its complex new economy.

The banking crisis landed hard here as the presidential contest was moving toward its close. As 2008 was ending, the state's unemployment rate climbed to 8.7 percent. Trouble in its core businesses pointed to long-term problems and little hope for economic growth. The mantra of tax cuts still played well with loyal Republicans, but that group was being offset by a growing coalition of independents and Democrats who were hit hard by the economic collapse. The question was whether the Bush record and a compelling Democratic candidate could pull the state into the blue column.

For John McCain, North Carolina was a "must win" place because it was such an integral part of the Republican party's "solid South" that victory seemed impossible without it. Most of those Southern states—South Carolina, Georgia, Alabama, Mississippi, Texas, Arkansas—were likely McCain victories. North Carolina and Florida were up in the air. But McCain needed them to offset weakness in places like New York, Pennsylvania, and the Pacific Coast states. At the same time there were many ways to parse an Obama victory that did not include North Carolina. The addition of North Carolina to the Democratic column would all but doom McCain and make a loud statement about the transformation of Southern politics.

Like a big part of North Carolina's population, Smithson is not a native. When I met her years earlier on a foggy night during Al Gore's 2000 presidential campaign, she had no idea she would end up living in a comfortable cul-de-sac home in what appears to be a suburban Charlotte model community.

We were at the University of Oregon with Jesse Jackson, who had either worked his way into or been invited into (one could never tell with Jackson) the Democratic campaign effort. He was there to stir up college students for Gore's great battle. Smithson was there because, no matter where she has lived, she has always ended up in the center of the most interesting political developments. She was already serving on the Democratic National Committee (on the Rules and Bylaws

Committee that sets regulations for presidential primary elections) and had a couple of state races behind her and a few more in front of her as a manager too. We swapped phone numbers and promised to stay in touch. I was a newspaper reporter and needed contacts who knew local politics to tell me how things were going as the election approached. It was a good match.

In smart presidential campaigns, state party organizations play a central role. They have the money and know where the votes are and how to get them. This is the point at which national politics and state politics click together (when it works) as though a machinist had milled the parts. Smithson was the most reliable and interesting political contact I had ever developed.

She remains angry about the election results in 2000, when Al Gore won the popular vote but lost the presidency when the Supreme Court decided to stop the recounting of ballots in Florida that gave the state's electoral votes to George W. Bush, sending the Texan to the White House. "I just felt like we were being robbed," Smithson said of the Gore defeat. She had met the vice president and was touched first by his kindness and then by the way he related to his family. There was nothing passive about his connection to his children, she said. But the Al Gore she knew when he was among friends or gabbing with her about family during car trips around Oregon wasn't the Al Gore the media presented. She said he would change around reporters, becoming much stiffer and a lot less warm. She believed that was because Gore was raised in a political family where the media were viewed as a potential enemy at worst and a risky companion at best. Reporters even speculated that Gore suffered some kind of disability in social settings, perhaps exhibiting signs of Asperger's syndrome. Maybe Gore was wisely protecting himself from reporters always primed to pounce on any mistake, however minor. Only the media would suggest a medical diagnosis for someone who was simply wary of their canine behaviors, as though it were an honor to be bitten on the leg by some bloviating pit bull.

Eight years afterward, Smithson was still angry about the outcome of the 2000 election. "At the end it was just like being hit by a truck in slow motion. I was so vehemently angry at Ralph Nader [the third-party candidate who, it was argued, stole votes from Gore]. What was so incredibly frustrating to me is that Al Gore clearly is an absolute god when it comes to saving the environment, and in my opinion, Ralph Nader was absolutely guilty of keeping him from office. And I am still angry about that. You know, if it weren't for Ralph Nader, we might not be in the war we are in. There are just so many feelings I have about that. It was difficult to watch Florida go through that turmoil, but I had that feeling we were going to get screwed in the end. I just knew it was going to end badly. We won our state, and I was proud of that, but it's not very exciting when you win the battle but lose the war."

After the election I tried to stay in touch with the Smithsons. Every couple of years Maria and John would come to Chicago for a medical convention, and she and I would meet for lunch. At one of our meetings she was angry with President Bush's tapping of evangelical votes. She thought he was a fraud and just using people. Then in 2003 she talked about moving to Charlotte.

Another lunch focused on her cancer. I was all geared up to talk about politics when Smithson announced she had cancer in what remained of her thyroid gland. I was taken aback. Then she declared her plan to take care of the cancer and get pregnant again, because she wanted more children and felt very close to family for the first time in years. It was just like that, at least on the outside. She would defeat her cancer and then have another baby.

"The doctor told me, here's what we're going to do, we're going to go back in and take the other half of the thyroid out, and you're going to have some radiation. I just sobbed and asked her the only thing

I could think of, 'Can I get pregnant?' And she said, 'We need to put that on the back burner for a while.' And that is what hit me the worst, the thought that I was not going to have a baby. You find out you have cancer, and it changes you."

When a doctor tells you that you have a 90 percent chance to live, she said, that might sound to an outsider like good odds. "Oh, you've got a *good* cancer! But you view it differently," Smithson said. "Ten people walk into a room, and one of them is not walking out." The experience reminded her of Shirley Jackson's 1948 short story "The Lottery," in which a young woman is the loser in a small American town's lottery. She is stoned to death by everyone in town, including her family, in a sacrifice to assure a good growing season. "You feel kind of that way," she said. "It's, 'Oh, shit, am I going to be the person who gets the card with the little black dot on it?' A 90 percent survival rate doesn't sound very good when you are the one who has to survive. It changed my perspective on politics too, to a large degree. It didn't become as important for me to run for office."

Her cancer treatment pushed her from abstract thoughts about how medical insurance for all would be a good thing to real thoughts about the people she met while she was undergoing radiation therapy. Some of them would not survive, some were not doing well. What happened to the ones who didn't have insurance to cover the $100,000 worth of doctoring demanded by even a thyroid cancer case?

"Most of the people you run into are either getting bone scans or radiation therapy, and I would sit there and think, well, I'm sure this whole thing is going to cost more than $100,000 by the time it's over—the two surgeries, the radiation doses. You get charged by every single doctor, even the ones you haven't seen who have just looked at your file. I remember thinking, 'I wonder what happens if they find a tumor and you don't have insurance? Does the hospital remove it knowing they're not going to get paid?' It's not like the emergency room, where they have to treat you. And then I thought, what if your child has cancer and you can't afford the treatment? Even though that had always been an issue I could talk policy on, I never felt it to my core."

Smithson knew the answer as well as I did. That child would probably die. It's the part of the cancer story people generally don't get to hear, along with the not-so-noble thoughts of people who are suffering with the treatment as well as the ailment. Smithson said she had absolutely no interest in hearing uplifting stories of people who went on to run marathons. "I've got cancer and I feel like shit and I might die, and I am not in a good mood. If that's a benchmark I have to hit, that I put a smile on my face so you can feel good, well, screw you." The people she wanted to sit with, she said, were those who told her, "Goddamn, this sucks."

She survived. Our long-distance relationship continued.

John Smithson had been raised in a family where politics was not discussed openly. He voted for Ronald Reagan in 1984 and George H. W. Bush in 1988, but found himself drawn to Democratic politics when President Clinton ran the first time. The joke in the Smithson household is that Maria required a party change from John before she would marry him. The reality is that he was drawn to Clinton, a Democrat with a global perspective, because his own career was becoming more global. After working in aerospace, he had shifted into the sale of dental supplies and ended up working with a politically conservative company in Portland. The end of Clinton's administration and the arrival of George W. Bush to the White House, followed first by 9/11 and then by the wars in Afghanistan and Iraq, troubled him. He did not believe the younger Bush was prepared to lead on the global stage. He wasn't comfortable at his old company anymore either. He knew there was an opportunity for him in Charlotte, and that's why he and Maria moved there.

It was hard for her to leave the Oregon political scene, where she was known and respected, not to mention a player, and shift into a whole new political world where starting over again was not a simple matter. North Carolina may well have changed, but politics everywhere remains local, as the late House Speaker Tip O'Neill of Boston said. And it takes a while for the locals to welcome you in. Maybe a long while. In retrospect, Maria said, it wasn't all that difficult. Moving to North Carolina was exciting, she said, like a vacation. In Portland the sun doesn't shine much. In Charlotte it becomes your fine backyard friend. You trade the grey skies of drizzly Portland for magnolias, early flowers, and azaleas to die for; the occasional chemical spritz to keep the fire ants where they belong; and the many sunny days that make North Carolina seem like a little green paradise.

This was a fortuitous coincidence for me. Hillary Clinton and Barack Obama were in a fight as the primary season played out. North Carolina, holding its primary very late in the season, on May 6, turned out to be one of those "must watch" states. The Obama campaign had been arguing since just after Super Tuesday in February that Clinton simply could not gather the convention delegates she needed to win the nomination, that it was over and had been over for some time. This was a convenient argument for the Obama camp because it was looking at some likely popular-vote losses down the road and needed to keep the focus on the numbers of delegates it had collected.

But the Clintons would not give up. They picked up some key primary victories, Pennsylvania in April among them. Still, Obama stayed ahead in delegates. Clinton could not make up the delegates she needed. The party's super delegates were also moving to Obama. In North Carolina the former president spent a lot of time in the countryside, hyperbolically chumming it up with rural voters, while Hillary worked the town people. Obama was not exactly floating above it all, but it was clear he would be winning the support of the state's African-American voters and lots of its well-educated relative newcomers, John and Maria Smithson among them.

The Smithsons started out supporting John Edwards because of his populism and campaign messages aimed at workers and their problems. They had met him and concluded he believed the proposals he was advancing. But Edwards failed to make much of a dent during the primary process, and after a dismal showing in the Iowa caucus he dropped out of the race. That was fortunate. He had built a deep well of respect around the nation in connection with his wife's struggle with cancer, but later the water ran out when it was revealed he had had an affair during the campaign. He apologized to his wife. The truth of it was that, affair or not, Edwards's message failed to connect in Iowa. Failure, not an exotic problem, forced him from the race. It wasn't hard for the Smithsons to move to a new candidate. Neither of them was drawn to Hillary Clinton. In Obama both of them found a new generation of politics with a different message, the message of hope so heavily emphasized by the candidate during the primaries.

Maria Smithson's reports on the North Carolina primary were like something you might get from a CIA analyst looking at developments in the former Soviet Union. She wrote: "It is clear that Obama is going to win this primary due to basic demographics. If you look at it like a three-legged stool, what makes up North Carolina's registered Democrats are African Americans, well-educated people, and blue-collar Democrats. Obama will easily win two of the three: African Americans and well-educated Democrats. I just don't see how [Clinton] can do it. What is interesting to me in the last few weeks before the primary is that Hillary doesn't seem to be even *trying* to persuade voters in the area where Obama has strength, and neither is Bill. All of their visits seem to be geared toward bringing out her base in the textile/tobacco belts, where the towns are more blue collar. As a campaign professional, I realize the importance of bringing in your base vote, but she loses without persuading voters to switch. She may have written North Carolina off, but you would think she would try to bring the numbers in closer."

All the communications with Smithson were like that one. She was looking far beneath the surface in a place that was still new to her. How does one develop that level of political interest? Smithson believes it all started before she was born, when her pregnant mother went to protests against the Vietnam War. She grew up in a political family where argument was served up with meat and potatoes at dinner each night. It took some talking with her about her connections to politics before she settled on the story that made her most aware, the story that welded her to the political process.

She was eleven years old when her brother, Hugh, died in a crash in John Day, Oregon. Much of the town turned out for the funeral or visited the family at their home. It was a small town, and people knew each another well. She remembers some of the local businessmen pouring whiskey for her father and offering condolences. Everyone knew and liked the family. It turned out that the friend who had driven the truck that killed her brother had been drinking beer purchased by an adult, who was convicted of supplying alcohol to minors. It surprised the family, she said, when the man and his brother later sought a license to open a mini-mart that would be selling beer and wine. They all went to the hearing to oppose the license. She was just twelve years old.

"When it was time for the two brothers' witnesses to get up, all of these business people got up and spoke in their behalf. And these were the people who had been at our house when my brother died. And the people my father, a small-town lawyer, had been working with. People who had been close friends of our family testified, supporting the license. And that was just devastating to my parents. That was my first real lesson in politics. It was the almighty dollar. It was so much more important to these people than what had happened to my brother."

One of her older brother's friends showed up and gave an impassioned speech. "I can't believe you are doing this," he said. Smithson recalls how "this made me a fighter." She became even angrier when the state liquor board overruled the hearing officer's recommendation and awarded the license. "I mean, it wasn't a defining moment in the sense that I said, 'Aha, I'm going into politics and change the world!' But it left an inspiration inside me that something had to be done to stop the bad guys."

Like so many other Democrats of her age, her first foray into presidential politics was in August 1992. The candidate was Bill Clinton. She was paid $150 a week as deputy press secretary for Clinton's Oregon effort. She got to do a lot of faxing and a lot of politicking with lesser party lights. Clinton was every bit the Rhodes scholar and policy wonk, but also genuinely empathetic to the people he met. She believed that he cared deeply about the lives of his constituents. He also came with an apparent attraction that affected everyone. When the young Bill Clinton walked into a room, everything stopped and people just looked. He could be instantly engaged and engaging, which made him a remarkable presidential candidate.

A process of osmosis was under way, she realized later. "It was like going to graduate school in campaigning," she said. At the same time she discovered she was pregnant with her first child. After Clinton won, many of her friends headed off to Washington to take White House and government jobs. "I really didn't want to leave Portland," she said. She was freshly married and had a new baby. That turned out to be an important decision. She gradually worked her way into a variety of Democratic campaigns for Congress or state office. She was elected vice chair of the state Democratic party and became part of the Democratic National Committee's rules-making process. She had a growing interest in watching over development of the state party. "You want to move in, gear it up, and make the party as strong as possible so that it's an organization that one of the major campaigns will just step in and take advantage of." That meant making sure every county was organized and had a good get-out-the-vote effort. This was a golden education in politics, one she would carry with her. She chose not to run for the vice chair again in 2003 when she and John decided they would move to Charlotte. She was ready to concentrate on raising her family—but she remained connected to the Democrats.

I asked her as a campaign professional to measure both candidates for me, Hillary Clinton first. "I think Hillary thought it was inevitable. I think she thinks she's entitled. I think she is somewhat out of touch, she's out of touch with people my age. And she's certainly out of touch with people younger than me. My God, I've been able to vote more than half my life. I think she has just lost touch with a lot of people, and that's killing her. She also hasn't done an effective job spending money. She's paid way too many people way too much money to be surrounding her and telling her what she wants to hear. That's a serious problem.

"She's also made a serious mistake in trying to be something she isn't. I think it's hard to respect her when she pretends to be soft, when she pretends to be touchy feely, when she says, 'I want to hear what you think.' It comes across as completely disingenuous. I think her biggest asset is her ass kicking. 'I'm going to kick butt, and I am real serious.' I think that's what people will expect from the first female president, and I'm certain that that would have boded well for her.

"You know, my brother has become a conservative, an angry Republican white male. Great guy, but angry. He told me a year or two ago he was supporting Hillary because she will kick ass. She's a hard ass and she'll kick ass, and he just thinks that's great. She should have stuck with that as opposed to trying to soften up and doing this horrible smile thing. I just don't understand it. Her eyes bug out of her head. It's blinding. I have to turn the TV off. She has been a terrible candidate. She has made mistake after mistake after mistake." All of that surprised Smithson because she visited the White House when Bill Clinton was president and found Hillary not only engaging but disarmingly kind and beautiful. It might have been a handling problem once she started her presidential campaign, because so much of what one saw of her seemed crafted for public consumption, which was not necessary. The real Hillary Clinton was certainly good enough.

"On the other hand," Smithson said, "Barack Obama has done everything right, and what amazes me is that he has done it without having to dumb down any of his language. He talks about policy in intricate ways, and it's inspirational. That hasn't happened in a while. I also think there is a generational thing happening here, maybe where the torch is being passed from the baby boomers to this next generation. He's more in tune with what's going on in our society overall, the modernization. He's also an incredible motivational speaker. You know, I listen to him and I feel a tingle. You feel like things could get better. And things have been so incredibly bad for the past eight years that he presents this possibility for change.

"I think what this country needs right now is an emotional milkshake, so to speak, and I think that's what he is giving the country in his campaign. People need to be woken up. They don't want to listen to policy stuff right now. I think we all need a kick in the ass, and I think that's what he's doing. I think we need somebody right now who can say, 'You know what, we can change this. It's going to be okay. We just have to put our hearts in the right place.' There's a certain amount of emotion in this election, and he's able to absorb that and send it back out. And the last thing—and I am sure Hillary would understand this too—is that the biggest thing presidents can

do to make themselves effective is the people they surround themselves with, and I think he understands that."

Heading into primary election day, the Clinton campaign claimed
to be delighted with polling results that showed Clinton and Obama
essentially even, within the range of a three-point margin of error.
This proved to be yet another object lesson in the flawed nature of
polling. If Clinton had her break in New Hampshire, where she was
down until the last minute and then won the contest, that wasn't going to happen in North Carolina. A last-minute flap occurred when it
was discovered that a feminist voting group in Washington had been
"robo"-calling African Americans well after the voter registration date
had passed, suggesting they would be getting a registration package
in the mail. That led to widespread confusion among people who
were already registered to vote. Misleading people about their access
to the polls can lead to felony charges. If you think you haven't been
registered when you are indeed registered, anything that implies you
are not, that you might as well not go out to vote, is illegal. It's a bad
old stunt used in the past to hold down black turnout.

Not to suggest that the New York senator had anything to do
with it, none of this worked to Clinton's advantage. Obama thumped
her in North Carolina by fifteen percentage points. As Smithson had
predicted, he put together a coalition of African Americans and well-
educated whites to push her out of the contest. John Smithson may
have offered the most astute assessment, boiled down into a simple
thought: "His heart was in it, and hers was not." Despite the Clinton
campaign's rhetoric, Obama's claim on the nomination seemed that
much stronger.

Smithson was happy about that. But her experience in the 2008
campaign was about to shift from the abstract to the concrete. She
would be running a campaign again. It would be a difficult contest
pitting Harry Taylor, a Democrat, against an entrenched Republican,

Sue Myrick, the former Charlotte mayor and one of the most conservative members of Congress. Myrick has been elected to Congress
every term since 1992. She won her first contest in 1994 by 65 percent, in 1996 by 63 percent, in 1998 by 69 percent, in 2000 by 69
percent, in 2002 by 72 percent, in 2004 by 70 percent, and in 2006
by 67 percent. Not much sign of weakness there.

The Democratic campaign was already in trouble when Smithson
signed on. The primary manager left after collecting some $70,000
in salary for an essentially uncontested race. But that would not be
the biggest problem. It was an interesting political challenge, taking
someone who had one of those "moments" that put him center stage
for a while and trying to translate that into a victory in a congressional
race. Smithson knew Obama had a lot of staying power in North Carolina, but what happens in primary elections doesn't always translate
into what happens in a general election campaign. The state's track
record was still strongly Republican at the presidential and federal
office levels. That didn't deter Smithson.

Harry Taylor literally popped up on August 8, 2006, at a community college event in Charlotte where President Bush was the
guest of honor. In what was clearly an unscripted moment, Taylor
told the president he had no question but wanted to make a statement. In brief, he said Bush and his administration were frightening
him by violating his rights, and they were oblivious to it. He wanted
to know whether Bush had the humility to be ashamed of himself for
the problems of his presidency. Bush said he wouldn't apologize, and
then it was on the news everywhere and Harry Taylor had his own
appreciation website with thousands of hits.

Most presidents screen audiences so rigorously that the chance
of a Taylor jumping up is minimal. That he was able to surface and
then give a little speech criticizing the president was news. Taylor
had been a Green party sympathizer for a while but had never run for
office. The response to his challenge to Bush was vast. Some friends

he knew through MoveOn.org began pushing for him to run for Congress against Myrick. After the primary the party approached Smithson because it sensed there was a chance, given Obama's campaign and the general tide against Republicans, to bump Myrick out of her seat. But it would take an aggressive, professional campaign to do that. This kind of calculation was being advanced all over the country as the Democratic Congressional Campaign Committee looked at Republicans who might be vulnerable. The Democrats had regained control of the House in 2006. No party had ever expanded its control over the House in two straight elections, but 2008 looked like a promising year.

Smithson's inner campaign manager clicked on right away. "My biggest concern was whether Harry would be able to stomach the game necessary to beat Myrick, which needed to be a highly negative attack campaign. You cannot beat a well-entrenched incumbent with a largely unknown newcomer with little money and no name identification without throwing some punches. Frankly, Myrick had it coming. The research on her showed some funky financial dealings in her previous campaigns. Her record was to vote with her people on religious and social issues, and against them on every financial aspect of their lives and communities, a common practice among a lot of Republican members of Congress throughout the nation. Myrick's way of keeping her voters angry and worshipping her was to demonize immigration, terrorists, and gays. In the Ninth Congressional District, it worked."

Smithson said she tried for five months to get Taylor to take on Myrick, but in the end, he could not. "Being a first-time candidate he had little appreciation for the hill we had to climb, and he didn't know how his name identification could be so low given the attention he got after the 'Bush Moment.' He had a great deal of anger for Myrick, but he didn't have the stomach for negative campaigning. He wasn't comfortable speaking publicly and avoided developing a fine-tuned message and a stump speech, despite the efforts of many individuals who tried to help." In short, Taylor's few minutes of fame were just that. It might have seemed like the lift of that event was enough to get the Congress capsule into orbit, but it wasn't. In many cases, congressional races are not so much about ideology as they are about personality. Anyone who has been a successful mayor in a city like Charlotte carries a familiarity that can transcend party lines, which obviously happened many times for Myrick given her track record as a 60 to 70 percent performer on Election Day. It's hard to unseat even a marginally successful member of Congress unless you have a set of issues, a scandal, or an aggressive candidate with a strong presence to change the dynamic of the election. Harry Taylor had none of that.

Still, there was that distant chance—a thought that settles on every campaign. It must have occurred with Clinton in North Carolina and with McCain and Palin too. Smithson knew what to watch out for, knew how those last couple of hopeful campaign days can affect your perspective.

"Finishing an unwinnable race is often like climbing Mount Everest," she said. "At some point toward the end of your climb, the adrenaline is waning but the endorphins have kicked in and a false sense of euphoria begins to bubble up. Oxygen deprivation at the higher elevations makes you see illusions, and you actually think you might pull it off. The last few weeks of a campaign usually have the same effect. Especially for first-time candidates, and sometimes their managers. But this time around I had a kick-in-the-head moment that made me realize we were screwed."

She was at a local library to campaign with early voters. Myrick's staffers were on hand too. A group of three black women showed up to vote. They didn't take any campaign literature going in. "Don't worry. We know how to vote," one of them exclaimed. On the way out, one of them gave the thumbs up and said, "We voted for Obama!"

And then one of them looked at a Myrick volunteer and said, "Don't worry, we voted for Sue too!"

"All three had voted for Sue Myrick, someone who had been serving Charlotte for a long time. A grandmother and a breast cancer survivor, she was someone they identified with. They probably couldn't have told you where she stood on welfare, unemployment, education, war, or anything. It didn't matter to them. They loved familiar ol' Sue Myrick. I knew at that moment it was over. We had not given them a single reason to question her service to the district."

It was not a happy Election Day for Smithson, but "the one saving grace was that it enabled me to help Obama through some of the outreach and fieldwork we did for Harry. That was a whole different inspiring parallel effort that made the election of '08 amazing and unforgettable."

"Unforgettable" would be one word for it. Everyone on the Democratic side knew it would be an uphill climb for Obama, not only in North Carolina, the red state with the blue insides, but also in a handful of other key battlegrounds where John McCain had spent most of his attention as the November confrontation approached.

Ironically, the kinds of places that played such large roles in 2000 and 2004 were not so much of an issue in the waning days of the campaign. The whole West Coast, from California to the Canadian border, looked like it was locked up for Obama. New York was beyond question. In the Midwest, he would obviously carry Illinois and Wisconsin, maybe Iowa and Michigan too, which had been flooded with campaign volunteers and staff. Florida was drifting his way. It was very close in North Carolina. Obama was sitting on tens of millions of dollars in campaign funds for use as needed. He was staffed up to the eyes, even in places where there was no doubt he would carry the day. His rolls of volunteers stretched into the millions. There was nothing more the candidate or the campaign or the party could have done. From midsummer to the end of the game, they had run the perfect presidential campaign. It was now settling on the nation that it might be sending the first black man in history into the presidency. All presidential elections are historic, of course. Not *that* historic.

The news could not have been worse for John McCain and Sarah Palin. It seemed that every time the Republicans tried to create a sign to show their concern about the economy—for instance, pulling off the trail for a day or so to go to Washington to help cobble together a response to the banking crisis—McCain looked that much more ineffective. It also emphasized the glaring dilemma the Arizona senator faced as a Republican candidate. He was being forced to run as a reformer after eight dismal years of Republican White House control. "Give us a chance to fix this mess. We know how. After all, we made it," isn't much of a clarion.

Palin was gesturing her way deep into comedy history as she seemed to mutate into a parody of herself, full of "you betchas," winks, arm-waving, and aspersion-casting on the campaign trail. Of course her audiences loved it. What would anyone expect when the only people who show up at a rally are the people who love the person on the platform? No one came out much after mid-September on either side to have their minds changed. It made it impossible to measure what impact, if any, Palin had on the contest. The media treatment she received was unfair. No one had much of an idea who she was in the first place, and in very short time the media on the left (with a little help from the media on the right) concluded she was an idiot. No one said that, of course. No one had to.

On that first Tuesday after that first Monday in November, people would watch closely to see how the electoral vote would break. It might have been a lingering sense of fairness that kept the media from just tossing their hands in the air and shouting, "Obama!" He was going into the election a couple of points up on McCain. Support seemed to be shifting, as it always shifts, in the days just before an election. Some of it was moving to Obama, less to McCain. But Obama seemed to have the advantage exactly where he needed it.

People had been so burned by the favorable exit-polling for John Kerry in 2004 that everyone in the media was reluctant to become too predictive. Of course there was always the behind-the-scenes assessment of the experts, the most expert of whom was sitting right beside Barack Obama.

"We always believed McCain's campaign was dead on arrival," said David Axelrod.

North Carolina would be one of the places to watch to see whether Axelrod had it right. The other, not surprisingly given its cantankerousness, ticket-splitting, and unconventional nature, geography, and demographics, was a place McCain and Palin seemed to be paying an undue amount of attention to late in the day: Pennsylvania.

10

NOVEMBER 4,
THE ELECTION KEYSTONE

SANDY STRAUSS measures success in small advances because of the nature of her work. As a minister, her calling is to lobby the state legislature on behalf of the Pennsylvania Council of Churches. This collection of some twenty denominations is not a muscle-heavy group in a state where the legislature is eager to respond in so many ways to clout, either in the form of simple raw strength applied by the special interests that populate commerce, or in terms of money, which is tossed around with abandon in connection with elections, legislative campaigns, issues, events—whatever presents the opportunity.

Many months before I met with Strauss on the eve of April's Pennsylvania primary election, she had signed on to the Obama campaign to do what she could to help him win the nomination and the presidency. This put her exactly where most of the Democratic political powers in the state, headed by Ed Rendell (the former Philadelphia mayor who is now governor), were not, as least in the primary campaign.

Like much of the Democratic party firmament around the country, they were backing Hillary Clinton, who thought she had everyone and everything wrapped up until the Illinois senator surfaced in a major and defining way as keynote speaker at the 2004 Democratic National Convention in Boston. Obama did have the support of Pennsylvania senator Robert Casey, Jr., a friend he had made as a fellow freshman in the Senate, the son of a political legend and a well-known figure across the state. But the institutional backing for Clinton was so substantial that she managed to beat Obama by a wide margin in the Pennsylvania primary. Obama carried an impressive number of supporters even in the counties he lost, predominantly white counties where backing for a black candidate seemed surprising and revealing at the same time.

Obama had something going in Pennsylvania, but it took a while to see it. It would be a decisive state in 2008, eclipsing Ohio, the focus of the 2004 contest, and Florida, the sad graveyard of wrecked ships and dimpled chads for Al Gore in 2000. On November 4 Pennsylvania was the place to watch, along with North Carolina. But back in April there was no way to anticipate what was going to happen.

Strauss and I sat and talked for a couple of hours in a sunlit room in an old seminary building in the center of Lancaster. Then we met her husband, David Arnold, also a minister but now a master woodworker, for dinner. We talked again later at their home in a tough section of uptown Harrisburg and went to an Obama rally downtown. Because I had covered the Pennsylvania legislature as a young reporter, Strauss and I had a lot to discuss. Most surprising to me was that the issues I thought had been resolved back in the 1970s—open government, campaign reform, lobbyists' disclosure, and the like—remained major issues to this day. Reform, it seemed, had a way of visiting the Keystone State for a while and then traveling to friendlier and more welcoming places. I was touched by Strauss's sense of patience. I had been part of a small army of overly aggressive Harrisburg reporters in the 1970s who shouted and poked away until the festering corruption, conflict of interest, and influence peddling became so embarrassing that something would happen. You could do that in the days when big newspapers in Philadelphia and Pittsburgh were not shy about kicking the butts of legislators whenever they could. By the time I sat with Strauss in Lancaster, those days were over. The *Philadelphia Bulletin*, which once had a trio of reporters in Harrisburg, was gone. The *Philadelphia Inquirer*, which had legendary investigators and reporters assigned to the state capitol and believed coverage of state government was crucial, was bankrupt and a sad shell of what it once had been. The *Harrisburg Patriot* had emerged as a quality paper covering state government, which was pleasantly surprising and unthinkable when I worked at that paper in the late 1960s.

With the aggressive big-city-newspaper voices of reform now muffled, Strauss (a progressive person of deep faith) was something of a voice in the wilderness in Harrisburg. She had her issues and her allies in the legislature—on health care, legislative reform, minimum wage, and an array of advocacies that flowed from commonly held Judeo-Christian values tied to some very old thoughts about the commandment to love God and love your neighbor as you love yourself.

But getting access to the top, to the legislative leaders who made the decisions, was tough. It is rare in this era to hear people talk about issues in the context of the New Testament. But Pennsylvania is one of those remaining churchgoing states where the description of "religion" stretches everywhere from the conservative Catholics of Philadelphia to the Mennonites and Amish in east central Pennsylvania, to the Bible-belt believers farther west, with lots of United Church of Christ members, Reform Church members, and Quakers with deep roots in between. Urban Jews, Muslims, Buddhists, agnostics, atheists—Pennsylvania has all of that. On most issues they don't have the clout of the manufacturers' association, AFSCME, or the Service Employees' International Union, but they do have a voice. Cobbling together coalitions from such a diverse group is no easy task. The official Catholics aren't going to be cuddling up to anyone who supports the right to choose or gay marriage, for example. Gay people welcomed in one church community, particularly in the United Church of Christ, may be spectacularly unwelcome at a UCC church down the road.

The state has its religious progressives along with its staunch religious conservatives. Some of them are certain about what kinds of behavior need to be enforced, and sometimes those issues pop up in the legislature. Sandy Strauss has never worked that way. She would much rather show how commonly held values and needs inform decisions about legislation. It is a thoughtful way of approaching a subject. In her view, the way to lobby a legislature is not to wine and dine its members (the traditional and successful strategy that defines much of lobbying at all levels) but to create a groundswell of support among constituents, who then make themselves and their positions known to their representatives.

What was most interesting to me about this approach was not its obvious ethical and tactical sense but the fact that it was exactly what Barack Obama and his staff had done in the two years that had led to this day, this November 4, when Sandy Strauss and her like-minded Obama backers in Pennsylvania would be at the polls and holding their breath to see whether once again something unanticipated had wrecked their best-laid plans. As in most other places, Obama's Pennsylvania effort had grown from the ground up and by November 4 was thriving in the face of all kinds of assumptions about what state voters were likely to do.

Around the nation Obama had constructed a strong organization. He had millions of people ready to volunteer, so many that in some places there wasn't enough work for them. He had raised three-quarters of a billion dollars, vastly more than any presidential candidate in history, a lot of it in small contributions from people who had never before participated. He had cruised through a brutal campaign without building an apparent sweat. He was calm, even in exasperating debate settings and even when his enemies tried to paint him as some kind of weird Manchurian candidate, black on the outside but Muslim and terrorist at the core.

He picked up a basketball, dribbled twice, and sank a three-pointer while visiting U.S. Army troops in a gym in Kuwait, his Blackberry at his waist and his shades hanging from a pants pocket. The near swoosh was the least remarkable aspect of the visit as he shook hands and joked and posed with dozens of soldiers in their grey ARMY T-shirts. We had never had a presidential candidate who was so cool and so comfortable. He adored his daughters and was not shy about it. He walked at the side of his strong, beautiful wife, again with no sense of awkwardness from either of them. He had no problem dancing on talk television. Or doing just a few little moves at campaign events. Even when he failed quite dismally at bowling in Altoona, he laughed it off. His blackness, of course, was apparent. But he ran as an American, not as a black candidate.

Within the context of this larger campaign, Pennsylvania was its own miniature collection of universes. Race was one of the big unknowns in the Keystone State, even though it had seemed to have been resolved in Iowa and in later primary victories in the South. Obama had drawn a great mass of white support along the trail. He had young people in his camp too. The money he had raised certainly didn't all come from the black community. But Pennsylvania's old reputation—a couple of liberal big cities with rednecks throughout the rest of the state—had people wondering.

All the myths about white people and black candidates were stirred up by this contest, including a lot of disproved theories in which whites were said to have lied when telling pollsters they would vote for a black. It was convenient to believe because it made the question cut-and-dried and reinforced lots of liberal thoughts about the inherent evil of being white. If you were predicting what might happen, race was the safety valve, the caveat you could always tack on at the end of each prognostication: "Of course, we don't know what impact race will have. . . . " It's hard to abandon old notions, no matter how compelling new experiences might be. If you signed on to the old theory of Pennsylvania, Obama would have to win big in Philadelphia and Pittsburgh to offset the good-old-boy nature of the rest of the place. But there was another way of looking at it: of course he would win in Philadelphia and Pittsburgh, but what would he pick up elsewhere? People wishing to make the conversation about race were overlooking the fact that, outside the big cities, Pennsylvania was solidly Republican in many areas. Before many voters even considered race, Obama would be a clear "no" solely because of party identity and ideology. It was a disservice to those Republicans to suggest that they had some problem with blackness when actually what they had was a passion for the Republican party, John McCain and Sarah Palin, tax cuts, and small government. Endorsing those things was not racial. If Obama picked up support outside the traditional Democratic strongholds and had a good showing in counties where the numbers were simply too strongly against any Democrat, he would be unbeatable.

Strauss and her friends were puzzled by the amount of attention the McCain-Palin campaign was paying to Pennsylvania in the remaining weeks of the contest. Obama had the numbers in most polls, but McCain's people continued to argue they could win the state—perhaps because conceding Pennsylvania before the election would have been conceding the election. No one wants to send a concession signal in a presidential election. You have to believe up until they start folding up the chairs at campaign headquarters and the mascara is tear-surfing down the cheeks of the most loyal volunteers. (By that time, most of the men are out getting hammered.) Still, there was no sign the Republicans were picking up traction. Philadelphia's suburbs, increasingly Democratic, were said to have been repelled by Sarah Palin's attack-husky persona. The cities had nothing for either

McCain or Palin, with Pennsylvania starting to look much like the rest of the nation. Its population centers were leaning toward Obama while its widespread collection of Republican counties, some of them thinly populated, were leaning toward McCain. What was the chance that someone might be planning one of those Election Day stunts that changes everything?

As November 4 dawned, signs pointed to a vague maybe. A week before the election Strauss had attended a conference in Philadelphia and heard from folks in the secretary of state's office (in charge of statewide elections) of reports that the shenanigans that had played a role in many previous contests were starting to blossom. Although these were like trying to track down smoke, word had it that Democrats in impoverished areas were being informed that so many people wanted to vote, the election had been stretched over two days. You could just show up on Wednesday and avoid the lines! There were also reports that state troopers would be on hand to arrest anyone with outstanding tickets, unpaid motor vehicle fines, debt problems, or overdue child support. These old turnout-suppression tricks keep surfacing because many people don't understand their voting rights. The tactics may affect people on the margins, and in a close election they may spell the difference. Could that be why the Republicans were still flooding the state with campaign visits and advertising? It's an interesting thought, but truly bold election fraud, in addition to being a felony, is a little hard to pull off these days. Elections are watched by so many layers of do-gooders, lawyers, and campaign volunteers, it's hard to imagine getting away with much of anything. Still . . .

There was another possibility at work too: Pennsylvania was all McCain and Palin had left. Ohio was probably locked up for Obama. Florida was also Obama's. Wisconsin? No way McCain could win it. Michigan—McCain had written it off and pulled out his forces. In fact, throughout the country everything had shifted from bad to much worse for Republicans.

Not only was President Bush's dismal performance scuttling the ship, the economy had gone from troubling to sickening. Retirement money (where lots of Republican support resides) was evaporating. Once again home ownership was becoming just home ownership, not a source of ever-increasing equity. Property values were plummeting almost everywhere, and the sense of well-being attached to what had been the best asset in the portfolio of average people was going south too. Clearly the federal government under Bush had no ready response to the banking crisis. Even the great-stone-face icon of numerous years of economic prosperity, former Federal Reserve chairman Alan Greenspan, had to face up to the bad news. Abandoning the obtuseness that had characterized much of his tenure as chairman, he admitted that mistakes were made. (Greenspan commented on October 23, 2008, "I made a mistake in presuming that the self-interest of organizations, specifically banks and others, was such that they were best capable of protecting their own shareholders.")

Despite these odds, McCain advisers held a lingering hope that a spark could be fanned into life in Pennsylvania, then used to make the argument that the contest really wasn't over, that the momentum had shifted to the Republican side. It was literally something to watch as the campaign mutated into a television ad war.

"Pennsylvania really was ground zero over the last weeks of the campaign, with many visits from all the candidates and barely a commercial break that wasn't a political ad," said Sandy Strauss in one of her election memos to me. "I was stunned by the utter lack of decency of the McCain ads. All sense of propriety seemed to have been jettisoned in the process. The ads were slanderous, full of lies, and just plain nasty. I worried that my husband might start throwing things at the TV. In the end, I think it all backfired. I think that decent folks that might have supported McCain (probably would have supported McCain) changed their minds in the wake of these ads. They showed a man who would do or say anything to get elected. After eight years of a president who would do or say anything to get his way, there might have been some reluctance to risk electing someone who exhibited similar tendencies."

Strauss said she didn't know enough about Sarah Palin to comment on her intelligence, but the vice-presidential candidate didn't seem prepared to move into the Oval Office. She said she was "flabbergasted" by Palin's apparent lack of knowledge of the issues in the presidential race.

She and a collection of friends and Obama supporters gathered on election night to await the results. She had voted and worked as an Obama volunteer early in the day, but there were so many Obama volunteers on hand, no one knew quite what to do with all of them (a good sign for the campaign). So she left the polling place and went home to wait for the results.

There are many ways to watch presidential election returns on cable television. One way is to start drinking beer and eating late in the afternoon, then have a party that runs until the last numbers are reported. The second is to sit alone nervously in front of a TV, trying hard to ignore all the ridiculous speculation and watching closely for returns from a handful of states that can determine victory or defeat. Or, in November 2008, if you lived close enough to Chicago, you could head to Grant Park, where the Obama campaign was planning a mammoth late-night rally. I took options two and three.

Television embraces unaccustomed caution on election night. It fears that predictions of victory or reports of early exit polls on the East Coast might somehow make people in middle America, in the Rockies, and on the West Coast decide to change their vote. Worse, they might decide it's all over and not vote at all, which sounds a lot to me like a felonious if unintentional suppression of voter turnout. If you're in television, it's best not to risk that kind of career bump. Too, everyone is afraid of that old "Dewey Defeats Truman" problem that so embarrassed the *Chicago Tribune*. The John Kerry problem in 2004, when early exit polls made it seem as though President Bush would be ousted, made big news for a little while, just long enough for everyone to become aware of how wrong the media could be. There were agreements this time around to keep the early predictions problem under tight control, generally by withholding results until polls closed in individual states.

What has evolved is coverage in which it seems everyone is just dying to get to the bathroom but somehow can't. They just have to live with the nervousness of it. While they're waiting for actual results to plug into their graphics and maps, they talk. And talk. And talk. And talk. Here's what John McCain needs to do. Here's what Barack Obama needs to do. Here's what race is going to do. Here's how the voters feel. The talk comes in layers, with banks of commentators (Carl Bernstein, Bill Bennett, and David Gergen in the same place!) and long tables of characters hiding behind opened laptops, as though there were something mysterious and revealing on the screen. It's confusing until you realize it's like a musical vamp designed to kill time before we get an explanation of something that's already well over.

*

Anyone paying attention as Election Day dawned knew from polling results that the entire West Coast—from Border Field State Park nestled down on the Mexican border all the way up to the Strait of Juan de Fuca off Seattle—would go big for Obama. That's 73 electoral votes locked up. There was not much doubt about most of the East Coast, either. From Maine down through New Hampshire, Vermont, Massachusetts, Rhode Island, Connecticut, and the bonanza state of New York, all were looking strong for Obama. That's another 65. Virginia adds 13, Maryland adds 10, and Pennsylvania adds 21. The District of Columbia adds 3. How many more do you need to collect the 270 electoral votes required to win the contest? Just 85. If you took the polls as your Bible on the night before the election, you were looking at an electoral college landslide for Obama.

Look to the Midwest. Illinois, Wisconsin, and Michigan were firmly on board for 48 more votes. Ohio was leaning toward Obama, and that's 20 more votes. All these safe places left Obama a handful of electoral votes away from the presidency. Assuming the McCain push in Pennsylvania was fantasy-based, either Florida or North Carolina would do it. There was no way you could construct the math to give McCain more than about 170 safe electoral votes from either the most Republican of places or places with tiny populations.

The more subtle measures were not looking good for Republicans either. More than six in every ten people thought the country was on the wrong track. Only 7 percent thought the economy was in good shape (who could they possibly have been?), and more than seven in every ten people expected the economy to grow worse. The bad economic news was relentless. Every drop of the Dow fueled headlines about the crisis. Every 401(k) report in the mail reinforced the downturn.

It's small wonder that for the Republicans the final days were desperate. McCain loves to gamble, but every single bet the party had made—that experience would win out over change; that a compelling war hero's story would be stronger than that of an unknown senator from Illinois; that the Democrats would fracture along sex lines once Hillary Clinton was rejected, providing an opportunity for the GOP to get the votes of women; that even unplayed, the race card would fall to their advantage; that the addition of an attractive wild card from Alaska would be a game changer—was wrong.

Obama had begun building his momentum the minute it was clear early in June that he had the nomination. He never looked back. Through debates, slanders, ignorance, through arrogant preachers, toothless old radicals, hyperbolic media blather, and even his own badly timed comments about guns, religion, and fear in rural America, he and his team pushed ahead while the Republicans floundered, desperate to dig up something that would give McCain the bump he needed to get his campaign rolling. They never found it.

Down in Pass Christian on the Gulf, Carmen Dedeaux decided to write a letter to Obama after he won the Democratic nomination and promise her support. Like almost everything she says and does, it was soulful and moving, a pleading voice asking for whatever help she could get with her primary mission: raising her children.

"I am a single mother with four children," Dedeaux wrote. "I have raised two college graduates. My oldest son is now in the Air Force. My oldest daughter is working on her PhD at Purdue. Her program has run out of money. She has been blessed to get an internship to substitute the funding. I also have a high school graduate and I have a fifteen-year-old son that is now in the tenth grade. I have tried to teach them all morals and values. God has always played a major part in our lives. I am proud of every one of them and all they have grown to become," she wrote. But there was a new problem. Her job at the Boys and Girls Club was among those eliminated as the organization nearly ran out of money.

"I am not a college graduate but I have made sure all of my children further their education. I now worry about being able to send my son to college. After almost depleting my savings, I worry about being able to provide for the only child I still have at home. I have followed this election since the beginning of time. With Obama's message of change, perhaps it won't be too late for a small business to hire me because of a tax deduction or maybe my son will be able to attend college by agreeing to serve his community or country. . . . I cannot imagine living through four more years of the same politics we have had to endure for the past eight years. Our state does not have early voting. Tuesday morning I will be at the polls at 6:00 a.m. to cast my vote for Barack Obama. No matter where I am Tuesday night, I will be there looking at history in the making. Wednesday morning, Barack Obama will be our next president of the United States. We will finally have the change we have needed and longed for. YES WE CAN!"

She wasn't kidding.

"I picked up my seventy-five-year-old mother and my twenty-year-old daughter and we went to the polls," Carmen wrote in her promised Election Day memo to me. "It was such a touching experience for me. My mother hadn't voted for eight years before she went to vote for Obama, yet she stood in the long line for over an hour hanging onto her cane and just waiting. I know how I feel but can only imagine how she must have felt. Some of our ancestors were slaves. . . . There were three generations of the Malley family standing in that line to vote that chilly November morning.

"We were blessed to be from a small town. My oldest daughter voted in Gary, Indiana. She, along with thousands of others, stood in line for over ten to twelve hours a day; some for four days just to vote. You see, in Gary there were only two voting machines to go around to be used by thousands of people in a four-day period. Even in Gary people were not going to give up. As I listened to the background noise as she continued to call me from her cell phone, I could hear people chanting and singing old Negro spirituals. I could hear poll workers crying and begging people not to be discouraged. As time was running out, I heard law enforcement officers come by and tell those same poll workers there could not be anyone left on the court-house grounds at 7 p.m. Some of these same people had already been trying to vote for the past three days. To be turned away on this day when it was their last chance to cast their vote would be devastating. The poll workers started crowding them into the courthouse like canned sardines until everybody was in. It wasn't about color that day. It was just about the right thing to do."

Marty Geraghty, that ardent Evanston conservative worried about the Republican party's drift away from its core values, voted early at

the Cook County Clerk's office next door to his own office in downtown Chicago. In the basement of the building, the clerk had set up
an orderly, efficient process to allow people to come in and vote. It's
one of the things in Chicago that work right. It took Marty just fifteen
minutes, mainly because of the long list of judges at the end of all
Cook County ballots. His wife, Maureen, voted early at the city hall in
Evanston and waited in line more than two hours to cast her ballot.

So on Election Day the Geraghtys were far away, enjoying a vacation in Prague. It's unlikely the election results put even a tiny damper
on their travel. Geraghty is a master of the grand gesture. Once while
my family and I were on vacation in Ireland, where we were running
in the hills and I was playing in a band, Geraghty showed up out of
nowhere in Connemara with a son in one hand and a jar of peanut
butter in the other. "We were in the area, and I thought you might be
needing this now," he said.

The day after the election, Geraghty said, they went to the Hole-
sovice train station to catch the 8:23 a.m. express to Vienna. "This
station is a dirty little hole of a place featuring a dingy waiting room
with a marginally useful television. Even if everyone on TV spoke
English, it would still be marginal. But the Czech language (unlike
German and the Romance languages) is one in which your basic English speaker cannot pick up even a single random word. So there I
was watching a crew of serious-looking anchors uttering unintelligi-
ble sounds while scenes of Grant Park and Phoenix, Arizona, played
behind them. Both Obama's and McCain's visages were serious and
I could not tell who had won, or even if anyone knew yet. This went
on for ten or fifteen minutes. It was very frustrating.

"But then the Czech newspapers showed *the map*. As the anchors
yammered on, I saw by this time (roughly 1 a.m. Central Time in the
U.S.) that Florida, Virginia, Pennsylvania, Ohio, and even good old
Indiana were blue. It was a kick in the gut. You know I have never been
enthusiastic about McCain, but I was, and remain, deeply worried

about Obama. And now, standing in this foreign city, I knew America and I had seen things very differently. I expect this to be one of the most consequential elections in my lifetime. And the consequences will not be good. One side note: my two Chicago-resident daughters (a Spanish teacher at an urban charter high school and a school psychologist in the suburbs) attended the Obama rally in Grant Park. Two weeks later, they are still nearly giddy about the experience."

Geraghty said he wanted to make a confession that his conservative friends would disapprove of: "At this moment, I am proud of America for having elected Barack Obama. Not 'gosh amighty, who'd a thunk it' proud, but more, 'I told ya so' proud. I'm not proud because I believe that previously racist America has overcome its internal devils and elevated itself above its innate racism. There are few, if any, such devils. Haven't been for several decades. There are surely more actual white racists out there than any society needs, but their presence does not make America racist any more than a number of gap-toothed people speaking bad English makes us a 'hillbilly' nation.

"Alas, we proved our post-racialism by electing the wrong black guy, but we did prove it. If it even needed proving."

In Evanston, Birch Burghardt made up her mind after we talked, and signed up to help Obama however she could. She voted for him enthusiastically. She did not rub it in by wearing an Obama T-shirt at home. True to her character as a person who does more than talk, she volunteered. Evanston was filled with Obama supporters who headed to Wisconsin, Michigan, Ohio, and Iowa for Election Day, to help out any way they could. Burghardt was dispatched to Cincinnati, where she stayed with a woman who heard of her from the woman Burghardt sat next to at the Obama headquarters telephone bank. "How nice is that?" she said.

"My alarm went off at 4:45 that morning, then a wake-up call came on my cell phone from John Kerry at 5 a.m. We had been through pretty extensive training in Chicago and Cincinnati, so I had my clipboard, maps, and forms on hand, as well as a huge bag of baked goodies that I had gotten from a Starbucks the night before (deeply discounted) for the election judges. And I'd scoped out the church that was my polling place the night before, so I knew how to get there. In Ohio, only Ohio residents are allowed to observe polls inside the polling places, so out-of-state observers had to be outside. I had been strongly instructed not to do any electioneering but rather to do what I could to improve voters' comfort and to report long lines or disruptions to local party headquarters. So that's what I did.

"I had a folding stool that I offered to infirm people when the line was long, and also loaned extra shawls and hats to folks who were shivering in the early-morning cold. I also told people what ID was required, so they wouldn't waste their time in line and then have to come back. In the early morning when there was a long line, it was really fun. There was a sense of excitement and warm community. I was in a pretty middle-class African-American neighborhood that was overwhelmingly Democratic, so there was also a sense of joint purpose there. In mid-morning, two judges, a Democrat and a Republican, came out to talk. The legality of my presence there had been challenged by the Republican observer, who had seen me talking with people in line. I showed them my credentials and explained that I hadn't been electioneering, which was supported by the people in the line who overheard what was going on. The judges listened sympathetically, said it was okay, and invited me to come in and use the facilities or share the treats that were inside any time I wanted. Whew!"

At day's end, Burghardt watched the votes being tabulated and bundled and then headed to her new friend's house, stopping off to pick up food and beer on the way. Just after she got back into her car, she heard on the radio that Obama had won Ohio "surely before the votes had been delivered."

"At the end of the day, I went back to the house, sat beside my hostess, and watched the results come in and the speeches as shown from Grant Park and we both wept. Too much joy to contain!"

In North Carolina, by Election Day Maria Smithson had come to view herself as "one of the hacks working the election." From her vantage point, running a congressional campaign and volunteering for Obama, she got a good education on how and why North Carolina had reached a turning point in its political history. She was touched, she said, by the number of new voters who had been registered. But being thoughtful about politics, she didn't let it sit there.

"One of my love-hates of this cycle was the number of first-time voters, primarily African-American, who registered and voted. On one hand it was really exciting to talk with so many people who had never voted and were excited to vote for Obama. One such person I talked to was a bagger at a grocery store who told me she had gotten herself, her husband, and her elderly mother registered to vote for the first time. She was so excited. And I met hundreds of people in North Carolina like her. As a political consultant, it was enjoyable to see the campaign get new voters to the polls en masse with relative ease because of the high motivation factor. But on the other hand, as someone who has worked in the trenches for decades trying to reach minority voters and the disfranchised to get out and vote for various Democratic candidates who best represent their needs, I also found myself being a bit angry. So many candidates of all colors have held the same beliefs and made the same promises that Obama was making, and were largely ignored by these people. Intellectually I know the reasons that these first-timers finally got involved and voted, but on some level I still feel like shouting 'It's about god-damned time!' So many of us have been fighting for these principles for so long, and yes it took someone like Obama to self-empower these voters, but they have held this ability all of this time and a lot of decent politicians and activists have been trying to improve their lives for a long time and have been completely ignored."

Smithson was a little angry, but not that angry. "As one of the hacks, I helped plan the official Democratic election night party. Essentially I called the owner of a huge bar/restaurant I know and asked if we could take over that night and give him huge sums of money for food and beer. He readily agreed. The two-story place, Dilworth Neighborhood Grill, was at full capacity and the crowd was largely black. Everything happened so fast, even though we were all there at 7:30 p.m. EST, and watched for several hours before the race was called for Obama, but with so many states getting called so quickly, it was just a constant celebration. Every couple of minutes, another round of cheering as another state went to Obama. The big moment was somewhat sudden and still shocking though. CNN called it literally 2.4 seconds before West Coast polls closed. In addition to a lot of cheering and screaming, I saw a lot of African Americans crying almost uncontrollably. Men included. For me, I was thrilled at Obama's election, thrilled that we had elected our first black president, but equally relieved that the horrible failure of the Bush administration, and 8 years of disastrous Republican domination, was finally coming to an end. I felt like I could believe in American democracy again. It restored my faith in American voters to make an intelligent choice."

Smithson was surprised to receive calls from Republican friends who reported they had voted for Obama or were happy he had won the election even though they had voted for McCain. "Usually, it was that they voted for Obama because they found him highly intelligent and capable. Sometimes it was because the choice of Sarah Palin made them realize John McCain was unsuitable to be president. If they didn't vote for Obama, they woke up with a sense of pride that America had just made a huge step forward in electing an African American. One of my dear friends, a military dad who supported Bush 100 percent all 8 years, and loved Sarah Palin, called to tell me on November 5, that, 'No matter what, Obama is now my commander-in-chief and I fully support him.' He went on to say how great it was that we had elected a black president. I have yet to hear anyone say anything negative about the outcome of this election."

That sentiment aside, North Carolina was a squeaker. Obama won by 13,692 votes in a contest in which the libertarian Bob Barr collected 25,419 votes. Obama increased Democratic participation by 6.3 percent over 2004. He rolled up huge majorities in the cities among young people and handily secured a large black vote. There were other signs of Republican distress in the results too. Elizabeth Dole, handpicked by President Bush to be the U.S. Senate candidate six years ago and an easy winner then, paid a high price for her connection to the troubled president. Democrat Kay Hagin won a landslide victory, beating Dole by 300,000 votes. North Carolina also elected its first woman governor, Bev Purdue, who beat Republican Pat McCrory by 140,000 votes. This Democratic tide, however, did little to help Smithson's House candidate. Harry Taylor was crushed by Sue Myrick, though she had less of a victory margin than usual.

Smithson called much later with a news report. Virgil Griffin, sixty-four and a member and leader of the Ku Klux Klan for forty years, had died at Gaston Memorial Hospital in North Carolina. He had lived in the congressional district where Taylor challenged Myrick. He had been Imperial Wizard of the Cleveland, North Carolina KKK in 1979 when Klan members, American Nazis, and the Communist Workers party had a street shootout at a rally in Greensboro that left five CWP members dead. The Communist Workers had moved to town in a bid to unionize (or radicalize, some would say) textile workers. After an array of charges, no one was convicted in the killings, though there was a $350,000 settlement in a civil action. Smithson thought the fact that her district was where old dead Virgil decided to hang his hood might help explain why Taylor had such an uphill fight.

The results meant North Carolina's 15 electoral votes were added to Obama's tally. Florida fell into place at about the same time. Obama beat McCain there by some 200,000 votes. It didn't exactly explode the state out of the Republican column, but it dragged it handily into Obama's camp.

The day was not shaping up well for McCain by any measure. If the view from space included that red/blue paint assessment that television so loves, you could see right away that the "solid" red Republican South had been fractured by the votes in Florida, North Carolina, Virginia, and Maryland. Much of the Plains down to Texas remained firmly Republican, but the color red in many cases masked an important distinction—hardly any people lived in a lot of those states. Two important blue states popped up as the night progressed. Colorado went firmly for Obama, by almost ten percentage points. The signs should have been clearly read when Obama stacked eighty thousand people into a sports stadium in Denver for his acceptance speech. Even factoring in created appearances of fervor (which both parties are good at), that's a lot of people. New Mexico went strongly for Obama by more than fourteen percentage points. Nevada slipped out of the Republican orbit, backing Obama by thirteen percentage points. All that work on the casino people helped, no doubt, as did the fact that real estate in Las Vegas was a shambles, and a state that anticipated much of its revenue from the longings of average Americans was taking a very cold shower as its building boom went bust and people stopped tossing money into the black hole that is, by design, gambling.

Vermont got little attention in election coverage because everyone knew what would happen there, just as they knew what would happen in once solidly Republican New Hampshire. Obama had blowout victories in both states. None of that dimmed Brian Vachon's passion:

"Never have I been more certain of a vote in my life, and that includes people who were running for office who were personal friends. Tuesday evening I went to the Democratic headquarters in

Burlington, where I had been invited to Senator [Patrick] Leahy's suite to watch returns. The great hall downstairs was filled with young, very happy, very loud enthusiasts. I felt a little old. And because I had been fairly certain for about a week that the election would be a landslide, I was pleased without being surprised. I paid my respects to Senator Leahy and to our congressman, Peter Welch, who won by an enormous amount, and went home.

"Nancy and I watched returns for a while in bed. By the time McCain conceded, Nancy was falling asleep. We found the CNN screen impossibly busy and difficult to read. MSNBC wasn't much better. I toyed with the idea of switching to Fox to see how unhappy they were, but that would mean breaking a pledge I had made to myself a year or so ago. So I didn't. At midnight I went downstairs to watch the acceptance speech, and I was moved more than I expected to be. I was sitting with my dog and cat, explaining to them what happened, and I started to weep. It was certainly weeping in complete relief and happiness, but I also cried because we've wasted too much for eight years, squandered such an incalculable amount of treasure and reputation and value. And we all let that happen. It wasn't the Bush administration's fault and it wasn't the Republicans' fault. America allowed it to occur. It's our shared stain on history. President Elect Obama was incredibly controlled. He could easily have whipped up a fervor, the crowd was ready to be uproarious, but he was measured and cool instead. I loved him. And I was enormously pleased that the election campaign had come to a close."

In New Hampshire, Ann Marie Banfield went to the polls in Bedford from 10 a.m. to noon to work for the McCain-Palin campaign. She had voted by absentee ballot before Election Day. Her job was to tally the voters so that Republican headquarters could telephone supporters who had not yet cast ballots.

From 1:00 to 1:30 p.m. she went to Adoration Chapel at the Catholic church to pray the rosary "for our country and for pro-life."

After that she had a parent-teacher conference with her youngest son's teacher. She finished Election Day with twenty other people holding "Pro-Life," "Palin," and "Country First" signs at the Bedford polls.

New Hampshire gave Obama 54 percent of the vote, with 44 percent going to McCain. In a state where the election had been projected as close earlier, Obama defeated McCain by more than sixty thousand votes.

In Milwaukee, Nick Giannini rose at 5:30 a.m. on Election Day and headed straight for Obama Volunteer Headquarters on Marquette's campus. The office was in the basement of an apartment building. The Obama campaign had rented it the Friday before the election so that students would have a handy way to volunteer.

Giannini was dispatched to the Sarah Scott Middle School, a polling place primarily for the community around Marquette. "I sat the entire day, taking only one hour for lunch, observing people coming in to vote. What makes this job a little more important than, say, an observing job in Illinois is that Wisconsin has same-day registration. So I sat and watched people coming in to register and then vote. It might seem boring, but I loved it, watching people come to vote for the first time. I saw elderly African Americans come to vote (I will speculate for Obama). They walked out of the polling place with the biggest smiles on their faces. I thought to myself how incredible it was to watch people come vote for an African-American candidate, which I'm sure some people thought they would never have the opportunity to do. . . . At one point in the afternoon, an elderly African American gentleman who was blind came to vote with the help of his aide. After this gentleman voted, he received his 'I voted' sticker, and that man wanted that sticker on his chest. It didn't matter that he couldn't see it, he wanted everyone to know he had voted. I saw moments like this all day. Just watching people participate in the democratic process was an amazing experience. I don't know what it was, but it brought a sense of wonderment to me, to think that we have these opportunities in this country, it is just incredible."

It was a long day, and as it came to a close, when the election officials at the school were printing out the tabulations, Nick began to worry a true college student's worry, that the party would be over before he had a chance to get to it. The results were coming in quickly and very strongly for Obama in Wisconsin. He ended up winning there by more than 400,000 votes.

"I ran back to my apartment about a mile away. My friends were already gathered. The party was sponsored by the Les Aspin Center, which is an internship program of which I am an alum. So we sat and watched, all of us knowing there was no chance for McCain to win, and as soon as the polls closed in the West and CNN called the race for Obama, we went nuts.

"Afterward I just sat there. I could not believe what just happened. I had put so much into this campaign, and to have Obama win was an incredible feeling."

In Florida, Colonel Chamberlain and his wife Sherry voted early because she was leaving to visit children in Germany. Chamberlain said he and his wife had a great time standing in the long line and talking to other people who were enjoying the moment. "God, it was a great election. I actually stayed up to watch the election returns and listen to the speeches, something I have never cared enough to do before. The line for voting was fairly long, and we had some great conversations of a nonpolitical nature with the people around us. The woman behind me, once she found out I was a retired army officer, did ask me about the war. I told her it was the dumbest thing we had ever done, and I explained why. She and her husband seemed surprised at my response but were in agreement. I suspect they voted for Obama also, as Sherry and I did when our turn finally came. We both felt good about that and see him as the best hope for our country these days.

"Several of our friends and family were upset that Obama won the election. We have taken the course of not discussing it unless asked, then are more than willing to tell them why we voted the way we did. I said last summer I would vote for whoever said they would end the war in Iraq, and that's exactly what I did. The financial crash and the economy in general made that all the easier to do. We can thank Bush *et al.* for all the deregulation that caused the whole damn thing to fall apart. Most people haven't figured that out yet, but it's as simple as that. Stupid bastards." Obama beat McCain by 200,000 votes in Florida.

There was little need for Angela Inzano—the Obama volunteer, Nick Giannini's friend and College Democrat president at Loyola—to head to a polling place in Chicago. That town was going to go big for the local. Instead she became the point person for the Obama phone bank on the Loyola campus. "On November 3, we made a lot of calls to Indiana and on November 4 they were to Pennsylvania," she said. "Most of the people there to volunteer were older. There weren't as many students as I had expected. I would say the response to the calls was pretty typical—a lot of annoyed people but also a lot of supporters. What was most interesting was that while we were making personal calls, the McCain campaign was using automated calls. Even if some people were annoyed at being called again, they seemed grateful that we took the time to use actual people. By the end of the day on November 4, even the youngest and most adamant staffers and volunteers were ready for this thing to be over. Two years is a long time!"

After they shut down the operation, Angela headed for Grant Park, where the crowds had been massing all afternoon. It was un-usually warm for a November day, delightfully warm actually. She stood in line from 8:00 until 10:45 p.m., waiting to be admitted to the area near the stage. "We really didn't mind all that much. Being sur-rounded by supporters, hearing the results come in through calls and texts, we all felt like we were in this thing together and were achieving something great as a unit. We were literally running into the crowd in the field as they announced he had won, which was unbelievable timing. Everything felt pretty surreal, and I can't quite believe that it is over and that we actually won. I say 'we' because I believe this is a victory for our whole country."

Inzano was upset about the setbacks on gay rights in ballot initiatives around the country. "For me, it feels like we broke down one huge barrier and yet strengthened another in the same night. I guess it just shows that while we have come far, we have far to go. I feel so invested in this presidency that I can't wait to see what happens. While I'm nervous about not only his safety but also the American people's impatience with the long process of change, I'm hopeful. I feel like I have a stake in the next four to eight years and I feel we are headed in the right direction."

It's interesting that the Obama campaign would use its Loyola volunteers to call likely voters in Pennsylvania just to make sure people there were casting their votes. It could be that, polling results aside, everyone was puzzled about what a complicated state might do when time came to decide whether to send the first black man to the White House. With all its money and volunteers, the Obama campaign had a luxury that eluded the McCain camp. It could add layers of support to its attack, almost at will. It was not enough in Pennsylvania to put the victory in a big box. The Obama people wanted to make certain it had a bow on it.

Obama's hot dog du mort in Altoona and his poor bowling did not help with the vote in Blair County, where McCain defeated him by 61 to 31 percent. That seems like a big victory, but there are not that many voters in Blair County. Philadelphia—now there was a big victory. Obama defeated McCain in Philadelphia 83 to 16 percent. That gave Obama a 461,670-vote buffer to carry into the state. He won Allegheny County (Pittsburgh) 57 to 42 percent. True to the

complexity of the state, he did well in several other heavily populated counties. He carried Cambria County, where Johnstown and
U.S. Representative John Murtha (who cannot seem to lose no matter
what he says or does) are both located, 50 to 48 percent. He carried
the collar counties around Philadelphia by huge margins. He carried
Dauphin County, home to the state capital, by nine percentage points,
and Erie by nineteen. He carried Centre County, home of Pennsylvania State University, by eleven percentage points. Altogether, in a
state where the cliché said Democrats did well in Philadelphia and
Pittsburgh and Republicans did well with the rednecks in between,
Obama won eighteen of sixty-seven counties and fell three votes short
of winning a nineteenth. Equally revealing, many of his losses were
not big, a couple of percentage points in some cases.

Pennsylvania was a 55-to-44 percent, 600,000-vote landslide, a
victory no one had anticipated in the early days of the campaign when
the fight was over guns, religion, and assumptions about Obama's
name, his early childhood education in Indonesia, his passing relationship with old radicals in Chicago, his loud former preacher,
whether he wore an American flag lapel pin proudly enough, whether
he was not black enough to draw black votes, whether he was too
black to draw white votes, whether he was not experienced enough,
whether the senator from New York was the inevitable and unbeatable Democrat, and whether the nation was ready to give its highest
elective office to a black man.

Around the nation, Obama ran away with the election, 365 electoral votes to 173 for McCain. In the popular vote, Obama won by
8.5 million. A nation that had been perceived as shifting solidly Republican only four years before had taken a 180-degree turn, embracing a black liberal Democrat from the Midwest with a thin federal
résumé but remarkable campaign skills, personality, and intelligence.

Was it Barack Obama's victory, or was it George W. Bush's loss
superimposed on the unfortunate John McCain, who finally got his

party's nomination after so many years of trying and with so many bitter frustrations along the way? There is no doubt that President Bush left the nation so damaged after two terms defined by terrorism, incompetence, unnecessary war, and economic collapse that it would have been nearly impossible for a Republican to achieve another victory.

But that explanation is too narrow to cover what actually happened on November 4. It's wrong to think that any Democrat who came along could have coasted into the White House. That was what Hillary Clinton and her backers were most likely thinking before Barack Obama came on the scene. She was the perceived "any Democrat" who was ready to take the prize. The only way to view her presidential fate is to see it as one of history's most unexpected losses. Some will argue she ran a poor campaign, that she might have won with better direction. They are wrong. She ran the best campaign she could, and she was a worthy contender. But a relative novice from Chicago came along and ran a campaign that was much better than hers in the primaries and immensely better than John McCain's in the general election.

One simply must admire the organizational skills of the Obama campaign, its finesse at finding new ways to collect a vast campaign treasury, to mobilize millions of volunteers, to flood the nation with money and street workers on Election Day as though the United States were nothing more than a big Chicago ward filled with ripe, eager voters. For those of us who admire that kind of politics, it's a nice thought—a Chicago stamp on a presidential election.

If you believe in democracy, with all its troubling warts and great blessings mixed up in one fabulous political festival, well, what could possibly be better? But this is a thought not big enough to hold the meaning of a campaign that was defined at its outset as a response to destiny's call.

After this long campaign it's fair to ask, where does our destiny come from, and how does it call us?

People who thought Obama was talking about his own destiny when he started his campaign in the shadow of Abraham Lincoln in Springfield were mistaken. He was talking about his country—our country—and its historic longing to live up to the promise close to its heart: the dream of opportunity for everyone, equality for everyone, and a government that sees a responsibility to respond to the needs of all its citizens, not just a privileged few. It's no surprise then when the nation, having felt lost and like it had long forgotten this dream, turned onto this path, which was so unexpected and in many ways so radical.

By the way he won the election, Obama redefined how presidential politics will look, sound, and move for all time. It's as though the promise of reform that was so important to the Democrats during their tortured journey from 1968 onward had finally come to life. In the face of a political agenda crafted by people who would not likely have recognized or embraced a black upstart from Chicago, the Democrats delivered a candidate who made his eloquent connection not with power brokers or with traditional special-interest groups but with a passionate new electorate noteworthy for its ability to respond and, most important, to answer the call.

We have always been more remarkable for our spectacular dreams than for our ability to achieve them. On November 4, 2008, the people of the United States went to vote and created one of those defining moments where the nation became, however briefly, everything that it said it wanted to be.

INDEX

A NOTE ON THE AUTHOR

Charles M. Madigan was born in Altoona, Pennsylvania, and studied at the Pennsylvania State University and at Roosevelt University in Chicago. He worked for the *Altoona Mirror* and the *Harrisburg Patriot*, and then for United Press International as a reporter in the United States and a foreign correspondent in the Soviet Union. With the *Chicago Tribune* from 1979 to 2007, he held a number of senior positions, including Washington news editor, national editor, and columnist. In 2000 his reporting on war crimes in Kosovo won an Overseas Press Club award. Mr. Madigan is now presidential writer in residence at Roosevelt University. He is married with three sons and lives in Evanston, Illinois.